Lucy & Desi

The Love Letters

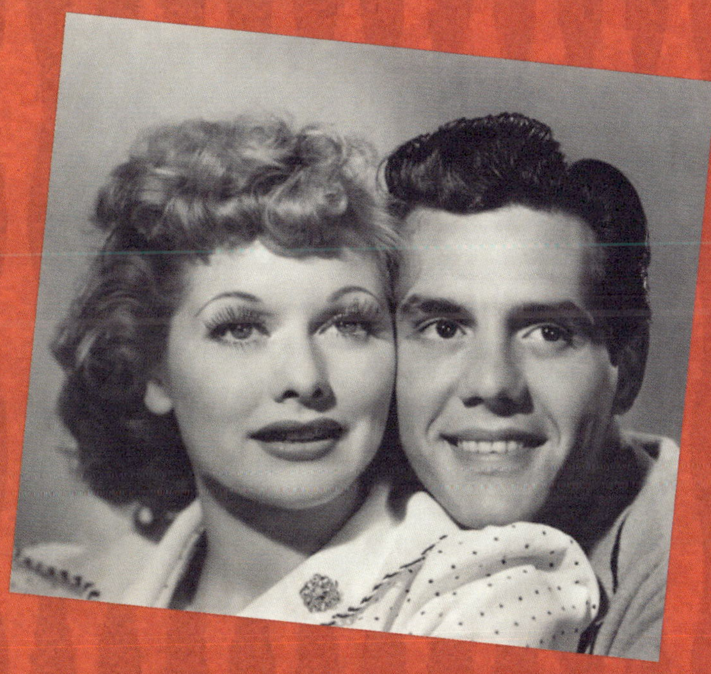

Private Desi Arnaz
Co. C. Group 496
S.C.U. 1950 Reception C
Arlington, Californi
spital

S.C.U. 1950 Reception
Arlington, California

CALIF. 1:30 PM 1943

Mrs. Lucille Ball Arnaz
19700 Devonshire Blvd

3

Private Desi Arnaz
Co. C. Group 496
S.C.U. 1950 Reception Ce
Califor

-MAIL

NEW YORK, N.Y. OCT 17 11-PM 1940

AIR MAIL
NEW YORK WORLD'S FAIR
6c 6c

Miss Lu
1403 No
Hollywoo
Calf

Pvt. Desi Arnaz
Co. C Group 496
S.C.U. 1950 Reception Center
Arlington, California

FORM 539

Free

CAMP ANZA MAY 27 1943 CALIF.

Mrs. Lucille Ball Arnaz
Devonshire Blvd.

AFTER 5 DAYS RETURN TO

UNITED STATES POSTAGE
SPECIAL DELIVERY
UNITED STATES POST OFFICE
10 TEN CENTS 10

AIR MAIL
6c U.S. POSTAGE 6c

CIAL-DELIVERY

VIA AIR MAIL

Miss. Lucille Ball
403 North Laurel
ollywood.
alifornia

NEW YORK, N.Y. OCT 27 1 AM G.P.O. 1940

Pvt. Desi Arnaz
Co. C. Group 496.
S.C.U. 1950 Reception Center
Arlington, California

Mrs. Lucille Ball
19700 Devonshire
Chatsworth, Califor

VAN NUYS MAY 1943 CALIF.

3

vate Desiderio A. Arna
Arlington Field
Arlington, Calif,
C. Group 496

Pvt. De
Co. C.
S.C.U. 1950 Reception Center
Arlington, California

ARLINGTON, CALIF. MAY 7 7:30 AM 1943

Free

Mrs. D. Arnaz.
19700 Devonshire Bl

Lucy & Desi

The Love Letters

COMPILED AND WITH AN INTRODUCTION BY

LUCIE ARNAZ

Historical Timeline and Notes by

ELISABETH EDWARDS

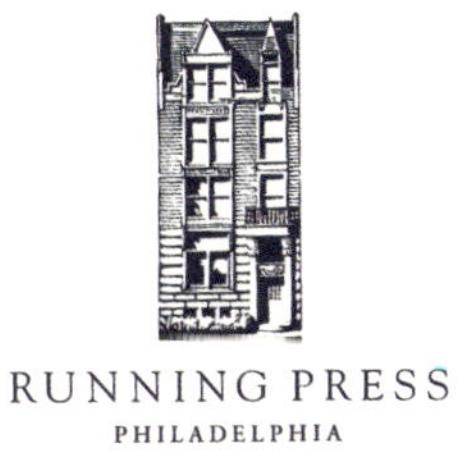

RUNNING PRESS
PHILADELPHIA

Running Press
Hachette Book Group
1290 Avenue of the Americas, New York, NY 10104
www.runningpress.com
@Running_Press

First Edition: November 2025

Published by Running Press, an imprint of Hachette Book Group, Inc.
The Running Press name and logo are trademarks of Hachette Book Group, Inc.

The Hachette Speakers Bureau provides a wide range of authors for speaking events. To find out more, go to www.hachettespeakersbureau.com or email HachetteSpeakers@hbgusa.com.

Running Press books may be purchased in bulk for business, educational, or promotional use. For more information, please contact your local bookseller or the Hachette Book Group Special Markets Department at Special.Markets@hbgusa.com.

The publisher is not responsible for websites (or their content) that are not owned by the publisher.

Print book cover and interior design by Susan Van Horn

Library of Congress Cataloging-in-Publication Data

Names: Ball, Lucille, 1911–1989, author. | Arnaz, Desi, 1917–1986, author. | Arnaz, Lucie, 1951– writer of introduction. | Edwards, Elisabeth, 1963– writer of supplementary textual content.
Title: Lucy & Desi : the love letters / introduction by Lucie Arnaz; historical notes by Elisabeth Edwards.
Other titles: Lucy and Desi
Description: First edition. | Philadelphia : Running Press, 2025. | Summary: "The real-life love story between the world's all-time-favorite TV couple, Lucille Ball and Desi Arnaz, is told through a collection of their own never-before-seen love letters, exclusive family photos, and text by Lucie Arnaz—the star daughter's first book on her parents!" —Provided by publisher.
Identifiers: LCCN 2024053756 (print) | LCCN 2024053757 (ebook) | ISBN 9798894140421 (hardcover) | ISBN 9798894140438 (ebook)
Subjects: LCSH: Ball, Lucille, 1911–1989—Correspondence. | Arnaz, Desi, 1917–1986—Correspondence. | Television actors and actresses—United States—Correspondence.
Classification: LCC PN2287.B16 A4 2025 (print) | LCC PN2287.B16 (ebook) | DDC 791.45092/273—dc23/eng/20250403
LC record available at https://lccn.loc.gov/2024053756
LC ebook record available at https://lccn.loc.gov/2024053757

ISBNs: 979-8-89414-042-1 (hardcover), 979-8-89414-043-8 (ebook)

Printed in China

1010

10 9 8 7 6 5 4 3 2 1

OPPOSITE: At home in Chatsworth in the early 1940s

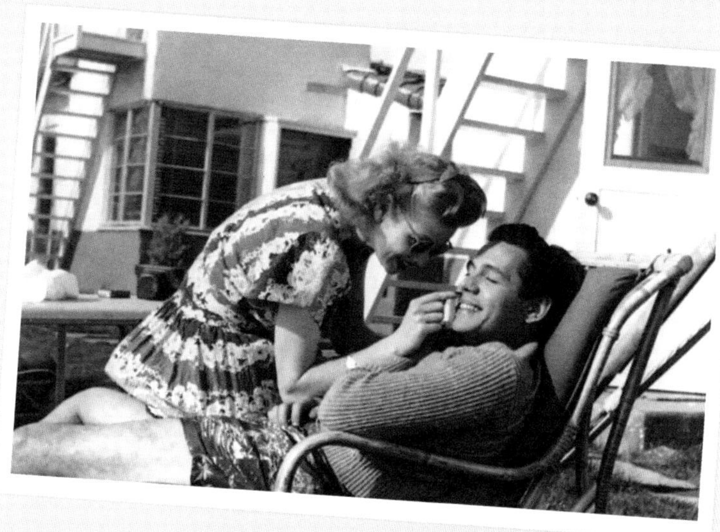

To each of my parents, for saving their priceless proofs of the passion they had for each other—especially my mother, for having the presence of mind to keep them all together even decades after she and my father were happily married to other people.

SAN DIEGO MAY 21 930 PM 1943 CALIF.

BUY WAR SAVINGS BONDS AND STAMPS

WIN THE WAR UNITED STATES POSTAGE

Desiderio A. Arnaz

Private Desi Arnaz (3)
Co. C. Group 496
S.C.U. 1950 Reception Center
Arlington, California
% Hospital
Camp Anza

Free

CAMP ANZA JUN 6 130 PM 1943 CALIF.

Mrs. Lucille Ball Arnaz
19700 Devonshire Blvd.
Chatsworth,
California

Pvt.
Co. C
S.C.
Arlington, California

CAMP ANZA JUN 4 130 PM 1943 CALIF.

SPECIAL DELIVERY UNITED STATES POSTAGE TEN CENTS 10

Private Desi Arnaz
Co. C. Group 496
S.C.U. 1950 Reception Center
Arlington, California
(3)

NEW YORK NOV 4 1130 PM 1940 GRAND CENTRAL

UNITED STATES POSTAGE 3 CENTS 3

UNITED STATES POSTAGE 2 CENTS 2

Special Delivery - Air Mail
Postage due 3 cents

Miss Lucille Ball
3403 North Laurel
Hollywood
California

Free

CAMP ANZA, CALIF. JUN 10 130 PM 1943

Co. C. Group 496
S.C.U. 1950 Reception Center
Arlington, California

Mrs. Lucille Ball Arnaz
19700 Devonshire Blvd.
Chatsworth

Private Desi Arnaz (3)
Co. C Group 496
S.C.U. 1950 Reception Center
Arlington, California

(3)
Private Desi Arnaz
Co. C. Group 496
S.C.U. 1950 Reception Center
Arlington, California

Free

Pvt. Desi Arnaz
Co. C. Group 496
S.C.U. 1950 Reception Center
Arlington, California

CAMP ANZA, CALIF. JUN 12 130 PM 1943

Mrs. Desi Arnaz
19700 Devonshire Blvd.
Chatsworth

Contents

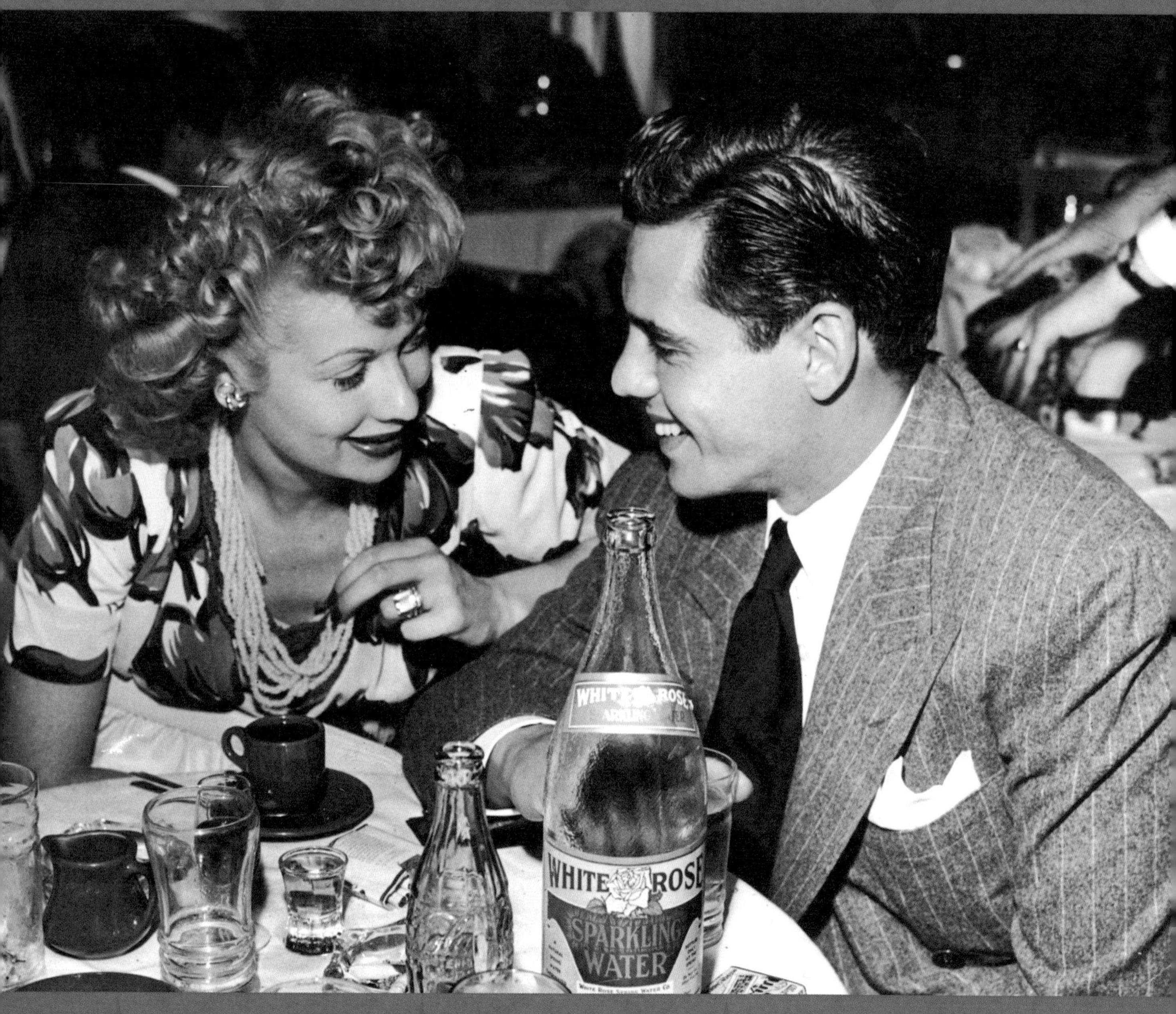
WHITE ROSE
SPARKLING
WATER

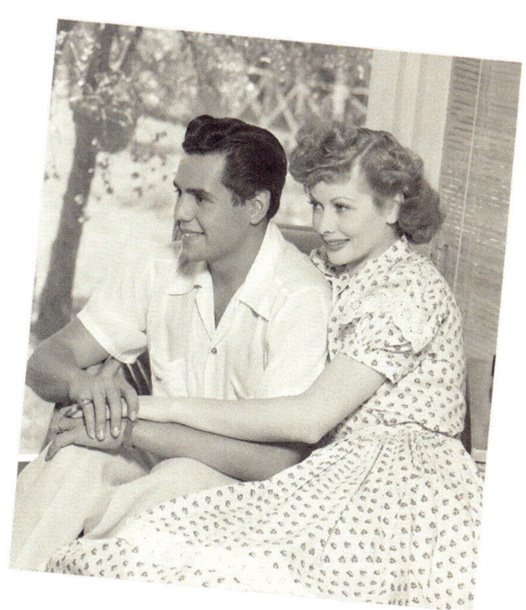

Introduction

ABOVE: At home together—their favorite activity

OPPOSITE: So in love

AFTER MY MOTHER DIED IN APRIL 1989 AND I STARTED going through her personal effects, I found a box with these meticulously saved, ribbon-wrapped, personal stationery letters from two people—herself and my father. They were, for the most part, written during World War II, when he was in the army and she was making movies in Hollywood. Those were the first few years of their marriage, and I discovered the letters showed their youthful, passionate, tempestuous, vulnerable, complicated relationship better than anything I've ever read about them anywhere else. For all that has been said and written about these two people who have captivated the world's attention both when they were at their peak starring in *I Love Lucy* and for the many decades since, there is nothing that captures their love story the way it's revealed through their own words.

Of course, at the time I found the letters, I thought they were very, very personal items that shouldn't be shared with just anyone, and so, for years, I kept them in a locked box not certain what I would eventually do with them. When we made our *Lucy & Desi: A Home Movie* in 1993, I used just a small sample of one from each of them to illustrate those years of loneliness when they were without each other, especially when my father was away in the army, much of the time in the hospital following a knee injury. But I hadn't known quite what to do with them since. I know they have to be preserved for historical purposes, but it also seems that people who love my parents might really enjoy experiencing them and seeing their handwriting—their personal handwriting—which is something we never really get a chance to see anymore, what with emails and typed letters and texts. You can understand a lot about a person by seeing the amount of space they take up on the page with their handwriting size, or the quality of the pen or maybe just a pencil that they had on hand. And there's a little snippet of history in every single one of the letters as well, when they talk about where they are, what they're doing, and what's going on in the world around them, whether it be a wardrobe fitting with a celebrated designer, getting a thank-you note from the commander of the US Army, or trying to buy *just the right* refrigerator to please your mother-in-law during wartime rationing. They almost come back to life in some respect, and I have so enjoyed reading and rereading these precious relics over the years to still feel close to my mother and father.

OPPOSITE: By the time my first birthday rolled around, *I Love Lucy* was already America's number-one television show.

Recently, it occurred to me that a lot of people might get some real value and benefit if I shared them. I wished I could share them exactly as they are—exactly as they look, how they feel, not just a typed version of their contents. So, as I have done in the past, I went to my friends at Running Press, who have made so many beautiful books with us, including the remarkable *Lucy & Desi: A Scrapbook*, which took actual items out of our family scrapbooks and digitized them in such a professional way that you'd swear you were holding the actual item. I asked my friend and editor Cindy Sipala at Running Press if she could visualize digitizing and transcribing them as part coffee-table/part art and historical reference book, and I was thrilled when she jumped at the chance.

But as much as I'd like the letters to be seen simply "as is," we realized some context could improve the experience. So, as you read through them here, keep in mind how different life was in the 1940s. At least in California, people could actually write a letter, put it in the mail early that morning, and the person they wrote it to—who may live hours away by car—would get to read it later that night. Sometimes Mom and Dad would write one, two, three letters to each other during a single day, as well as call each other nearly every night, so they hardly ever put a date on these letters. You'll see they might say "Saturday, 4:00 P.M." or "Sunday morning," which is charming. When I tried to put them in chronological order, it was a bit difficult to decipher the faded postmarks on the envelopes to see which letter came first. But that's also part of the charm and historical accuracy of the way these letters were written—so, too, are their occasional misspellings and imperfect grammar. We've also added a historical

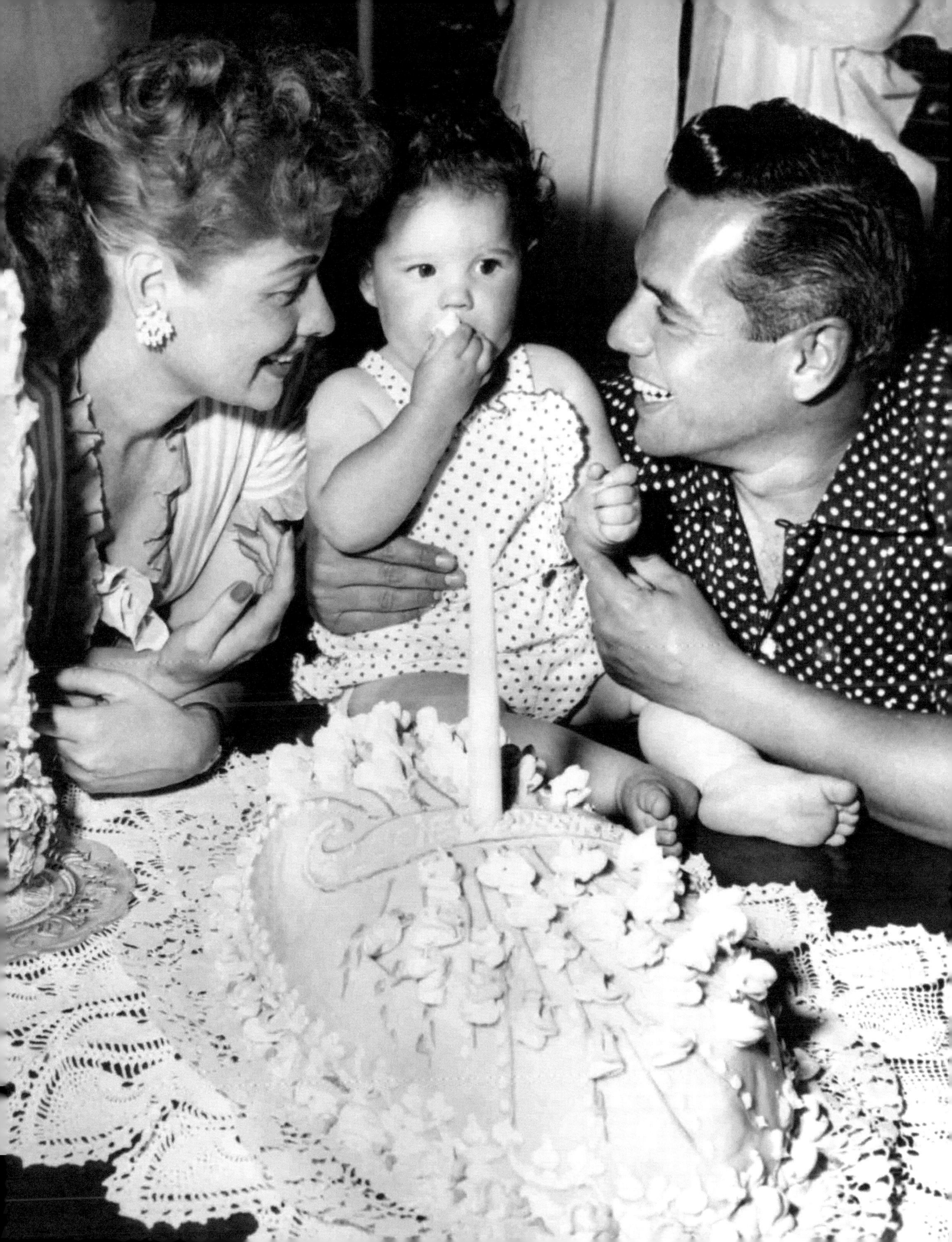

timeline starting on page 1 and notes toward the end, on page 209, to help readers understand who or what they're talking about, if in fact I even know.

My parents were married for almost twenty years. The fifty-ish letters in this book were written during a relatively small chunk of that time but are representative of their entire relationship in many ways. The early ones written during their courtship show passionate people in a budding romance. But the first decade of their marriage was defined by separation, because of work—Dad toured as a bandleader and Mom had a stable gig in Hollywood as a continuously working, if not big-time, movie star—and by world events. How that affected them is illustrated in the bulk of these letters written during wartime. In 1951, they started *I Love Lucy* as a show they hoped would keep them working and living life together and hopefully have some success with it, never expecting that it would be regarded as one of the best and most influential shows of all time more than three-quarters of a century later. Behind the scenes their marriage crumbled. You even get a glimpse of that in the last few letters of this collection.

I'm hoping that, like me, after reading these, you will feel closer to them and understand them as people even better. Because, as much as the world enjoyed them as Ricky and Lucy McGillicuddy Ricardo, they were not those people. But the people they were, were absolutely fascinating.

—*Lucie Arnaz*

Historical Timeline

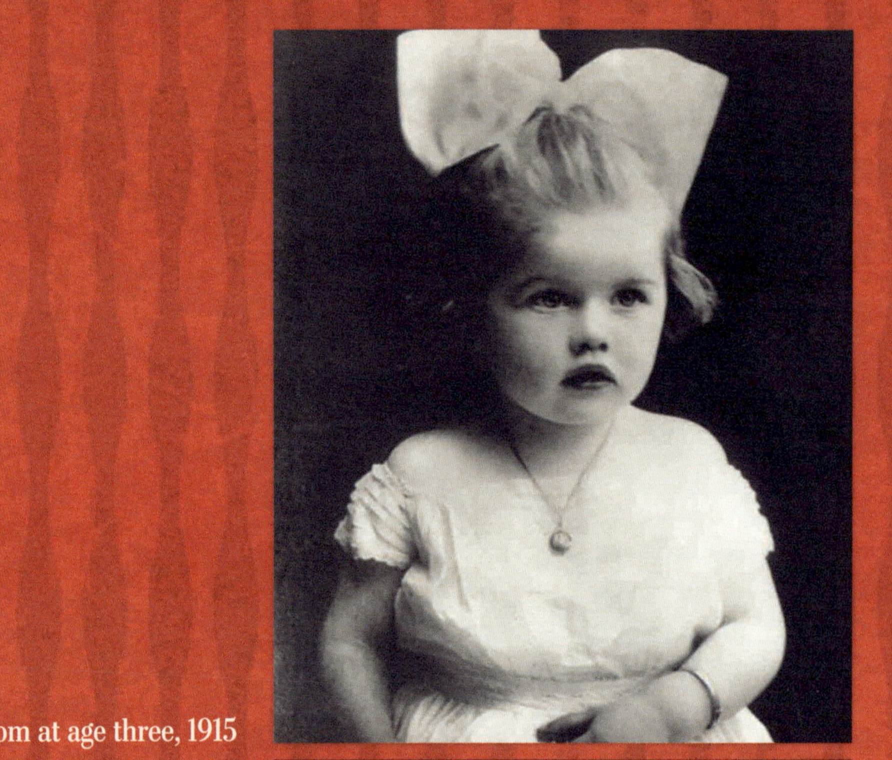

Mom at age three, 1915

1911

August 6: Lucille Desirée Ball born in Jamestown, New York.

September/October: Lucille Ball and her mother travel to Butte, Montana, to join father/husband Henry Durrell Ball.

1912

April 30: Universal Pictures is formed.

May 8: Paramount Pictures is founded.

1913

April 24: The Woolworth Building opens in New York; at the time it was the tallest building in the world.

October 13: The Lincoln Highway, a road stretching from Times Square in New York to Lincoln Park in San Francisco, is dedicated.

1914

February 13: The American Society of Composers, Authors and Publishers (ASCAP) is established in New York to protect copyrighted music.

July 28: A telegram declaring war between Austria-Hungary and Serbia is sent, the official start of World War I.

1915

January 25: The first transcontinental telephone call occurs between Alexander Graham Bell in New York and Thomas Watson in San Francisco.

February 28: Lucy's father, Henry Ball, dies of typhoid fever in Wyandotte, Michigan.

July 17: Lucy's brother, Frederick Henry Ball, is born in Jamestown, New York.

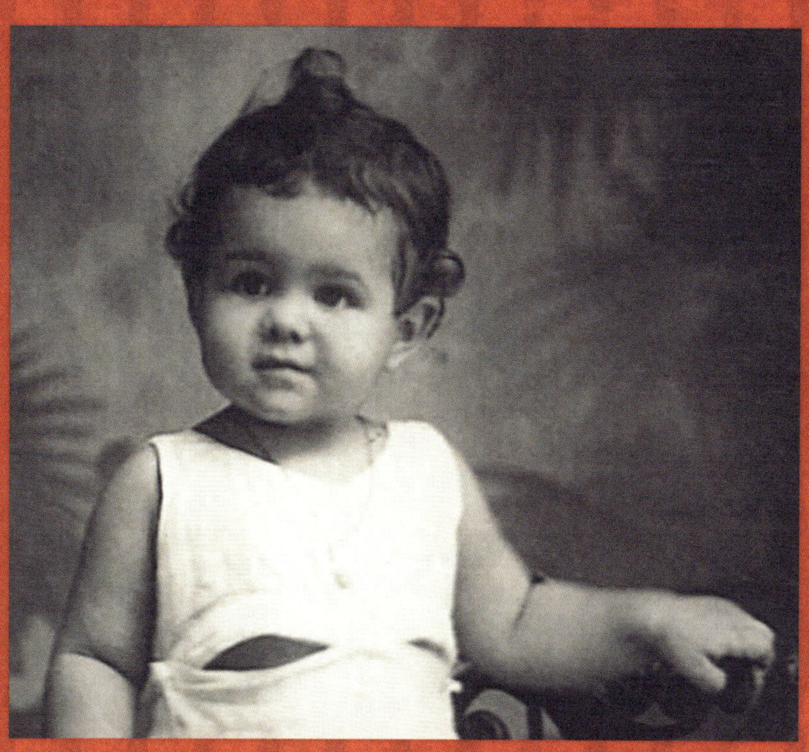
Dad at age three, 1920

1916

June 24: Mary Pickford is the first movie actress to sign a one-million-dollar contract, becoming one of the world's highest-paid individuals.

1917

March 2: Desiderio Alberto Arnaz III is born in Santiago de Cuba, Cuba.

April 6: The United States declares war on Germany, leading to its entry into World War I.

1918

May 15: The United States Post Office begins regular airmail service.

September 18: Desirée Hunt Ball marries her second husband, Edward Peterson, in Jamestown, New York.

November 11: An armistice is declared between Germany and the allied countries, officially ending World War I.

1919

February 5: United Artists is incorporated by Charlie Chaplin, Douglas Fairbanks, D. W. Griffith, and Mary Pickford for the purposes of film production and distribution.

September 1: The Communist Party of the United States of America (CPUSA) is established.

1920

August 18: The 19th Amendment to the US Constitution is ratified by Congress, giving women the right to vote in elections

1921

July 29: Adolf Hitler becomes head of the Nazi Party in Germany.

1923

December 29: The first US patent for "television systems" is filed by Vladimir Zworykin.

1925

October 2: John Logie Baird successfully transmits the first television picture from his laboratory in England.

September/October: Lucille leaves Jamestown to study at John Murray Anderson-Robert Milton Dramatic School in New York City.

1927

July 3: As the sole adult present during the accidental shooting of a neighbor boy, Lucy's grandfather was held responsible for the tragedy, leading to the loss of the Hunt family home and breakup of the family.

September 18: CBS is formed in the US with 47 radio stations.

1928

May 11: The first regular schedule of programming—consisting of farm and weather reports—begins on GE's television station W2XB in Schenectady, New York.

Mom made her film debut in *Roman Scandals*, 1933.

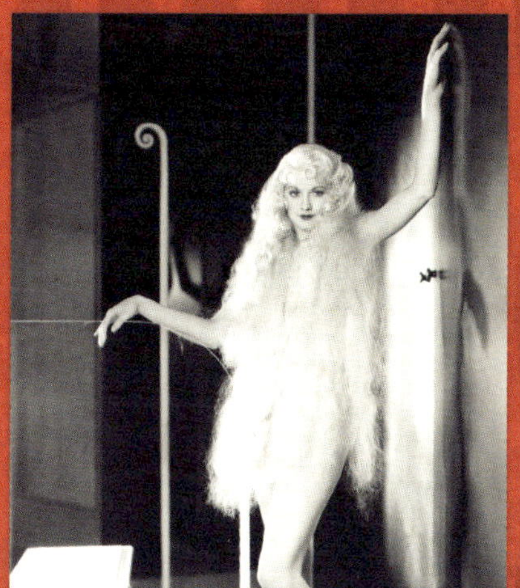

My father in Santiago, Cuba, in 1933

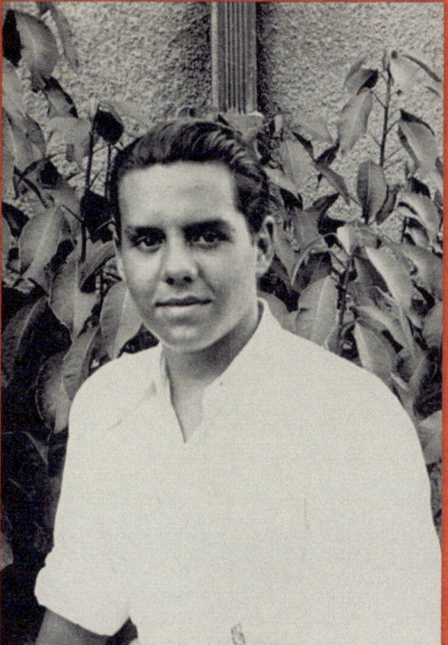

On the set of *Kid Millions* (1934)

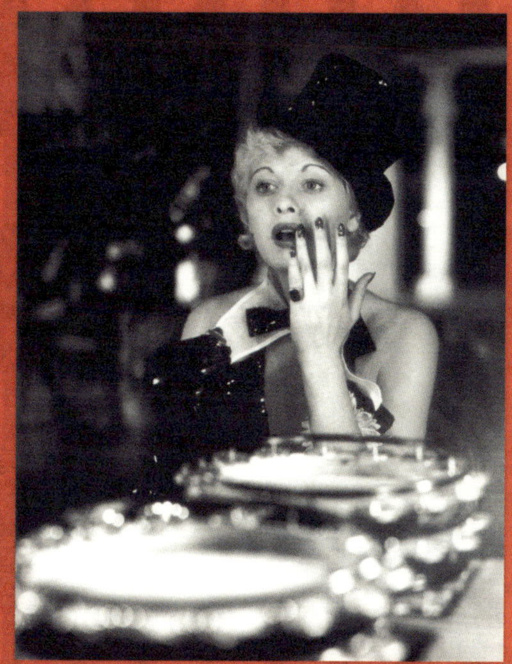

1929

October 24: The beginning of the Wall Street Crash, leading to the Great Depression.

1932

November: Desi's father, Desiderio Alberto Arnaz II, is elected to congress in Cuba under the presidency of Gerardo Machado.

1933

July: Lucy is offered a chorus girl role in the movie *Roman Scandals*, leading to her departure from New York for Hollywood to become a Goldwyn Girl.

August 12: Desi's home in Vista Alegre and all the Arnaz family farms and ranches are burned to the ground during a violent revolution. The Machado government collapses, Desi and his mother flee to Havana, and his father is imprisoned for a period of six months.

November 27: Samuel Goldwyn Productions releases *Roman Scandals*.

1934

Spring: Lucy rents a home at 1344 North Ogden Drive in Los Angeles, intent on bringing her family together under one roof.

June 27: Seventeen-year-old Desi arrives in Florida, reuniting with his father, who had been exiled there after his release from prison. The two settle in Miami, where Desi would work and finish high school.

Now a contract player at RKO

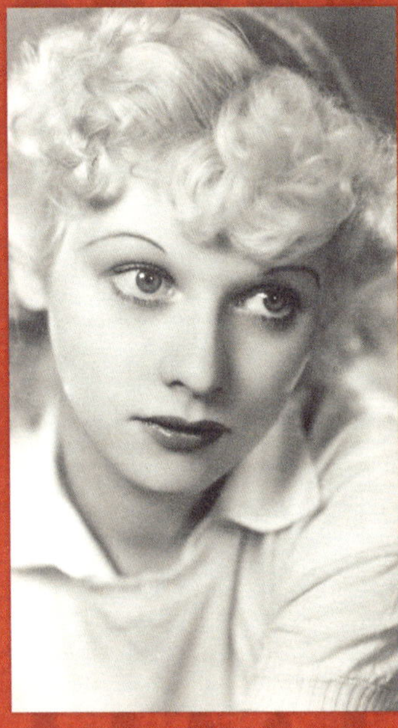

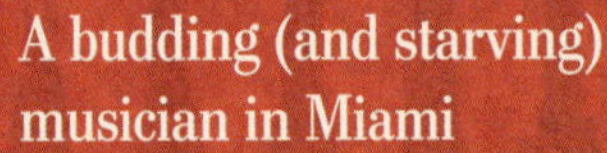

A budding (and starving) musician in Miami

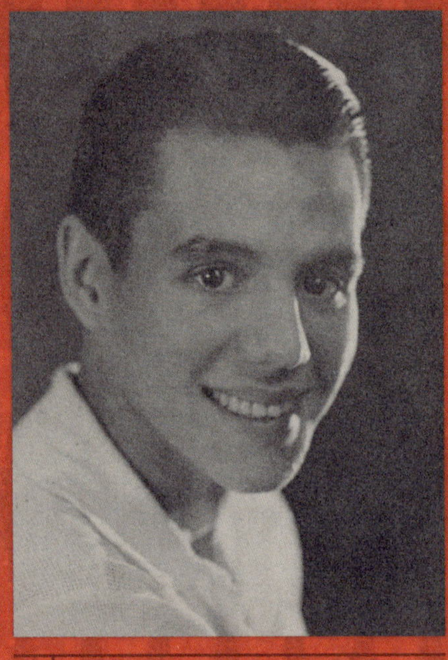

1935

March 20: Lucy signs a contract with RKO Radio Pictures for the weekly salary of $75. Her first credited role under this contract is in the movie *Follow the Fleet* starring Fred Astaire and Ginger Rogers and featuring an early appearance by future star Betty Grable.

1936

October 25: The Rome-Berlin Axis, a pact between Nazi Germany and fascist Italy, is formed, a major step on the road to World War II.

Winter: Desi is hired to work at the Roney Plaza in Miami Beach, playing in a band, The Siboney Septet. They are paid $39 a week.

1937

May 30: Desi graduates from St. Patrick's High School in Miami Beach, Florida.

Summer: Desi is hired by bandleader Xavier Cugat and leaves Florida for New York.

October 8: RKO releases the film *Stage Door*, starring Katharine Hepburn and Ginger Rogers. This is Lucy's breakout role, playing the part of Judy Canfield, a budding actress living at the Footlights Club.

December 27: Desi gets his first job with his own Latin band at Bobby Kelly's in Miami Beach. He introduces the conga (his "dance of desperation") to the United States, and it (and he) becomes such a hit that they change the name of the club to La Conga.

1938

March 12: Austria is annexed, becoming part of Nazi Germany.

September 21: The Marx Brothers' film *Room Service*, featuring Lucille Ball, is released.

September 29: The Sudetenland in Czechoslovakia is annexed and becomes part of Nazi Germany.

November 9: Kristallnacht (the night of broken glass, wherein Jewish businesses, homes, and people endured grave attacks) takes place in Germany.

November 30, 1940, happily Mr. and Mrs. after eloping to Connecticut

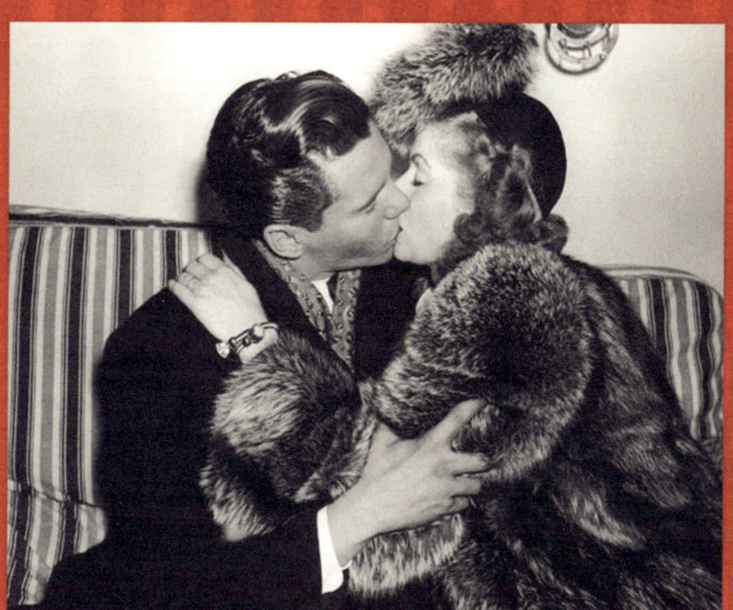

At home with their cow, named the Duchess of Devonshire

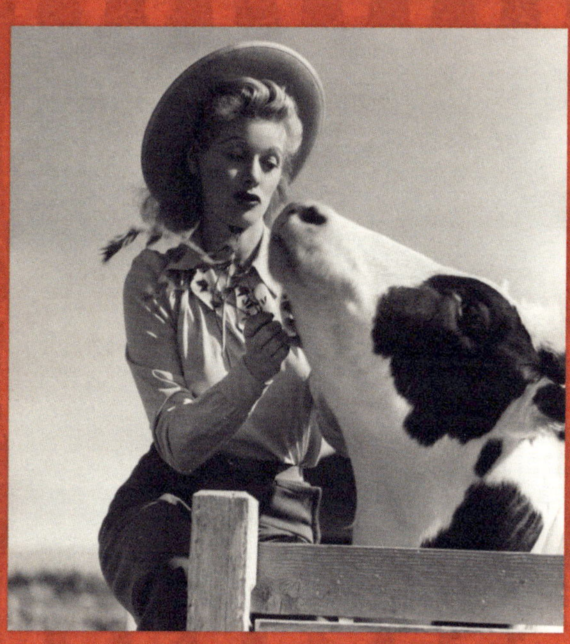

1939

September 1: Nazi Germany invades Poland, starting World War II.

October 18: Desi Arnaz makes his Broadway debut in the Rodgers and Hart musical comedy *Too Many Girls* at the Imperial Theatre.

November 6: *Hedda Hopper's Hollywood*, starring the gossip columnist, debuts on radio.

November 8: CBS television conducts test transmissions from the top of the Chrysler Building in New York.

1940

June: Lucy and Desi first meet on the set of RKO's *Too Many Girls.*

November 5: Franklin D. Roosevelt is reelected president of the United States for a third term.

October 8: *Too Many Girls* is released in US movie theaters.

November 30: Lucille Desirée Ball and Desiderio Alberto Arnaz III are united in marriage by Judge John J. O'Brien at the Byram River Beagle Club in Greenwich, Connecticut.

1941

March: Lucy and Desi find their new home in Chatsworth, California.

May 15: Desi is hired by RKO Radio Pictures to perform in two movies, which resulted in his appearances in *Four Jacks and a Jill* and *The Navy Comes Through*. After that, Desi is fired from RKO.

July 1: CBS Television begins commercial operations on WCBW in New York.

December 7: The US fleet at Pearl Harbor, Hawaii, is bombed.

December 8: The US and other Allied powers declare war on Japan.

December 11: The US declares war on Germany and Italy.

Publicity pose for their mutual studio, RKO

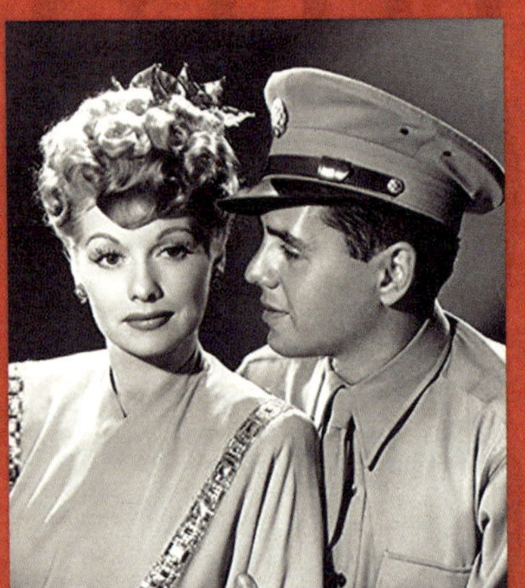

Dad, Mom, and my great-grandfather Fred Charles Hunt, in Los Angeles

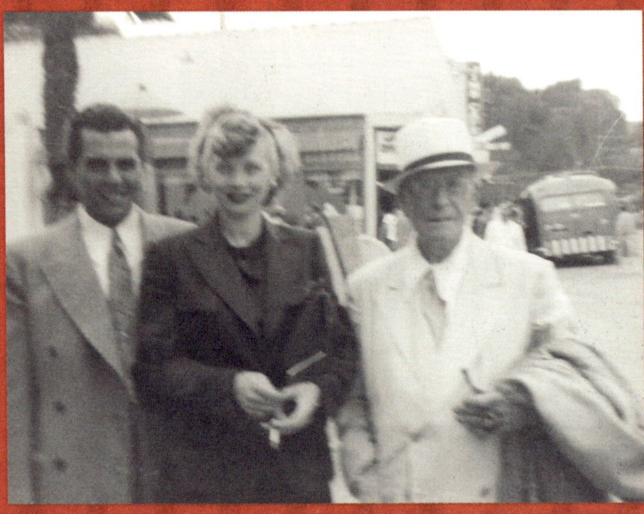

1942

January 16: Returning from a tour promoting war bonds, actress Carole Lombard (Lucy's mentor) is killed in a plane crash near Las Vegas.

April-May: Desi tours with the Hollywood Victory Caravan. Shortly thereafter, he meets with Louis B. Mayer and is picked up as a contract player for MGM.

1943

May: Desi receives his military draft notice.

May 23: Desi injures his knee in a baseball game while waiting to leave for bombardier training. Having passed all his tests for admittance into the US Air Force, he is very disappointed when this injury forces him to drop out of training.

June 3: Desi's MGM wartime movie, *Bataan*, is released.

October 1: Desi becomes a naturalized US citizen.

1944

January 9: Grandpa Frederick C. Hunt dies in Los Angeles, California, aged 78.

June 6: D-Day, the landing of Allied forces in France.

1945

April 12: President Franklin D. Roosevelt dies in Warm Springs, Georgia.

April 30: Adolf Hitler commits suicide in Berlin, Germany.

May 8: V-E Day, the official end of the war in Europe.

August 15: V-J Day, the official end of the war in Japan.

December 1: Staff Sergeant Desi Arnaz is honorably discharged from the US Army. For his service, he was awarded the Good Conduct Medal, the American Theater Campaign Medal, and the World War II Victory Medal.

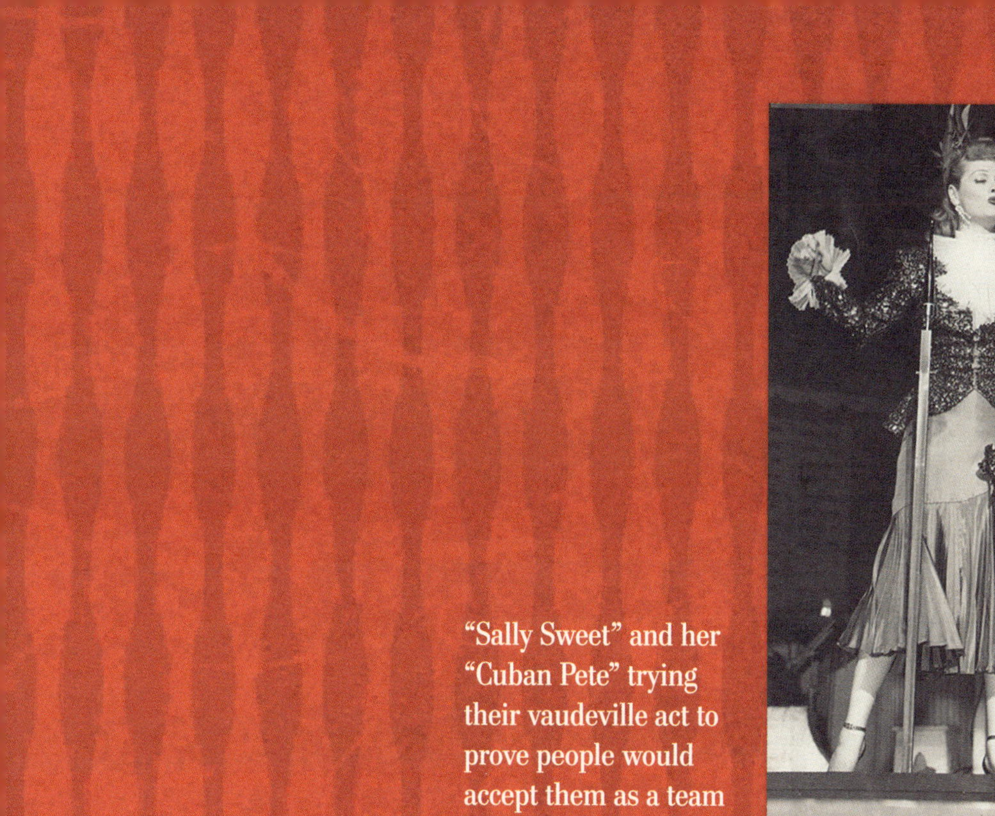

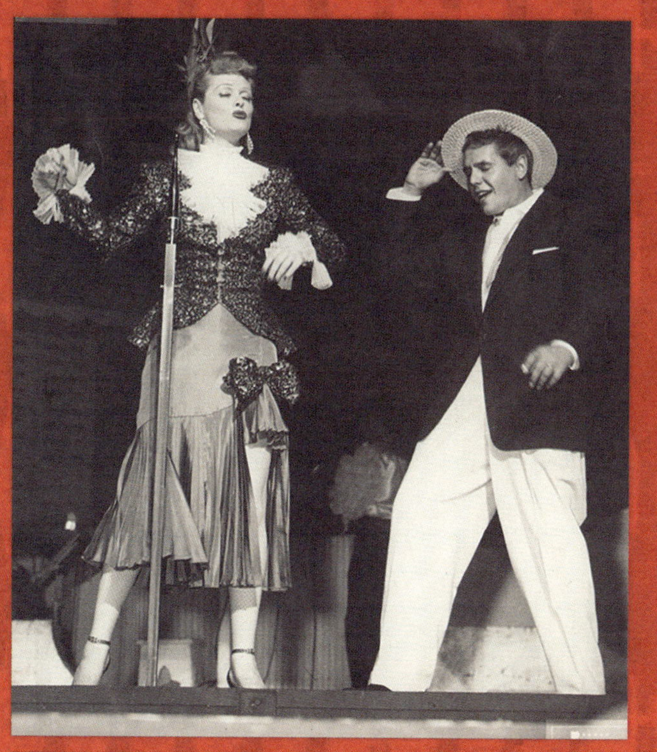

"Sally Sweet" and her "Cuban Pete" trying their vaudeville act to prove people would accept them as a team

1947

April 16: A TV camera zoom lens is demonstrated in New York.

November 17: The Screen Actors Guild (SAG) enacts an anti-communist loyalty oath for members.

1948

April 19: ABC begins broadcasting television programs.

July 5: The "audition" (pilot) episode of *My Favorite Husband* starring Lucille Ball and Lee Bowman premieres on CBS Radio. The series will debut a month later with Lucy and Richard Denning in the starring roles.

1949

June 23: Lucille Ball opens in *Dream Girl* at the McCarter Theatre in Princeton, New Jersey.

1950

June 2: Lucy and Desi's vaudeville act, showcasing them as a comedy duo, opens at the Chicago Paramount Theater. They will tour the show across the country.

October: The Starlite Room at the Chi Chi Club in Palm Springs opens with Desi Arnaz as the headliner.

1951

March 2: The pilot for *I Love Lucy* is shot (also Desi's 34th birthday).

March 31: The final episode of *My Favorite Husband* airs on CBS Radio.

July 17: Lucie Desirée Arnaz is born in Los Angeles, California.

August 6: Lucille Ball's 40th birthday.

September 3: First reading of an *I Love Lucy* script with the cast.

September 8: First episode of *I Love Lucy* is filmed.

October 15: *I Love Lucy* premieres at 9:00 P.M. on CBS.

In their cabbage rose haven in Chatsworth, California

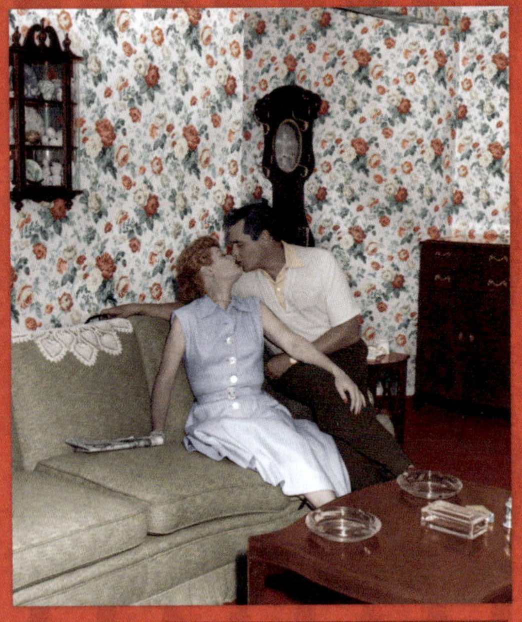

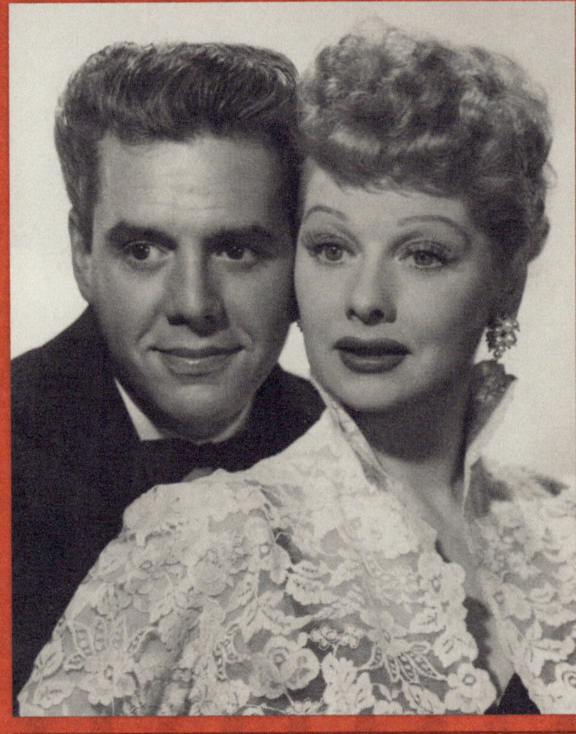

Imagine this was considered a "mixed marriage" in 1951!

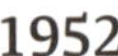

1952

February: *I Love Lucy* is the number one show for the first time.

April 3: Lucy testifies in her first confidential meeting before HUAC (the House Un-American Committee) about voting for communist candidates in 1936. She testifies that she registered communist to please her aging grandfather, Fred Hunt.

April 7: The American Research Bureau announces that an *I Love Lucy* episode ("The Marriage License") was the first television show in history to be seen in ten million homes.

June 18: Louella Parsons announces in her gossip column that there is a second Arnaz baby on the way.

July 29: Season two of *I Love Lucy* commences production early, with scripts approved by a priest, a minister, and a rabbi.

October 3: The first "pregnancy" episode, "Lucy Is Enceinte," using the French word for "pregnant," is filmed.

1953

January 19: Desiderio Alberto Arnaz IV is born in Los Angeles, California; Ricky Ricardo Jr. is born in New York City via CBS. The episode "Lucy Goes to the Hospital" garners record high television viewing with more than 44 million viewers and a 71.1 rating.

February 2: MGM announces plans for Lucy and Desi to star in a Technicolor movie comedy entitled *The Long, Long Trailer.*

February 5: *I Love Lucy* wins the Emmy for "Best Situation Comedy."

September 4: Lucy is asked to appear at a second confidential closed-door HUAC meeting. When shown a document appointing her as a delegate to the Communist State Central Committee, Lucy questioned the legitimacy of the document as she had not signed it, did not recognize it, and her name was misspelled. She did not remember voting. She stated, "I am not a Communist now. I have never been. I never wanted to be." She was cleared of all charges.

September 7: Walter Winchell's nationally syndicated radio show announces Lucy's HUAC testimony to the world.

September 11: Lucy and Desi report to the *I Love Lucy* set for filming of the first episode after the Communist announcement. They are overwhelmed with relief when CBS and MGM executives, sponsors, and audience members make it known that they are clearly behind them.

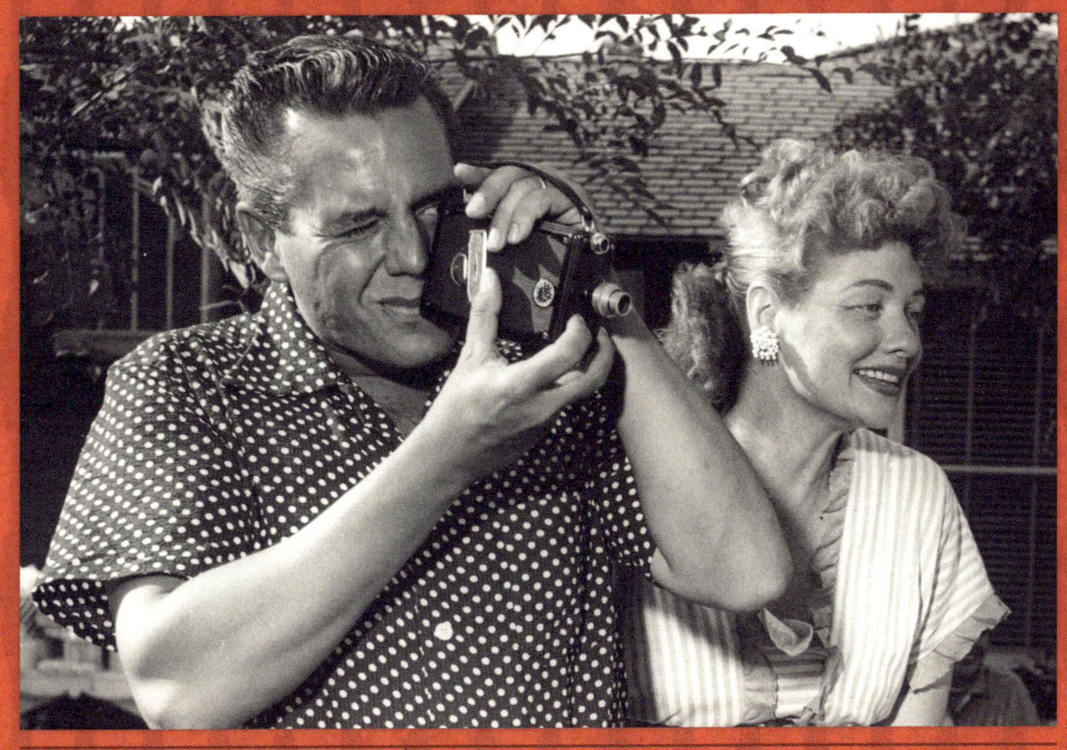

With this little Kodak 16mm color film camera (without sound) they preserved hundreds of hours of wonderful memories.

1954

February 18: MGM's *The Long, Long Trailer* is released in US theaters.

December: Lucy and Desi buy a house at 1000 North Roxbury in Beverly Hills, giving up their beloved Chatsworth ranch.

1955

June 14: Lucy and Desi begin filming *Forever Darling* for MGM.

1956

February 9: MGM's *Forever Darling* is released in US theaters.

October 1: Desilu sells all episodes of *I Love Lucy* to CBS for $4.3 million.

1957

March 2: Desi Arnaz's 40th birthday.

May 6: The final episode of *I Love Lucy* ("The Ricardos Dedicate a Statue") airs on CBS. Four-year-old Desi Arnaz Jr. makes a cameo appearance.

November 6: The first of 13 hour-long episodes of *The Lucille Ball–Desi Arnaz Show* airs on CBS.

December 11: Lucy and Desi purchase RKO's Gower Street and RKO-Pathé's Culver City lots, with its 457 furnished offices and 26 sound stages, for $6,150,000.

1959

May: In an attempt to salvage their failing marriage, Lucy and Desi, and the children, sail to Europe aboard the French liner *Liberté* for a six-week European vacation. Despite their good intentions, the trip did nothing to improve their relationship and rumors of divorce began to circulate around Hollywood.

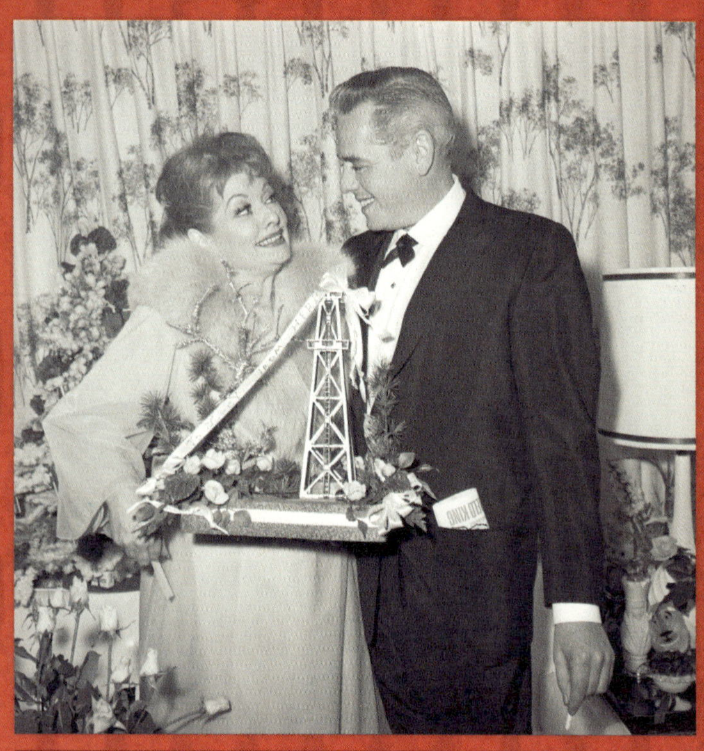

Dad continues to produce Mom's shows, including her Broadway musical, *Wildcat*.

1960

April 1: The final episode of *The Lucille Ball–Desi Arnaz Show* airs on CBS.

May 4: Lucy and Desi's divorce is finalized.

September: Lucy, her mother, and the children move to New York for her starring role in the Broadway musical *Wildcat*.

December 16: *Wildcat* opens at the Alvin Theatre.

December: Lucille Ball is introduced to comedian Gary Morton.

1961

May 24: Lucy's final performance in *Wildcat*.

November 19: Lucille Ball marries Gary Morton at the Marble Collegiate Church in New York.

1962

October 1: The first episode of *The Lucy Show*, starring Lucille Ball and Vivian Vance, premieres on CBS.

1963

March 2: Desi marries Edith Mack Hirsch.

1967

September 10: The Desi Arnaz series, *The Mothers-in-Law*, premieres on NBC.

Mom, in the film version of the Broadway musical *Mame*

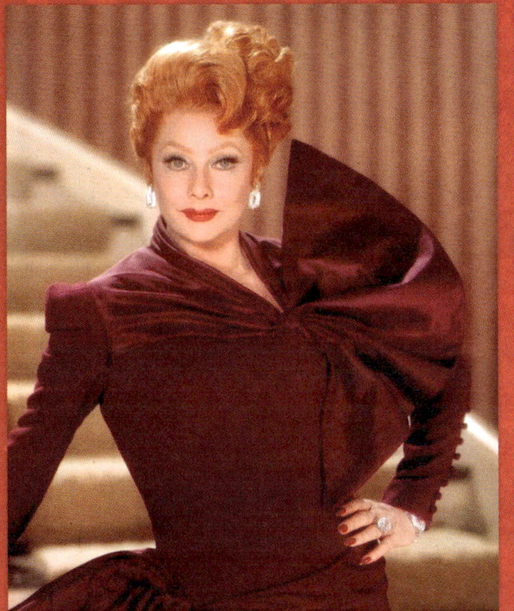

With my brother, Desi, and me, promoting her third TV series, *Here's Lucy*

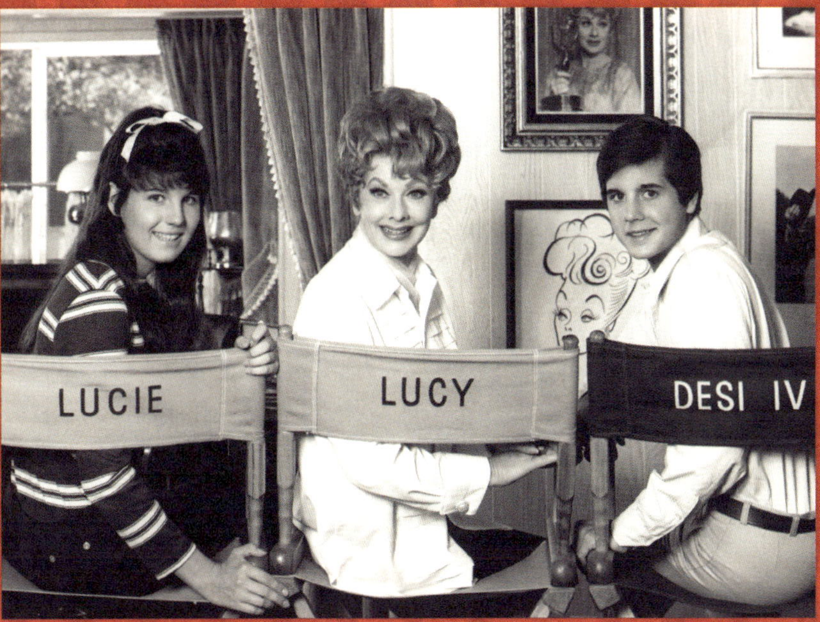

1968

March 11: The final episode of *The Lucy Show* airs on CBS.

April 24: The United Artists film *Yours, Mine and Ours*, starring Lucille Ball, Henry Fonda, and Van Johnson, is released in the US.

September 23: *Here's Lucy*, starring Lucille Ball, Gale Gordon, Lucie Arnaz, and Desi Arnaz Jr., premieres on CBS.

1969

April 13: The final episode of *The Mothers-in-Law* airs on NBC.

1974

March 7: Lucy's last movie, *Mame*, is released in the US.

March 18: The final episode of *Here's Lucy* airs on CBS.

1976

January 1: *A Book*, the autobiography of Desi Arnaz, is published.

1980

June 22: Lucie Arnaz marries actor Laurence Luckinbill in New York.

December 9: Simon Thomas Luckinbill, son of Lucie Arnaz and Laurence Luckinbill, is born in Los Angeles.

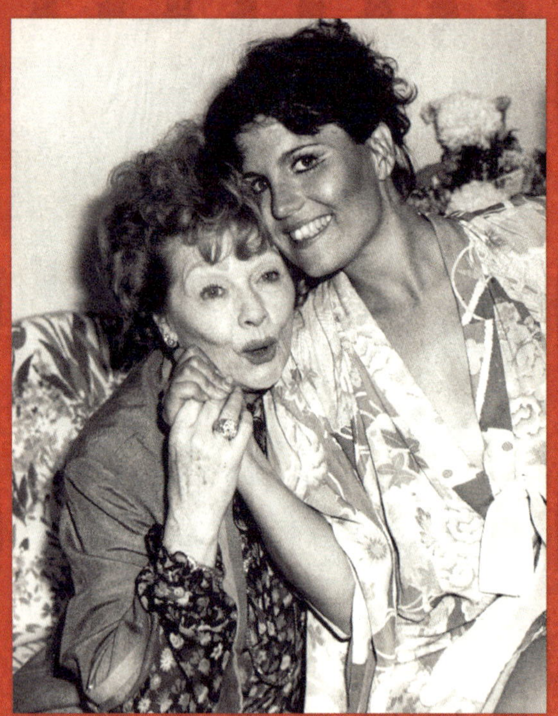

Mom and me backstage after my pre-Broadway opening in *They're Playing Our Song*

1982

December 31: Joseph Henry Luckinbill, son of Lucie Arnaz and Laurence Luckinbill, is born in New York.

1985

January 11: Katharine Desirée Luckinbill, daughter of Lucie Arnaz and Laurence Luckinbill, is born in New York.

March 25: Edie Arnaz passes away from cancer.

1986

September 20: *Life with Lucy*, starring Lucille Ball and Gale Gordon, premieres on ABC.

November 15: The final episode of *Life with Lucy* airs on ABC.

December 2: Desi Arnaz passes away from lung cancer in Del Mar, California.

1989

March 29: Lucille Ball makes her last public appearance at the Academy Awards at the Shrine Auditorium in Los Angeles, with longtime pal Bob Hope.

April 26: Lucille Ball passes away from complications following heart surgery in Los Angeles, California.

Love Letters

AIR-MAIL

NEW YORK, N.Y. OCT 17 11-PM 1940

AIR MAIL 6¢ NEW YORK WORLD'S FAIR

Miss. Lucille Ball.
1403 North Laurel

> The inevitable has happened: Lucille Ball and Desi Arnaz will be co-starred in a Gene Markey flicker. Lucille planes East later this month to eat her Thanksgiving turkey off Desi's fork.

Desi Arnaz

Monday.
5 P.M.

It was wonderful talking to you last nite (I mean this morning) you sounded as if you were next to me and I was trying to get you up to go to the studio. You are such a baby darling and I adore you, you monkey.

I'm enclosing a little something that was on Killgallen's column today, I don't know how she got it but I do hope it was true.

I just got back from M.C.A. and had a long talk with Lurow. Tomorrow at noon he is meeting Foyer, the man that handles Marion and we are definitely trying to get out of the show. Keep your fingers crossed. Will let you know.

…much that I
…do that show
…ld go out to the
…th you and
…cture, that I'm
…inking that I might
…o work it out, and
… here in New York
…y, and then you'll
… and this time
… or seven months,
… terrible, why can
…hat they really
… life is so short
… miseries, and
… you have a chance
…few happy years,
… to worry about con-
… money, and what's
…what's not good for you
…nderstand now why all
…rries about, it's to keep
working … as many pictures
as he can get in and make

Monday, 5 P.M.

It was wonderful talking to you last nite, I mean this morning, you sounded as if you were next to me and I was trying to get you up to go to the studio. You are such a baby darling and I adore you, you monkey.

I'm enclosing a little something that was on Killgallen's column today, I don't know how she got it but I do hope it was true.

I just got back from M.C.A. and had a long talk with Jurow. Tomorrow at noon he is meeting Foyer, the man that handles Marion and we are definitely trying to get out of the show. Keep your fingers crossed. Will let you know.

This spread and next: Sent from Meurice Hotel, West 58th Street, NYC to Hollywood, October 17, 1940.

Newspaper clipping attached: "The inevitable has happened: Lucille Ball and Desi Arnaz will be costarred in a Gene Markey flicker. Lucille planes East later this month to eat her Thanksgiving turkey off Desi's fork."

I wish so very much that I didn't have to do that show and that I could go out to the Coast and be with you and make that picture, that I'm going nuts thinking that I might not be able to work it out, and I will see you here in New York for a few days, and then you'll be gone again and this time it'll be six or seven months, oh honey, it's terrible, why can people do what they really want to do, life is so short and full of miseries, and then when you have a chance to spend a few happy years, you have to worry about contracts, and money, and what's good and what's not good for you.

I can understand now why all Carlson worries about, it's to keep working in as many pictures as he can get in and make the money he can, without worrying about being a star or bettering his career with stage play, and personal and so on. I think he got the right idea about life and that's why they're so happy. God bless them. By the way, how is their house coming along, I certainly hope they be very happy in it.

Don't let this lousy letter make you feel too bad, I guess I'm in a bad mood, but I'll snap out of it and become once more the smiling kid to whom everything looks beautiful and promising and the future it's something for the suckers to worry about.

I do love you. Desi P.S. I just found out that "Too Many Girls" is opening here around Thanksgiving at the "Criterion". Isn't that great? Damn it, damn it and you damn it once for me, will you? The CRITERION of all the God damn theaters in New York that will certainly help me the hell of a lot, I hope I'll be out of town by then. Sorry sweet, I'm in a worst mood now, but thank God, I still love you very much and I hope you love me—

Desi Arnaz

the money he can, without worrying about being a star or bettering his career with stage plays and personal and so on. I think he got the right idea about life and that's why they're so happy. God bless them.

By the way, how is their home coming along, I certa[...] they be very happy [...]

Don't let this lou[...] make you feel b[...] guess I'm in a ba[...] I'll snap out of it a[...] once more the [...] to whom everyth[...] beautiful and prom[...] future it's somethi[...] to worry about.

I do love y[...]

Desi Arnaz
Mevina Hot[...]
West 58th St
N. Y. C.

P.S.

I just found out that "Too Many Girls" is opening here around Thanksgiving at the "Criterion".

Isn't that great?

Damn it, damn it and you damn it once for me, will you? The CRITERION of all the god damn theaters in New York. That will certainly help me the hell of a lot. I'll be out of town by then.

Sorry sweet, I'm in a worst mood now, but thank God, I still love you very much and I hope you love me —

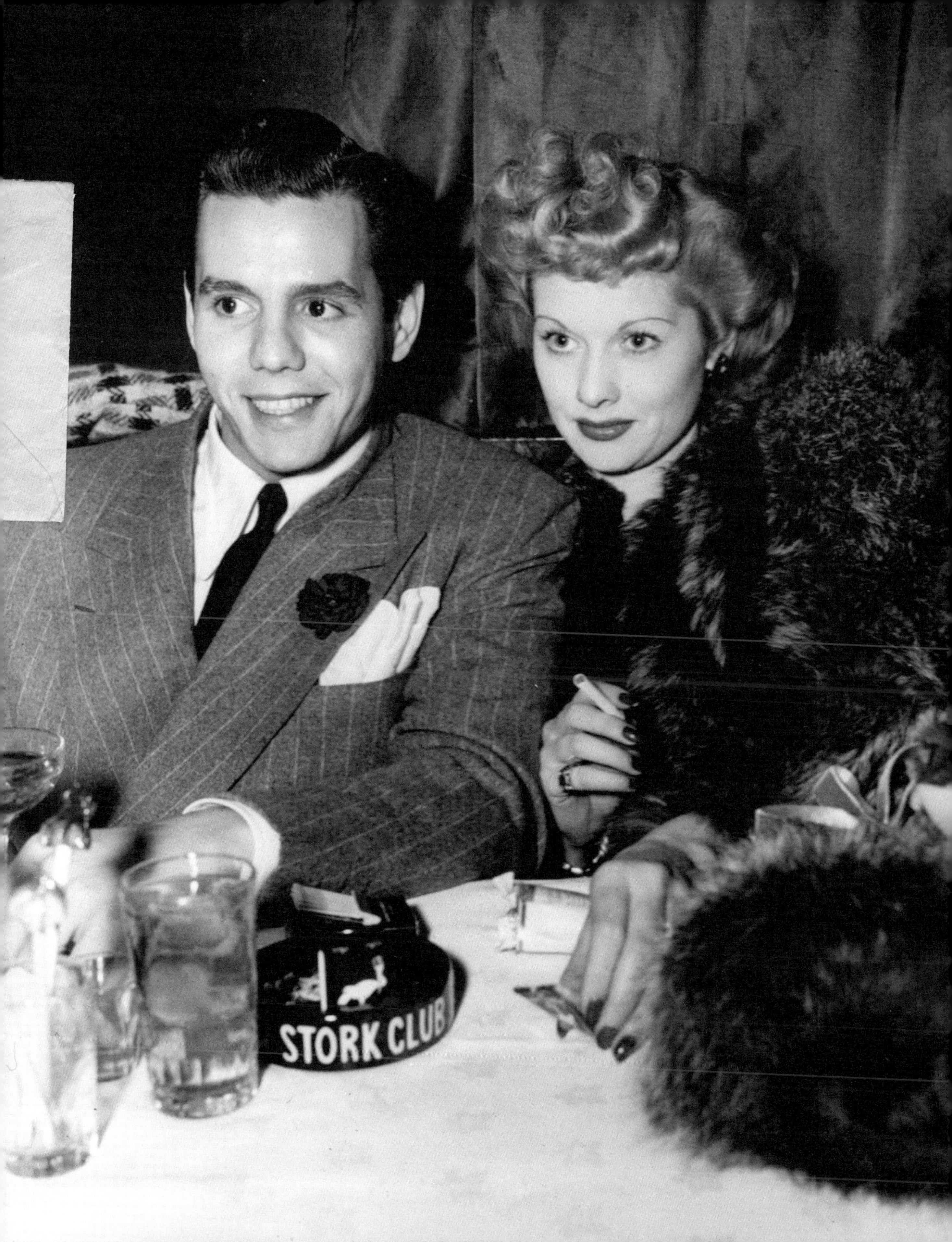
STORK CLUB

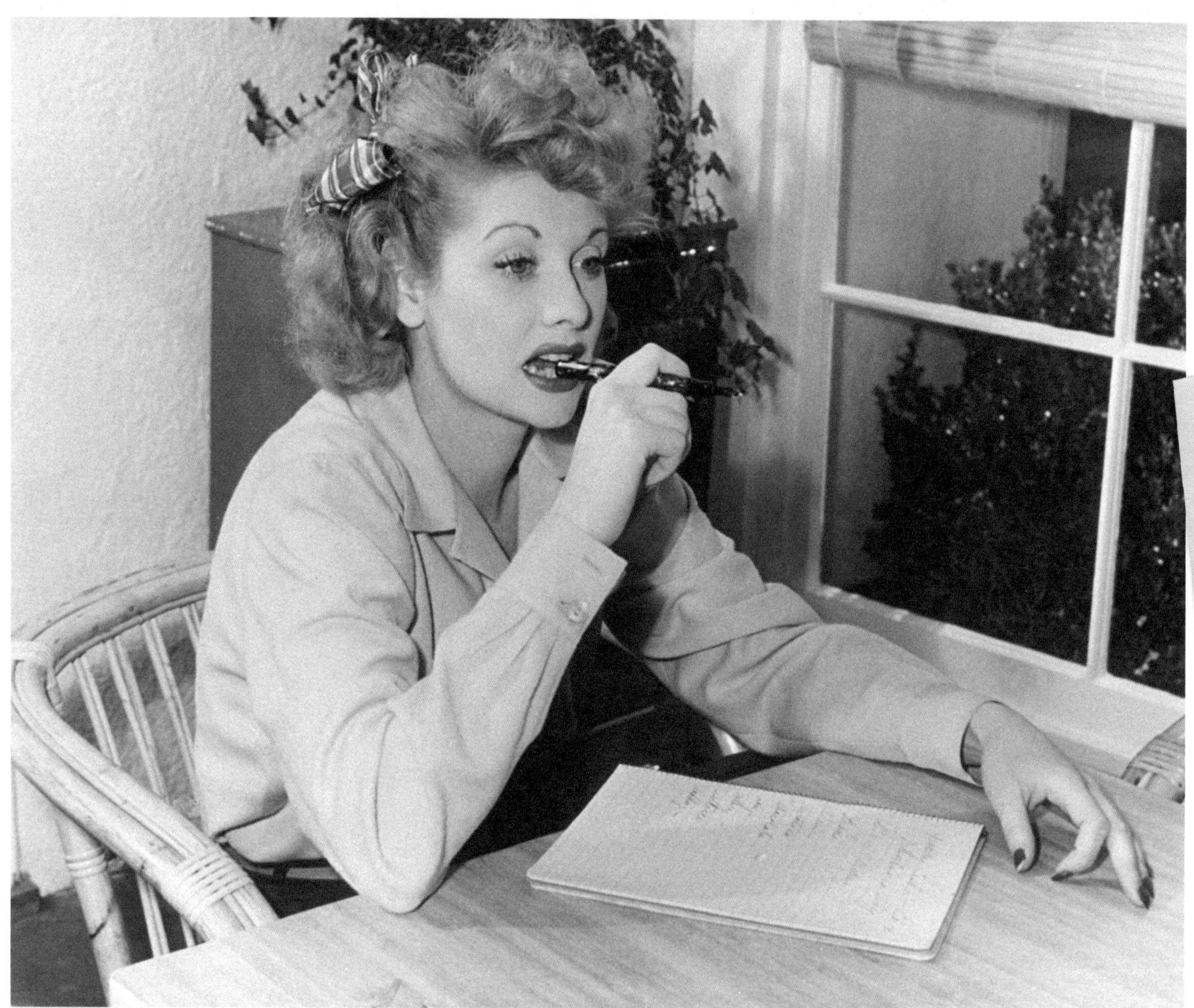

Tuesday

Good morning my Baby–

October 27, 1940

This is 7:35 A.M.—under a dryer—before breakfast—but I have already been thinking of you—let's see—for—exactly—one hour and twenty minutes. I think of you instantly upon waking—all day—all nite—until I go to sleep again. Maybe that's why you sounded so kinda sad + bored with me last nite.—I think of you so constantly—I wear you out—mental telepathy—maybe it's the same as being around me too much—I'd hate to risk that too—

Anyway—I'm going to send you a wire today—hoping you'll get an answer back by this afternoon telling me you are not as sad as you sounded—because Desi Baby listen—

Tuesday

Good morning my Baby –

This is 7:35 A.M. – under a dryer – before breakfast – but I have already been thinking of you – let's see – [illegible]tly – one hour and [illegible]nutes. I think [illegible]nstantly upon [illegible] all day – all [illegible] I go to sleep [illegible] Maybe that's [illegible]

[illegible]ast nite. – I think of you so constantly – I wear you out – mental telepathy – maybe it's the same as being around me too much – I'd hate to risk that too –

Anyway – I'm going to [illegible] you a wire today – hop[illegible] you'll get an answer bac[illegible] this afternoon telling [illegible] you are not as sad [illegible] you sounded – beca[illegible] Desi Baby listen

There are so many wonderful things in store for us – we neither of us should be sad for a moment – I know that now – you were trying to convince me of it – a while back – you are a little confused and indecisive these days so I'll tell you what you told me – only 20 times louder.

Separately or together – we both have so much

to look forward to in the almost *immediate* future—
We are going to have *so* much fun—make money—
Well — anyway—even if you wander away from me—I'll even be able to [illegible] —(of course [illegible] a little piece [illegible] my heart—along [illegible] so will you [illegible]lly—but while [illegible]

have fun together —
There — it's a little involved the way I wrote it—due to so many interruptions but you get the idea—
I'm "on the set" now—freez[illegible] to pieces—beautiful wint[illegible] we're having now—
I almost freeze ~~to~~ ev[illegible] nite—could you do any[illegible] about that do you thin[illegible]
Desi Arnaz—you ne[illegible] answer *anything* in my

letters! Do you throw them away and forget what I write about?
I'm trying to get this wir[illegible] off to you—and I'll be all sad myself tonite if I haven't had a wire in answer—
Gee Baby—for the firs[illegible] time—I'm beginning to see the "light"—This picture *will* end—it

won't go on forever —

I will see you ag
soon — some place
I will be able to kis
you again — as lon
as I can hold you

Darling — I love
so much this mornin
You will probably
this in the middle of
afternoon and not be
mood l
at all —

know how much I love yo
in the morning — try
and think of it when you
read this — because I'm
mad about you this A.M.

I tried to imagine you
right beside me before
I climbed out this early
dawn — but I'm afraid
do but the
do you

dislike reading this
stuff — tell me if you
do — or don't. — —

Tomorrow you say you
might get the answer on
your show status — mine
remains as before — so far
my vacation is as I asked
for it — from the day
I finish until Jan 3 —
If I have to pull a
phony breakdown — I'll
get some time off —!

There are so many wonderful things in store for us—we neither of us should be sad for a moment—I know that now—you were trying to convince me of it—a while back—you are a little confused and indecisive these days so I'll tell you what you told me—only 20 times louder.

Separately or together—we both have so much to look forward to in the almost immediate future—We are going to have so much fun—make money—

Well—anyway—even if you wander away from me—I'll even be able to survive that—(of course you'd take a little piece right out of my heart—along with you) and so will you survive—naturally—but while it's fun—we might as well have fun together—

There—it's a little involved the way I wrote it—due to so many interruptions but you get the idea—I'm "on the set" now—freezing to pieces—beautiful winter we're having now—

I almost freeze every nite—could you do anything about that do you think?

Desi Arnaz—you never answer anything in my letters! Do you throw them away and forget what I write about?

I'm trying to get this wire off to you—and I'll be all sad myself tonite if I haven't had a wire in answer—

Gee Baby—for the first time—I'm beginning to see the "light"—this picture will end—it won't go on forever—

I will see you again soon—some place—I will be able to kiss you again—as long as I can hold you down.

Darling—I love you so much this morning—You will probably receive this in the middle of the afternoon and not be in a mood like mine at all—but you know how much I love you in the mornings—try and think of it when you read this—because I'm mad about you this A.M.

I tried to imagine you right beside me before I climbed out this early dawn—but I'm afraid noting will do but the real you!

I wonder—do you dislike reading this stuff—tell me if you do—or don't—

Tomorrow you say you might get the answer on your show status—mine remains as before—so far my vacation is as I asked for it—from the day I finish until Jan 3—If I have to pull a phony breakdown—I'll get some time off—! unless they want me to work with you—then in that case—I'll snap out of it quickly—if I have the strength—really I am tired—and would so welcome a vacation—

unless they want me to
work with you — th
in that case — I'm
out of it quickly
I have the strength
really I am tired
and would so we
a vacation —
Palm Springs wou
be wond

if I can have you —
otherwise I won't —
Please don't jeopardize
the next few months
with those awful dames
I dislike so — Please
don't prefer them instead
me — really darling
won't be worth it —

try & make you happy —
without counting ev
hour with you — li
two condemned cr

This little item I
enclosing originat
New York as you a
so don't know wh
offender is — but
sort of thing tha
me — "Miss Bal
publicly stated sw

that she — etc etc etc" —
I've never heard of the
show — & who the hell
wants to work with Max
Baer!?

Evan Frankel came in
to take a look at you
last nite, didn't he? He
couldn't stand it any longer.
He called me & told me
how good you were — and
wanted my assurance that
I really loved you —

was true about ... married — I quieted his fears in that direction — ... thought you were ... ally something ... — but like all ... good friends — ... ut to see me ... etc for 15 min. ... eciate his interest ... wish

people wouldn't remind me constantly about how unhappy you are going to make me — I hope I've been so unhappy over you as I can get — I don't know h... can top that ... week I put ... please tell ... I've never, ... unhappy over ... Please tell

No — I can't say goodbye yet — have a few more minutes I think — tell ... darling — can't you ... just a little more ... in your letters — yo... next one — and tell ... really what you a... about us — whil... bouncing around ... Can't you tell me ... on in your mind ... one day — as I tell you —

not just ... & when you ... but — jus... you so often ... what plea... thinking — ... I mean — ...

Gotta ...

All ... to you...

Palm Springs would be wonderful Desiderio. I know you'd love it so if that is as far as I can get I'll be satisfied—if I can have you—otherwise I won't—

Please don't jeopardize the next few months with these awful dames I dislike so—Please *don't* prefer them instead of me—really darling it won't be worth it—

Are you taking care of yourself? *Are* you getting any rest? Wish I could really have a chance to *try* to make you happy—without counting every hour with you—like two condemned criminals.

This little item I'm enclosing originated in New York as you can see—so don't know who the offender is—but it's the sort of thing that "burns" me—"Miss Ball has *publicly* *stated* *several* times that she—etc etc etc"—

I've never heard of the show—+ who the hell wants to work with Max Baer!?

Evan Frankel came in to take a look at you last nite, didn't he? He couldn't stand it any longer. He called me + told me how good you were—and wanted my assurance that I really loved you—Wanted to know if it was true about our getting married—I quieted his fears in that direction—

They thought you were swell—really something special—but like all my really good friends—don't want to see me hurt etc etc for 15 min. I appreciate his interest + I'm glad he liked you so much—but I do wish people wouldn't remind me constantly about how unhappy you are going to make me—I hope I've *been* as unhappy over you as I can get—I don't know how *anything* can top that suicidal week I put in—please tell me Precious. I'll never, *never* be that unhappy over you again.

Please tell me—Bye—

No—I can't say goodbye yet—have a few more minutes I think—tell me darling—can't you be just a *little* more explicit in your letters—your next one—and tell me really what you do think about me—while you're bouncing around New York. Can't you tell me what goes on in your mind even one day—as *I* tell *you*—not just what you do + when you do it—but—just as I ask you so often out here—what *please* are you thinking—about us I mean—

Gotta go now—all my love to you my baby

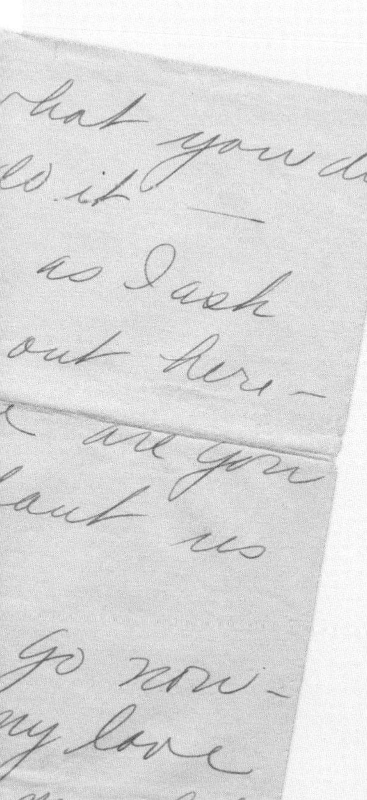
hat you do
do it —
as I ask
out here —
are you
about us
Go now —
my love
my baby.

Sunday

Hello darling:

I have slept all day today and here in the club now is that I'm writing to you. Away from the mob, downstairs. It's awfully crowded and I should be very happy about the whole thing, but I'm not, I'm tired of clubs, tired of people, of New York and most of all, I'm awful tired of being away from you, but everything has an ending and I guess, we'll just have to wait a few more weeks.

This uncertain situation in which I find myself, has me very worried. This show that I'm supposed to do and which looks very, very indefinite at the moment, without anybody knowing who's the producer or the cast, or the backers, or where do they start rehearsing, or anything.

Larry Hart had a long talk with me about it and he said I should have never signed under these conditions. I don't know if you remember or not, but I had a hunch that something wasn't right, I should have played my hunch as I've done in the past always, I guess, I was counting too much on my good luck.

I'll be here at the Versailles until the 14th of Nov., after that I don't know what's what, I know I must keep working, and I will, someplace, somewhere, but just now I don't know. I'm terribly sorry I have to keep you guessing where I'm going to be and what I'm going to do, but sweetheart, really it's not my fault, and I would be very happy if I could tell you.

My mamy doesn't want to go to Cuba now, in a way I don't blame her, it's really not very nice for her to front all of her friends after her divorce and so on, but she must go sometime to fix her paper, so I might convince her to go now and get it over with.

If she doesn't go, I'm going to try not to be in New York for your vacation, and maybe you can spend it someplace else wherever I'm at. Because I want to be with you and be with you all the time, without having to tell lies and be watching the clock all the time.

As you know, I'm trying to get out of this damn show and I hope I can. I'm writing Wasserman a long letter explaining the whole thing and asking him about the possibilities of a picture as soon as possible.

Sweetheart please be patient for a few more days and I assure you that I could tell you something more definite soon.

I have to go downstairs and say hello to a few of the mob, I'll finish this later, if not tomorrow.

So long darling, I love you very much.

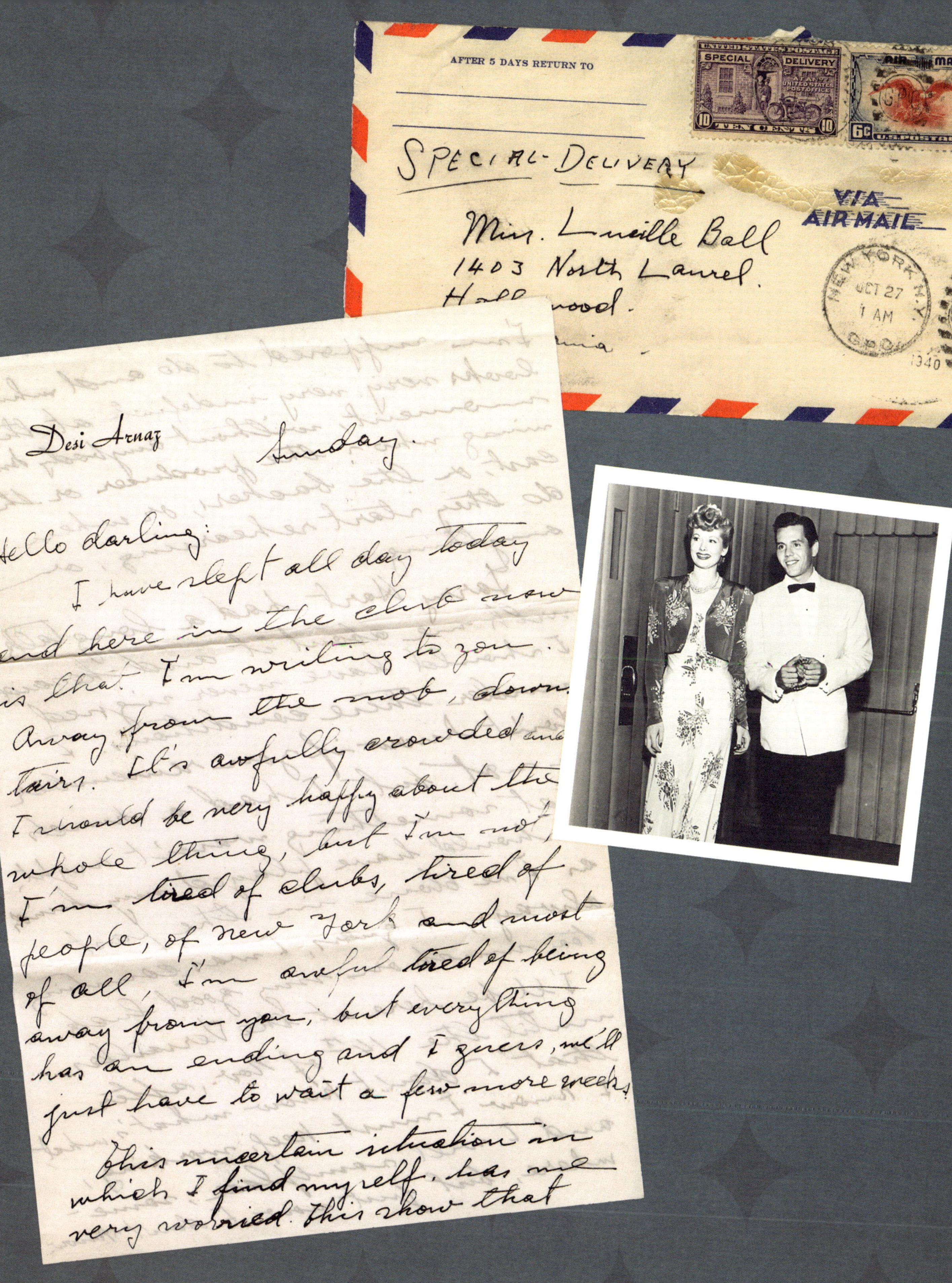
AFTER 5 DAYS RETURN TO

UNITED STATES POSTAGE SPECIAL DELIVERY AT ANY UNITED STATES POST OFFICE 10 TEN CENTS 10

AIR MAIL 6c U.S. POSTAGE

SPECIAL-DELIVERY

VIA AIR MAIL

Miss. Lucille Ball
1403 North Laurel.
Hollywood.
California

NEW YORK N.Y. OCT 27 1 AM 1940

Desi Arnaz

Sunday.

Hello darling:

I have slept all day today and here in the club now is that I'm writing to you. Away from the mob, downstairs. It's awfully crowded and I should be very happy about the whole thing, but I'm not, I'm tired of clubs, tired of people, of New York and most of all, I'm awful tired of being away from you, but everything has an ending and I guess, we'll just have to wait a few more weeks.

This uncertain situation in which I find myself, has me very worried. This show that

I'm supposed to do and which looks very, very indefinite at the moment, without anybody knowing who's the producer or the cast, or the backers, or where do they start rehearsing, or anything.

Larry Hart had a long talk with me about it and he said I should have never signed under these conditions. I don't know if you remembe[r] or not, but I had a hunc[h] that something wasn't rig[ht] I should have played my h[and] as I've done in the past always, I guess, I was coun[ting] too much on my good luc[k]

I'll be here at the Versaille[s] until the 14th of Nov., afte[r] that I don't know what I know I must keep worki[ng] and I will, someplace, so[me]where, but just now I do[n't]

Desi Arnaz

I'm terribly sorr[y to] keep you guessing [what's] going to be and wh[at I'm] to do, but sweethea[rt it's] not my fault, a[nd I'd] be very happy if I

My mammy doesn't w[ant] now, in a way I [know] her, it's really not for her to front all after her divorce a[nd] but she must go ro[und] her paper, so I mig[ht] her to go now an[d] with.

If she doesn't go, I'm not to be in New Yor[k] vacation, and mayb[e] spend it someplace el[se] I'm at. Because I wan[t] you and be with you time, without havin[g]

lies and be watching the clock
all the time.

As you know I'm trying to get
out of this damma show and
I hope I can. I'm writing
Wasserman a long letter
explaining the whole thing and
asking him about the possibi
lities of a picture as soon as
possible.

Sweetheart please be patient
for a few more days and
I assure you that I could tell
you something more definite
soon.

I have to go downstairs and
say hello to a few of the
mob, I'll finish this later,
if not tomorrow.

So long darling, I love you
very much.

I have to
here I'm
t I'm going
, really it's
t I would
ould tell you.

t to go to Cuba
it Hama
ery nice
t her friends
d so on,
time to fix
t convince
t it over

oing to try
for your
you can
whenever
to be with
all the
to tell

This envelope approved by the U. S. Post Office Dept.
for Air Mail Only. Use for other purposes not permitted.

And Good morning My
Handsome Little Man—
This is Wed—under that
same damn dryer—one
hour out of dreamland—
and I hasten to say—
you had better get back
to me—or I had better
get to you—but soon!
(If you don't mind my
mentioning it—) my
dreams are so realistic about
you—it makes waking up a

...le dis-appointment.
...ay—you get the
...s trying to convey—
though you apparently
don't get the dreams—
you never mention them
anyway—
In case you're interested—
I do think I'll wait—
for you— as if you
didn't know I would—
Wish you could honestly
say the same— S'easy

And Good morning my Handsome Little Man–

This is Wed—under that same damn dryer—one hour out of dreamland—and I hasten to say—<u>you</u> had better get back to me—or I had better get to you—but <u>soon</u>!

(If you don't mind my mentioning it—) my dreams are <u>so</u> realistic about you—it makes waking up a horrible disappointment.

Anyway—you get the idea I'm trying to convey—though you apparently don't get the dreams—you never mention them anyway—

In case you're interested—I do think <u>I'll</u> wait for you—as if you didn't <u>know</u> I would—wish <u>you</u> could honestly say the same—S'easy to see what mood I get up with these days isn't it? S'awful to be writing such things to <u>anyone</u>—but what-the-hell—I'm in love—

Late October 1940

This letter was written about a month before their marriage. The photo captures the new Mr. and Mrs. Arnaz on their wedding day.

Today you're s'posed to find out about your show. You probably won't be able to know exactly what's to happen—for days—<u>So</u> more indecision to worry about.

Am enclosing your horoscope—not anything to get excited about—but here it is—

Papers today said "R.K.O. has turned down Argentine Producers who wanted to do a stage musical with Desi Arnaz + Lucille Ball."—Every day there is something—and thank God—<u>some</u> of it is alright—

Going on the air tomorrow nite. "Hollywood for Roosevelt" program—I'm not politically minded but am working with Groucho Marx + the spot seems to be very funny—so—

I'll probably wire you about it before you get this—if everything goes alright at rehearsal tonite—

Got a card from Tessie—says she's been very ill—why don't you call her—I'm going to write her—please give her my love in the meantime. The other kids too—if you see 'em—

Please please please answer some of my questions in my other letters—if you still have the letters—and here's one to answer in particular—what do you do with my letters? Do you have to tear them up or what—

Some of the things I very much want answered—your Mom going to Cuba? What are you going to do with your car? What + how do you think about us? What about your show? Did you get yourself some nice new clothes? etc etc etc—

to see what mood I get up with these days isnt it? S'awful to be writing such things to anyone — but what-the-hell — I'm in love —

Today you're s'posed to find out about your show. You probably won't be able to know exactly what's to happen — for days — So more indecision to worry about.

Am enclosing your horoscope — not anything to get excited about — but here it is —

Papers today said "R.K.O. has turned down Argentine Producers who wanted [to] do a stage musical [wi]th Desi Arnaz & Lucille [Ba]ll." — Every day [the]re is something — and [tha]nk god — some of it [is] alright

Going on the air to~~t~~nite. "Hollywood for Roosevelt" program — [I'm] not politically minded [but] am working with Groucho Marx & the spot seems [to] be very funny — so — I'll probably wire you about it before you ge[t] this — if everything go[es] alright at rehearsal tonite —

Got a card from

Jessie — says she's been very ill — why don't you call her — I'm going to write her — please give her my love in the meantime. The other kids too — if you see 'em —

Please please please answer some of my questions in my other letters — if you still have the letters — and here's one to answer in

particular – what do you do
with my letters? Do you have
to tear them up or what –
~~Some of the things I very~~
want answered – Your Mom,
to Cuba? What are you go
to do with your car? Wh
& how do you think abo
What about your show?
you get yourself some n
new clothes? etc etc et

My God – don't even
the tour until you

have to! I don't want
that to think about. You
mentioned my being able
to go with you – Of course
I couldn't – my God it
would be three times cheaper
for me to bring you here
with me – for both of us.
Anyway ———

Please write again –
a long letter this time –
please darling –

Didn't you like Evan
Frankel – the jerk?

I'll tell Edington wha
you said about the S
press preview yesterday
I think they are begin
to give me the pressure via
the publicity dept – about
that Butler picture I
said I didn't want to do
in favor of a vacation –
I dunno for sure – but –

Do you know when you
seem very, very close to
me – anytime I'm in these
places – you do not seem
3000 miles away – 1st my bedroom – and damn that
phone – 2nd my dressing room
and ditto the phone –
3rd a movie – any movie –
4th the makeup dept – I can
hear you there every morning
5th The recording stage – 2A or B –
6th And the Still gallery –

My God—don't even think of a tour until you just have to! I don't want that to think about. You mentioned my being able to go with you—of course I couldn't—my God it would be three times cheaper for me to bring you here with me—for both of us.

Anyway—

Please write again—a long letter this time—please darling—

Didn't you like Evan Frankel—the jerk?

I'll tell Edingtow what you said about the S.A. press preview yesterday.

I think they are beginning to give me the pressure via the publicity dept—about that Butler picture I said I didn't want to do in favor of a vacation—I don'no for sure—but—

Do you know when you seem very, very close to me—anytime I'm in these places—you do not seem 3000 miles away—1st my bedroom—and damn that phone—2nd my dressing room and ditto the phone—3rd a movie—any movie—4th the makeup dept—I can hear you there every morning—5th the recording stage—2A or B—6th and the still gallery—

—¤¤¤—

Desi Darling

This is still Wednesday. 1:30 P.M. Wrote you this morning already—but just found these proofs and wanted you to see them—on your honor to return them all to me immediately for my scrapbook.

I love them all—they make me very, very lonesome for you this afternoon—I'm still in the same "mood" I was in this morning incidentally—

Dick and I were talking about you when that one was taken—

I love the one with you in the background—not aware of the photog—

Be sure darling—return them to me pronto—thanks—

I'm on the set now—no time to write—

Everyone says hello to you every day—I love you—

Gonna talk with Wasserman today I hope—will tell you more about the Markey picture as soon as possible—

Perry Lieber just came + told me I am to go to Milwaukee the 24th or 25th—

My God—

More plans!

Goodbye

Desi darling
This is still Wednesday -
1:30 P.M. Wrote you this
morning already - but
just found these proofs
and wanted you to see
them - on your honor
to return them all to me
immediately for my scrap
book.
I love them all - they
make me very, very lonesom

for you this afternoon -
I'm still in the same "mood"
I was in this morning
incidentally -
Dick and I were talking
about you when that one
was taken -
I love the one with
you in the background -
not aware of the photog-
Be sure darling - return
m to me pronto -
Thanks -

I'm on the set now -
no time to write -
Everyone says hell
you everyday - I
Gonna talk with
Wasserman today I
Will tell you more
the Markey picture a
as possible -
Perry Lieber just c
& told me I am to go
Milwaukee the 24 or 25th
My God -

More plans!

Goodbye

Desi Arnaz Thursday. 8:30 P.M.

Darling:

I received your letter about
1 o'clock this aft
was wonderfu
three times alrea
feel a little a
you talk. I
I love you very
very happy about

I just got
arrangers, we wa
about two hour
it's going to
number, I hope
we and Rodgers and
it turns out to be
we are going to wor
Spanish and then
repertoire set, at

---

with.

I'm flying to Knoxville, Tennessee, Saturday morning to arrive there in the early afternoon, and coming back 2:30 A.M. Tuesday to be able to rehearse with the orchestra at the Versailles Tuesday afternoon.

Wednesday we are having a cocktail party at the Versailles with about fifty debutants, but darling, honestly God, I'll be a good boy, I promise.

Thursday it's the opening and I'm very glad the Hartmans are opening with me.

Peter Lind Hayes opens at the Versailles, Friday, cause Sheilla Barret has a bad throat and he will be there for six days until we open.

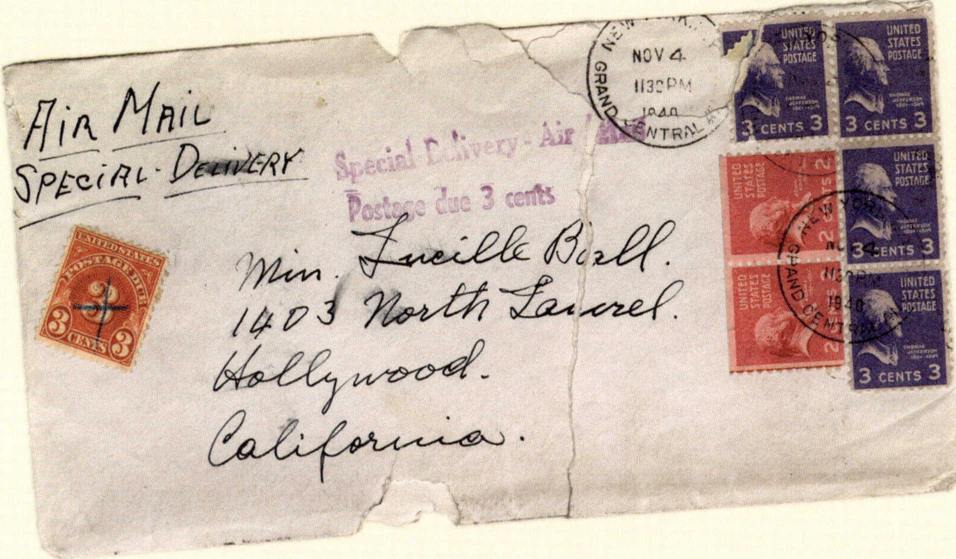

Thursday, 8:30 P.M.

Darling:

I received your letter about 1 o'clock this afternoon, and it was wonderful, I've read it about three times already, it makes me feel a little as if I was hearing you talk. You know something, I love you very much, and I am very happy about it.

I just got home from my arrangers, we worked on Tabú about two hours and I think it's going to make a swell number, I hope so. Yesterday we cut Rodgers and Hart medley and it turn out to be fine, tomorrow we are going to work on Spic and Spanish and then I'll have my repertoire set, at least to start with.

Written from Meurice Hotel, New York

November 4, 1940

I'm flying to Knoxville, Tennessee, Saturday morning to arrive there in the early afternoon, and coming back 2:30 A.M. Tuesday to be able to rehearse with the orchestra at the Versailles Tuesday afternoon.

Wednesday we are having a cocktail party at the Versailles with about fifty debutants, but darling, honesty God, I'll be a good boy, I promise.

Thursday it's the opening and I'm very glad the Hartmans are opening with me.

Peter Lind Hayes opens at the Versailles, Friday, cause Sheila Barrett has a bad throat and he will be there for six days until we open. I read the script and think it's swell, I'll get one to send to you as soon as possible.

Darling, don't make excuses about writing too much, thank God you want to write because I love receiving and reading your letters and the longer and oftener the better.

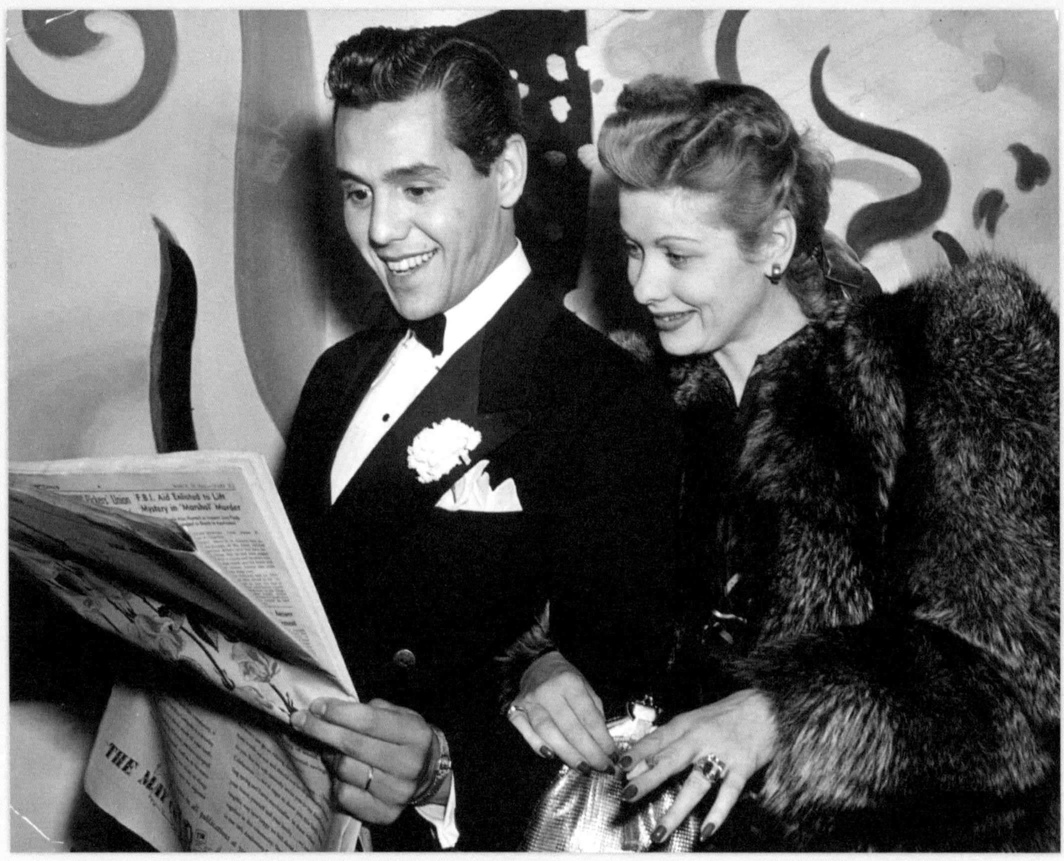

ABOVE: Reading a great review of Dad's club act, 1940

I love you sweetheart, I love your eyes, and your skin and your body and your feet, and the way you talk, your smartness, the way you think every little bit of you I love and I'm afraid I'll always will, but really I'm not afraid I'm happy immensely happy, because I think you and I are going to be very, very happy.

I'm very glad about your contracts being all set and I'm terribly excited about your coming next month, we'll really have some fun. You go ahead and buy all those pretty clothes and rest and look your best, I want to show these New Yorkers off. I'm going to be very proud of you and I know and feel it that every month that passes by I'm going to be more so.

Work hard darling, don't drink please, and DON'T stay up late, allright? I'm doing it, so you should too.

Give my best to your mama and all the fellas at the studio.

I miss you too much and I can't love you any more.

Desi

P.S. No more long distance calls, darling, save your money, we'll need it for the swimming pool.

P.S. No more long distance calls, darling, save your money; we'll need it for the swimming pool.

Desi Arnaz

I read the script and think it's swell, I'll get one to send to you as soon as possible.

Darling don't make excuses about writing too much, thank God you want to write, because I love receiving and reading your letters and the longer and oftener the better.

I love you sweetheart, I love your eyes, and your skin and your body and your feet, and the way you talk, your smartness, the way you think every little bit of you I love and I'm afraid I'll always will, but really I'm not afraid I am happy immensely happy, because I think

Desi Arnaz
Menrice Hotel
N.Y.C.

LOS ANGELES CALIF. NOV 2

NEW YORK N.Y. NOV 5 1 AM G.P.O.

… going to be
… y.
… about your contracts
… I'm terribly
… coming next
… really have some
… ahead and buy
… ty clothes and
… your best, I
… these New Yorkers
… to be very proud
… know and feel it
… uth that passes by
… to be more so

Work … darling, don't drink
please, and don't stay up late, allright?
I'm doing it, so you should too.

Give my best to your mammy
and all the fellas at the studio

I miss you too much and
I can't love you any more

Desi.

(1)

Desi Arnaz Tuesday
Aboard plane.

Darling:
We are about half an hour from New York yet and so far the trip has been wonderful and very smooth flying.

I send you
Chicago telling
well your pi
last night, I
derful rest.
baby. I love yo
God damn
getting funny
I shouldn't h

(2) Desi Arnaz

so soon. It's not too bad though.

Get Picture Play, the one that came out today, it has that story I told you about.

I already miss you very much and sincerely hope that you can be in New York next month, we'll have *the* *hell* of a time.

Work hard baby and be good, I promise to do the same.

Soon you will be a great star and I'm going to be awfully proud of you and I hope you can be proud of me too.

Loving you immensely
Desi.

Tuesday aboard plane

Darling:

We are about half hour from New York yet and so far the trip has been wonderful and very smooth flying.

I send you a wire from Chicago telling about how well your pills worked last night, I had a wonderful rest. Thank you baby. I love you.

God damn, it's just getting bumpy now, I shouldn't have talked so soon. It's not too bad though.

Get Picture Play, the one that came out today, it has that story I told you about.

I already miss you very much and sincerely hope that you can be in New York next month, we'll have the hell of a time.

Work hard baby and be good, I promise to do the same.

Soon you will be a great star and I'm going to be awfully proud of you and I hope you can be proud of me too.

Loving you immensely, Desi

Tuesday, 10:00 A.M.
Back on this damned location

And you—Desi baby—are—I hope—sleeping peacefully—a few hours from New York—

Watching you fly away from me last nite was—well—I can't put it into words this morning—any more than I could talk last nite—

I didn't cry—I was too dead for tears—I didn't talk all the way home—that guy never stopped talking but I didn't even hear him.

I went right to Mother's until 10:30—and was in bed when you said you would be—Slept as though I'd been hit over the head—Harriett had to excavate this morning to get me out.

Missing you is more poignant this morning—There are so damned many things about you to miss—more about that later—no point in breaking myself up this morning so early———or is there?

Gee—I'm so grateful for all the plans we've managed to make from now until the 1st of the year. It gives me so many things to think about—right away—

Can hardly wait until I get in off this ghostly rathole called a "ranch"—so that I can start "things"—

I got right out of the car here at my corner hot box—and started for the third time to say good morning to you—I tried to write under the dryer—but tore them all up—Haven't said hello up front as yet—am in the next shot—have only gotten a sickening glance at O'Brien—can't stand that jerk!

Have been thinking houses all morning again. Coming through that valley does that. Wish I liked the valley better—guess that's the only place anyway—and they say you learn to like it very quickly.

Harriett just told me you gave her something when you left—sneaking things behind my back eh? You'll never have any money—you'll give it all away—and while I'm on the subject briefly—give yourself a course of instruction in not picking up all the checks always—and darling—you won't have to worry about being called cheap—really you won't—just relax a little in that dept. Lecture over for this morning—Don't feel like lecturing you today at all—

Feel like kissing the breath out of you—

Gee—I repeat (after five minutes lapse of time for day dreaming) there are so many things to miss about you—

They're calling me—

Bye—

Gosh! Your wonderful.

Tuesday
10:00 A.M.
Back on this
damned location.

And you - Desi baby - are - I hope - sleeping peacefully - a few hours from New York - Watching you fly away from me last nite was - well - I can't put it into words this morning - any more than I could talk last nite - I didn't cry - I was too ... for tears - I didn't talk all the way home - that guy never stopped talking but I didn't even hear him.

I went right to Mothers until 10:30 - and was in bed when you said you would be - Slept as though I'd been hit over the head - Harriett had to excavate this morning to get me out.

Missing you is more poignant this morning - There are so damned many things about you to miss - more about that later - no point in breaking myself up this morning so early — — — or is there

Gee - I'm so grateful for all the plans we've managed to make from now until the 1st of the year. It gives me so many things to think about - right away -

Can hardly wait until I get in off this ghostly rathole called a "ranch" - so that I can start "things" -

I got right out of the car here at my corner hot box - and started for the third time to say good morning to you - I tried to write under the dryer - but tore them all up - Haven't said hello up front as yet - am in the next shot - have only gotten a sickening glance at O'Brien - can't stand that jerk!

These planes flying overhead are driving me daffy – reminds me constantly that you are so damned far away from me – and that I'm not going to find you at home or at the studio when I get in.

You are just about getting in to New York if you are on time – Your mind is going like a whirl wind – you've so many things to get done – I wonder if you've had maybe a fleeting thought of me – just a tiny one. You won't have much time for weeks to think of me – but maybe – just once in awhile you'll manage –

Maybe I'll go to a movie tonite with Peggy – no – just asked her – she can't – I'll take Mom –

Everyone is of course kidding me today about not having you here anymore – & how I can't do my work well today etc etc But at the same time – everyone has been talking about you today – about how much they like you – how much different you seem – when they have a chance to really know you – In short – everyone thinks your swell – and headed for so many wonderful things — they're telling me!

Honey

Your wire just arrived. I loved it — Glad the sleeping nugets worked – I almost kissed the driver who brought the wire out.

It's 4:15 – I'm finished – and for a couple of days Thank God! Or maybe I should want to work so

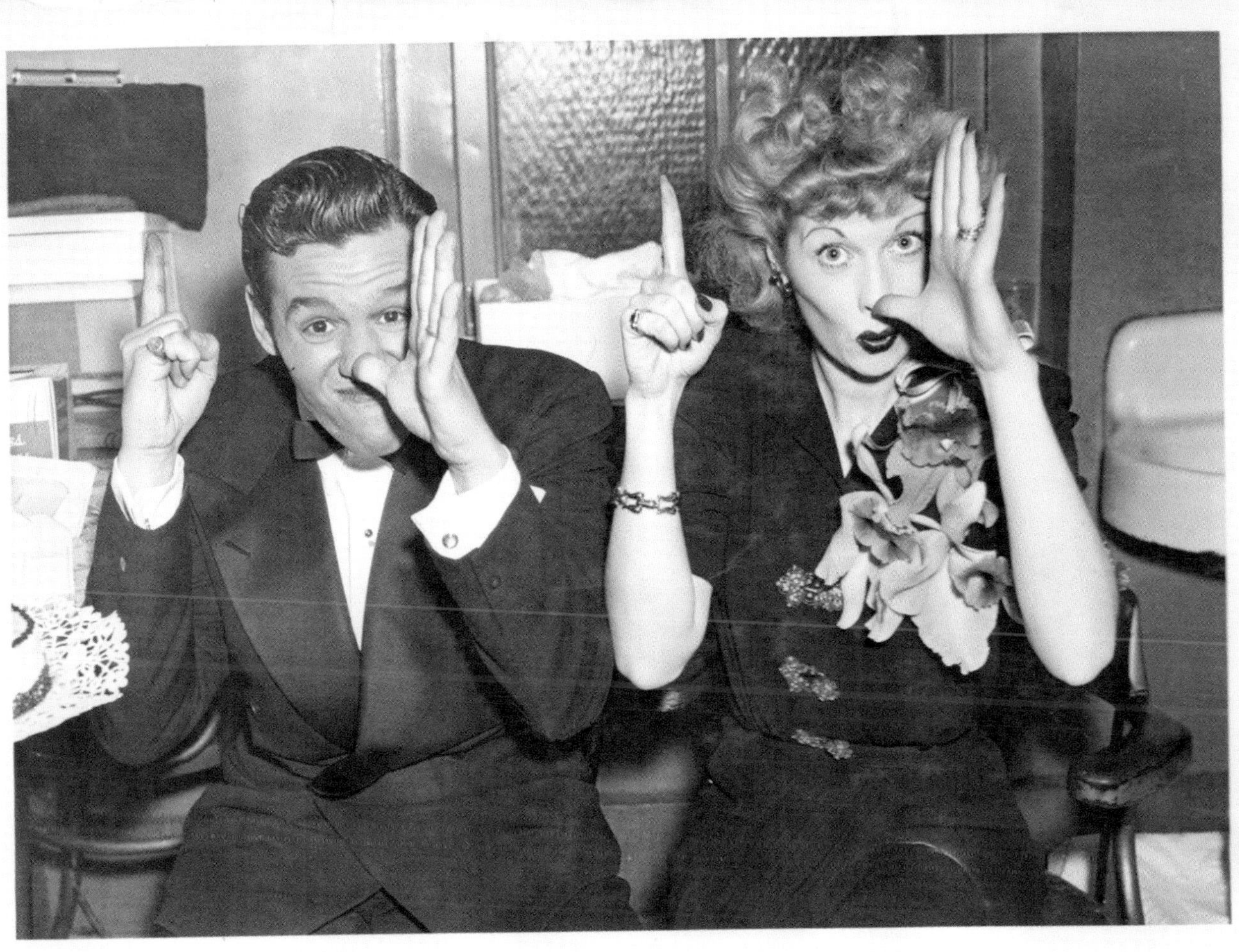

—¤¤¤—

It's 2:30 now—hotter then hell—I've finished my "falls" and I didn't enjoy them a bit!

Peggy Carroll is here—George Murphy + Peggy + I are sitting around trying to keep cool for a few minutes. I expect to finish early today—and won't have to work for a couple of days unless that Duke Wales catches up with me—

These planes flying overhead are driving me daffy—reminds me constantly that you are so damned far away from me—and that I'm not going to find you at home or at the studio when I get in.

You are just about getting into New York if you are on time—your mind is going like a whirlwind—you've so many things to get done—I wonder if you've had maybe a fleeting thought of me—just a tiny one. You won't have much time for weeks to think of me—but maybe—just once in awhile you'll manage—

PAGE 47: Thumbing their noses at the naysayers while celebrating their first wedding anniversary, November 1941

—¤¤¤—

Maybe I'll go to a movie tonite—with Peggy—no—just asked her—she can't—I'll take Mom—

Everyone is of course kidding me today about not having you here any more—and how I can't do my work well today etc etc. But at the same time—everyone has been talking about you today—about how much they like you—how much different you seem—when they have a chance to really know you—In short—everyone thinks your swell—and headed for so many wonderful things—they're telling me!

—¤¤¤—

HONEY!

Your wire just arrived. I loved it!—glad the sleeping nugets worked—

I almost kissed the driver who brought the wire out.

It's 4:15—I'm finished—and for a couple of days. Thank God! Or maybe I should want to work so I don't have so much time to think—

—¤¤¤—

I don't have so much time to think —

5:00 P.M.

There! I'm back in the studio. Going to get into some pants and start my campaign — my traveling campaign — will keep you posted —

Gee I love this picture of you. So damned glad I have it — Harriett is so funny — I ask her every day if she doesn't

think it's a wonderful picture and she gives me that take'em — "Yes, Miss Ball it's a wonderful picture."

If I only had a little button I could push and make the picture come to life —

Anyway —

Here I go —

I'll be writing often I guess — It makes me feel closer to you — so I guess that's the

thing to do —

But darling — you don't have to answer them all — just when you feel like it. Each one doesn't have to be accounted for — I do think I feel a letterwriting streak coming on though — I hope you can take it.

I love you — love you — love you —

Mad about you —

Please be good —

220 West 81 St

Have been thinking houses all morning again. Coming through that valley does that. Wish I liked the valley better — guess that's the only place anyway — and they say you learn to like it very quickly.

Harriett just told me you gave her something when you left — sneaking things behind my back eh? You'll never have any money — you'll give it all away — and while I'm on the subject briefly — give yourself a course of instruction in not picking up all the checks alway — And darling — you won't have to worry about being called cheap — really you won't — just relax a little in that dept. Lecture over for this morning — Don't feel like lecturing you today at all —

Feel like kissing the breath out of you —

Gee — I repeat (after five minutes lapse of time for day dreaming) there are so many things to miss about you —

They're calling me —

Bye —

Gosh! Your wonderful.

It's 2:30 now — hotter than hell — I've finished my "fal

and I didn't enjoy them

bit!

Peggy Carroll is here — George Murphy + Peggy +

I are sitting around try

to keep cool for a few minu

I expect to finish early

today — and won't have

work for a couple of day

unless that Duke Wales

catches up with me —

5:00 P.M.

There! I'm back in the studio. Going to get into some pants and start my campaign—my traveling campaign—will keep you posted—

Gee I love this picture of you. So damned glad I have it.

Harriett is so funny—I ask her every day if she doesn't think it's a wonderful picture and she gives me that take 'em—"Yes. Miss Ball it's a wonderful picture."

If I only had a little button I could push and make the picture come to life—

Anyway—

Here I go—

I'll be writing often I guess—It makes me feel closer to you—so I guess that's the thing to do—

But darling—you don't have to answer them all—just when you feel like it. Each one doesn't have to be accounted for—I do think I feel a letter writing streak coming on though—hope you can take it.

I love you—love you—love you—

Mad about you—Please be good—

United States Army letterhead and envelope

May 7, 1943, from Arlington, California

Wednesday morning

Dearest baby:

By the time I got back to my barracks last night and fix my bed and cleaned and undressed, they turned out the lights and I couldn't write to you. We just had breakfast and are back in our barracks; the day's work here doesn't start until eight o'clock and is about seven thirty now so I have a little time.

The trip over here in the bus was allright, everybody kind of homesick and wondering what next.

I love the country very much, but <u>this</u> <u>is</u> <u>ridiculous</u>. I need a notarized photostatic copy of our marriage certificate, also and affidavit by two friends, not family, that my mother is my dependent 100%. Get Ed and Andy.

Get this things and keep them at the house until I send for them or the government might send for them.

The beds are fine, I didn't sleep too good but it wasn't the bed's fault; just not settled yet that's all.

Got up at five thirty this morning, made my bed, boy, am I good,! cleaned up dressed, stood at inspection had breakfast consisting of one orange, wheaties, scrambled eggs and mashed potatoes, toast, marmalade and butter, coffee and two glasses of milk, all of this without a ration book.

I just saw Cully Richards after breakfast outside the mess hall; Gee, it certainly was nice to see someone you knew, he is going to come over tonight after dinner and maybe go see a movie here at the fort, of course there's no other place to go, but it'll be nice to talk and compare experiences and plans and ideas.

Today seems to be going to be the busiest and most important day of all. I will talk to you tonite and let you know. Gosh I really missed you last nite.

Here we go, so long.

—¤¤¤—

Pvt. Desiderio A. Arnaz
Co. C. group 496
S.C.U.-1950 Reception Center
Arlington, California.

Free

ARLINGTON, CALIF. MAY 7 7:30 AM

Mrs. D. Arnaz.
19700 Devonshire Blvd.
Chatsworth

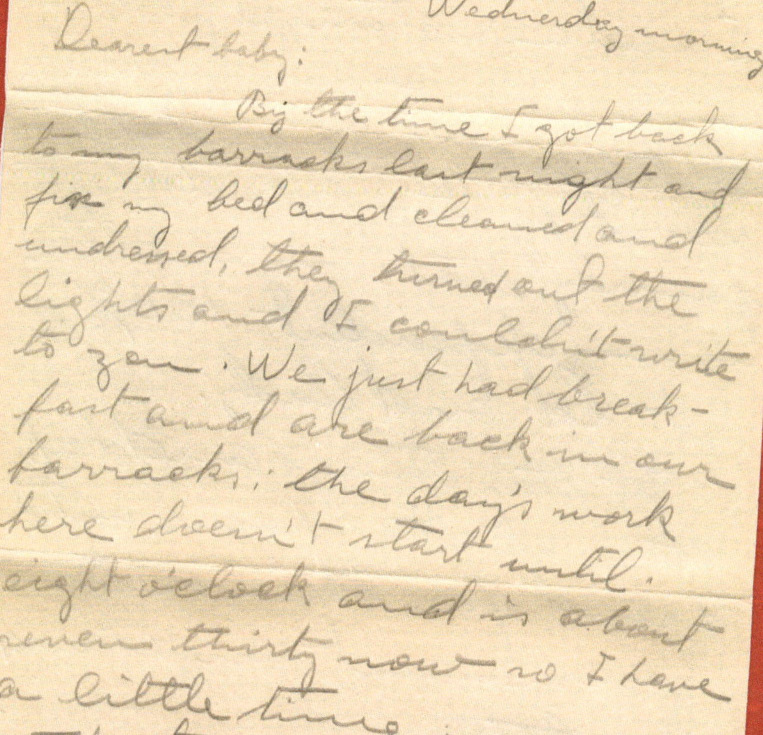

UNITED STATES ARMY

Wednesday morning.

Dearest baby:

By the time I got back to my barracks last night and fix my bed and cleaned and undressed, they turned out the lights and I couldn't write to you. We just had breakfast and are back in our barracks; the day's work here doesn't start until eight o'clock and is about seven thirty now so I have a little time;

The trip over here in the bus was allright, everybody kind of homesick and wondering what next.

need a notarized phot
atic copy of our marria
rtificate, also and affi
avit by two friends, no
amily, that my moth
s my dependent 100%
et Ed and Andy.
Get this things and
them at the home
I send for them or
government might
for
Th
didn'
it w
just

3

UNITED STATES ARMY

Got up at five thirty this
morning, made my bed,
boy, am I good, cleaned up
dressed, stood at inspection
had breakfast consisting
of one orange, wheaties,
scrambled eggs and mashed
potatoes, toast, marmalade
and butter, coffee and
s of milk

---

after dinner and maybe
go see a movie here at
the post, of course there's
just no other place to go, but
it'll be nice to talk
and compare experiences
and plans and ideas.
Today seems to be going
to be the busiest and most
important day of all.
I will talk to you tonite
and let you know.

Gosh I really missed you last
nite

Here we go, so long.

Thursday Morning
Believe it or not I haven't
been able to write one
more more to this
thing since yesterday

UNITED STATES ARMY
5

I could have done i
nite, but would
missed talking
It's so wonderf
hear your voice,
God I can't beli
see you Saturd
I do hope noth
goes wrong.
I feel so much
after passing my
and having a li
clearer picture of
going on and
want, I know
the Air Force
be it.

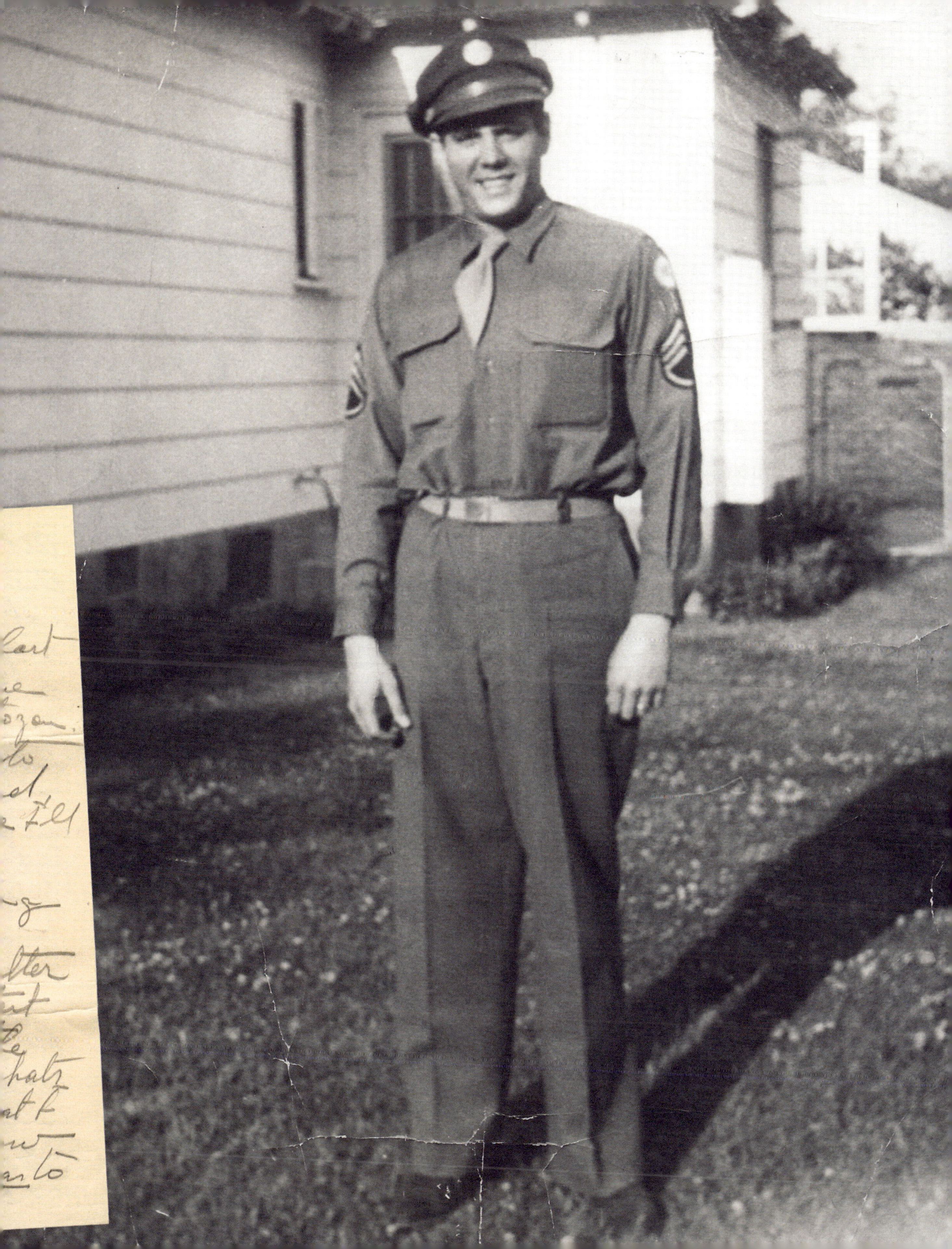

Thursday morning

Believe it or not I haven't been able to write one more word to this thing since yesterday. I could have done it last nite, but would have missed talking to you. It's so wonderful to hear your voice, and God I can't believe I'll see you Saturday. I do hope nothing goes wrong.

I feel so much better after passing my test and having a little clearer picture of what's going on and what I want, I know now the Air Force has to be it. All the interviewers thought I was nuts for not having somebody request me for liaison or intelligence or Special Service, they say a guy like me have no right or place in this outfit, they say they are just looking everywhere for fellows with my qualifications, but at the same time those are all specialties and they have no authority here to send me there unless somebody requests me. I'm sure it'll work out all right.

PAGE 55: Dad in his Army uniform, 1943.

Darling, I love you so very much and I miss you so terribly, I will say this same two things a million times probably, but they won't just be repetition, every time I'll mean them just as much or more, and I don't seem to be able to express my feelings at this moment in any other better way. Boy Oh Boy!!!

I'll see you Saturday

Whoopee!!!

Give my love to Ed and Eba.

Give a kiss to mother and as far as you are concerned just hold everything till Sat.

So long here we go again.

Love,
Desi

6

All the interviewers
thought I was nuts for
not having somebody
request me for liaison
or intelligence or Special
Service. they say a guy
like me have no
right or place in th
outfit, they say they are
just looking everywhe
for fellow
qualifi
the
are all
they ha
here to
unless
me. I'
work

UNITED STATES ARMY

9

Darling I love you
so very much and
so terribly
this same
a million
ly, but they
e repetition,
mean
uch or
don't
able
feeling
ent in
tter way

Boy Oh Boy!!!
I'll see you Saturday
Whoopee!!!

Give my love to Ed and
Cha.

Give a kiss to mother
and as far as you are
concerned just hold
everything till Sat

So long here we
go again

Love

Den

LUCILLE

Thursday
9:00 P. M.

My Baby—

You called about an
hour or so ago. Am ki
lonesome tonite — kind
lost again — wonder
long I'm going to feel
this way. Probably
be worse when you
in San Be
I wont th
It's going

on you down there I'm
afraid — so I shouldn't
squawk.

Am happy you are going
to come back with me
Sunday nite anyway.
Because with you making
a change in camps and
me starting a picture —
few weeks
together.
here
moon

LUCILLE

as yet — but so cool
and quiet. If only
those damn frogs would
shut up! But they are
just getting worse every
nite. Tried to think of
some way of getting rid
of them tonite — and
even took several of them
out of the pool with that
long wire thing — and dragged
them out into the back

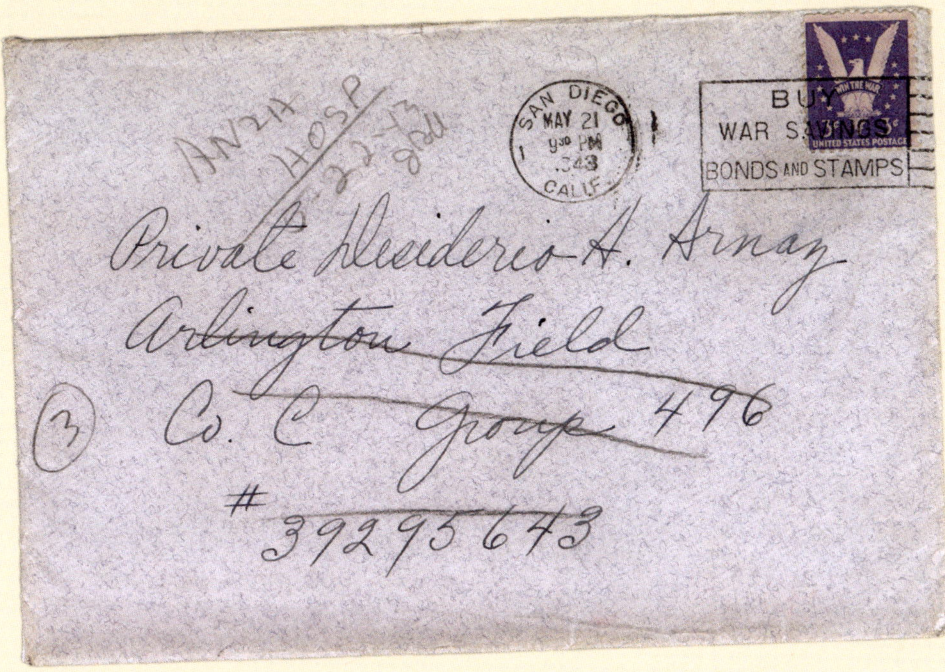
SAN DIEGO MAY 21 930 PM 1943 CALIF.
BUY WAR SAVINGS BONDS AND STAMPS
ANZA HOSP 5-22-43

Private Desiderio A. Arnaz
Arlington Field
Co. C Group 496
39295643

May 21, 1943, San Diego postmark. Addressed to Arlington, forwarded to Anza Hospital

Thursday 9:00 P.M.

My Baby–

You called about an hour or so ago. I'm kinda lonesome tonight—kinda lost again—wonder how long I'm going to feel this way. Probably will be worse when you are in San Bernardino but I won't think about it. It's going to be tough on your own there I'm afraid—so I shouldn't squawk.

Am happy you are going to come back with me Sunday nite anyway. Because with your making a change in camps and me starting a picture it may be a few weeks before we get together.

Gee it's beautiful here again tonite. No moon as yet—but so cool and quiet. If only those damn frogs would shut up! But they are just getting worse every nite. Tried to think of some way of getting rid of them tonite—and even took several of them out of the pool with that long wire thing—and dragged them out into the back lot and was going to kill them but then I lost my nerve and dragged them all back again + put them back into the pool!! I did kill one little one + I s'pose that'll haunt me now for weeks.

19700 Devonshire Boulevar
Chatsworth, California

lot and was going to kill them but then I lost my nerve & dragged them all back again & put them back into the pool!! I did kill one little one & I s'pose that'll ...nt me now for weeks.

...lled Annie 5 times. ...nswer tell Cully. ... Marion –

LUCILLE

5:00 P.M. N.B.C. didn't you?

If you only knew ... I hate to fly to Sa... tomorrow. Don't ... which I hate wors... flying – or mak... speech! But so... I'll learn how to s... Hope you reach ... by phone tomorro...

but if you don't – please don't be angry with me – because I haven't any idea where I'll be at what time. Grant Hotel eventually to sleep – that's all I know – and you may rest assured I'll be there as soon as I possibly can! I hate San Diego – sailors – bond rallies – and Don Wilson & his wife!

LUCILLE

Amerillo is staying here with me tonite. as I told you.

Freddy arrives Mo[illegible] Tues. Is inducted W[illegible] You'll probably see h[illegible] I called Dick + Ed [illegible] both places for Tues[illegible] A.M. [illegible] we pa[illegible] the [illegible]

Ask for it to be back by the end of this week even before Tuesday.

Try to listen to Groucho program – though it [illegible] the worst I've [illegible]n. Sat nite [illegible]o I think.

[illegible] People" doesn't [illegible] all – wish [illegible] me a decent

LUCILLE

leading man. Would like to have Geo. Murphy – But no one likes him over there – isn't that awful –

Desi darling – Please don't worry about me here at the ranch. You know I'll do all I can to do the right thing. Believe me honey – for the duration and forever I wouldn't

LUCILLE

late - so came home right
after rehearsal - got the
papers - walked around
the yard for awhile
in the moonlight
"The Boys" and "girls" -
of you - and us -
wished to God the
was over - and was
thankful you were
so close.
I love you Desi

do anything I shouldn't -
or do anything to make
you unhappy - if you
are going to do the right
thing as concientiously as
we have nothing
about. Please
that.
weren't seen a
was going to

LUCILLE

you seem to forget it
so often.

Please keep nice thoughts
about me for awhile -
perhaps you'll trust me
more - and I sure
would appreciate that -
All my love
Forever & ever -
Your wife -

Called Annie 5 times. No answer tell Cully. Talked with Marion—she's very happy about Sunday—you said 5:00 P.M. N.B.C. didn't you?

If only you knew how I hate to fly to San Diego tomorrow. Don't know which I hate worse—flying—or making the speech! But someday I'll learn to say no!

Hope you reach me by phone tomorrow nite but if you don't—please don't be angry with me because I haven't any idea where I'll be at what time. Grant Hotel eventually to sleep—that's all I know—and you may rest assured I'll be there as soon as I possibly can! I hate San Diego—sailors—bond rallies—and Don Wilson and his wife! Amerillo is staying here with me tonite as I told you.

Freddy arrives Mon or Tues. Is inducted Wed. You'll probably see him. I called Dick + Ed—O.K. both places for Tuesday A.M. We are doing all we possibly can about the birth certificate. Ask for it to be back by the end of this week even before Tuesday.

Try to listen to Groucho program—though it is one of the worst I've ever been on. Sat nite around 6:00 I think C.B.S.

"Meet the People" doesn't thrill me at all—wish they'd give me a decent leading man. Would like to love Geo. Murphy—But no one likes him over there—isn't that awful—

Desi darling—Please don't worry about me here at the ranch. You know I'll do all I can to do the right thing. Believe me honey—for the duration and forever I wouldn't do anything I shouldn't—or do anything to make you unhappy—if you are to do the right thing as conscientiously as I am—we have nothing to worry about. Please believe that.

I still haven't seen a movie. Was going to see one last nite but thought I'd better get home before it got too late—so came home right after the rehearsal—got the papers—walked around the yard for awhile in the moonlight with "The Boys" and "girls"—thought of you—and us—and wished to God the war was over—and was very thankful you were still so close.

I love you Desi—and you seem to forget it so often.

Please keep nice thoughts about me for awhile—perhaps you'll trust me more—and I sure would appreciate that.

All my love forever and ever—
Your wife

Tuesday 10:00 A.M.
Beauty Salon

My Baby–

Sorry angel I missed your call last nite. When Freddy and I got to the ranch it was cancelled. Hope you call tonite. Going home right from studio so I won't miss it. Saw the Jean Arthur picture "The More the Merrier" One of the best comedies I've ever seen + I cried + cried when it was over—cuz it was so cute—and made me think of you! It was the climax to a very nerve wracking day. The kind of a day I hope I don't have again for a long time—or I'll blow my topper. Briefly—your mother practically drove me nuts! I don't think she realizes how unreasonable she is—+ as yet I haven't told her—and I hope I don't have to—but she certainly understands just so much—and no more—I'm sure it'll all straighten itself out when she gets moved + settled but in the meantime you may be calling me from a sanatorium. She doesn't seem to realize I have to work most every day at the studio + and from today on—absolutely every day—making last week + yesterday my only days to get her a stove and refrigerator—+ I think you understand how nearly impossible it is to find either of those items.

It means scanning the ads at nite—the few that might be there + rushing out at the crack of dawn for me to get to the address + take a look at the stuff. It's usually gone when you get there—or much too large for her house or too expensive—the rest of the time I've spent on the telephone—+ leaping back + forth at Dept stores + gas Co—You have to catch anything electrical or mechanical in midair—Anyway I'm certain that you know what I'm talking about. How many hours and hours of the few days I've had these last 3 weeks, I've spent running around trying to get her set up before I start the picture. Well—I finally with the aid of Andy H.—Al Cohen at the furniture Co—Barker Bros—+ Mother—located a stove—right price—size—good condition—etc + took Lolita to see it—way to hell—+ gone down town—and what do you think she said—"it's the wrong color"! It's cream color instead of pure white! The right color she has to have yet! Well—she took it finally + then called me up + was wondering if I could get rid of it + keep looking for a white one etc etc etc—until I'm nearly batty. That's only one of her little episodes—I won't tell you any more—I just hope I can hold my temper—because I know you want me to.

VAN NUYS
MAY 26
6 30 PM
1943
CALIF.

(3)

Private Desiderio A. Arnaz
Arlington Field
Arlington, Calif,
Group 496
[illegible]5643 % Hospital

LUCILLE

Tuesday 10:00 AM.
Beauty Salon

My Baby -

Sorry angel I missed your call last nite. When Freddy & I got to the ranch it was cancelled. Hope you'll call tonite. Going home right from studio so I won't miss it. Saw the Jean Arthur picture "The More the Merrier"

One of the best comedies I've ever seen & I cried & cried when it was over - cuz it was so cute - and made me think of you! It was a climax to a very nerve wracking day. The kind of a day I hope I don't have again for a long time - or I'll blow my topper. Briefly - - your Mother practically drove

LUCILLE

me nuts! I don't think she realizes how unreasonable she is — as yet I haven't told her I hope I don't have to — but she certainly understands just so much — and no more — I'm sure it'll all straighten itself out when she gets ...

may be calling me from a sanatorium. She doesn't seem to realize I have to work most every day at the studio & from today on — absolutely every day — making last week & yesterday my only days to get her a stove & refrigerator — & think you understand how nearly impossible it is to find either of those

LUCILLE

It means scanning the ads at nite — the few that might be there & rushing out at the crack of dawn for me to get to the add & take a look at the ... It's usually gone when I get there — or much too large for her house or too expensive — the rest of the time I've spent on the telephone — &

leaping back & forth at Dept stores & gas Co — you have to catch anything electrical or mechanical in mid air — Anyway I'm certain that you know what I'm talking about. How many hours & hours, of the few days I've had these last 3 weeks, I've

LUCILLE

trying to get her set up before I start the picture. Well - I finally with the aid of Andy + - Al Cohen at the furniture Co - Barker Bros - + Mother - located a stove - right price - size - good condition - etc + took Lolita to

see it - way to hell - + gone down town - and what do you think she said - "it's the wrong color." It's cream color instead of pure white. The right color she has to have yet! Well - she took it finally + then called me up + was wondering [illegible]

LUCILLE

could get rid of it + keep looking for a white one etc etc etc - until I'm nearly batty. That's only one of her little episodes - I won't tell you any more - I just hope I control my temper - because I know you want me to

She cried + carried on when she found you were hospitalized - as I knew she would. And made a big thing about getting the hospital on the phone immediately + talking to you - Told her I'd take her down first time I go of course - if I'm still

LUCILLE

sane.

You hate me when I tell you anything at all about your Mother but god Desi – when my Mother drives me batty I talk about it to you so I don't know why you think your Mom is perfect –

They all of them have their wonderful moments But believe me – when you are not around – Your Mother's dissappears with me anyway.

And of course the way she continues to ignore Des is anything but pleasant & or

LUCILLE

congenialness provoking.

So much for all that. I'll try to keep her satisfied but believe me it isn't a cinch job – it's a 24 hour duty. She's dissatisfied with everything the painters have done & they are her painters so I'm glad of that!

Called Bill last nite. Was worried about you. He said everything was O.K. Gee hope you call tonite – he told me the visiting hours – will come down first chance I get.

Unless this letter makes you so angry you don't want to see me – if it does – tell me when you call.

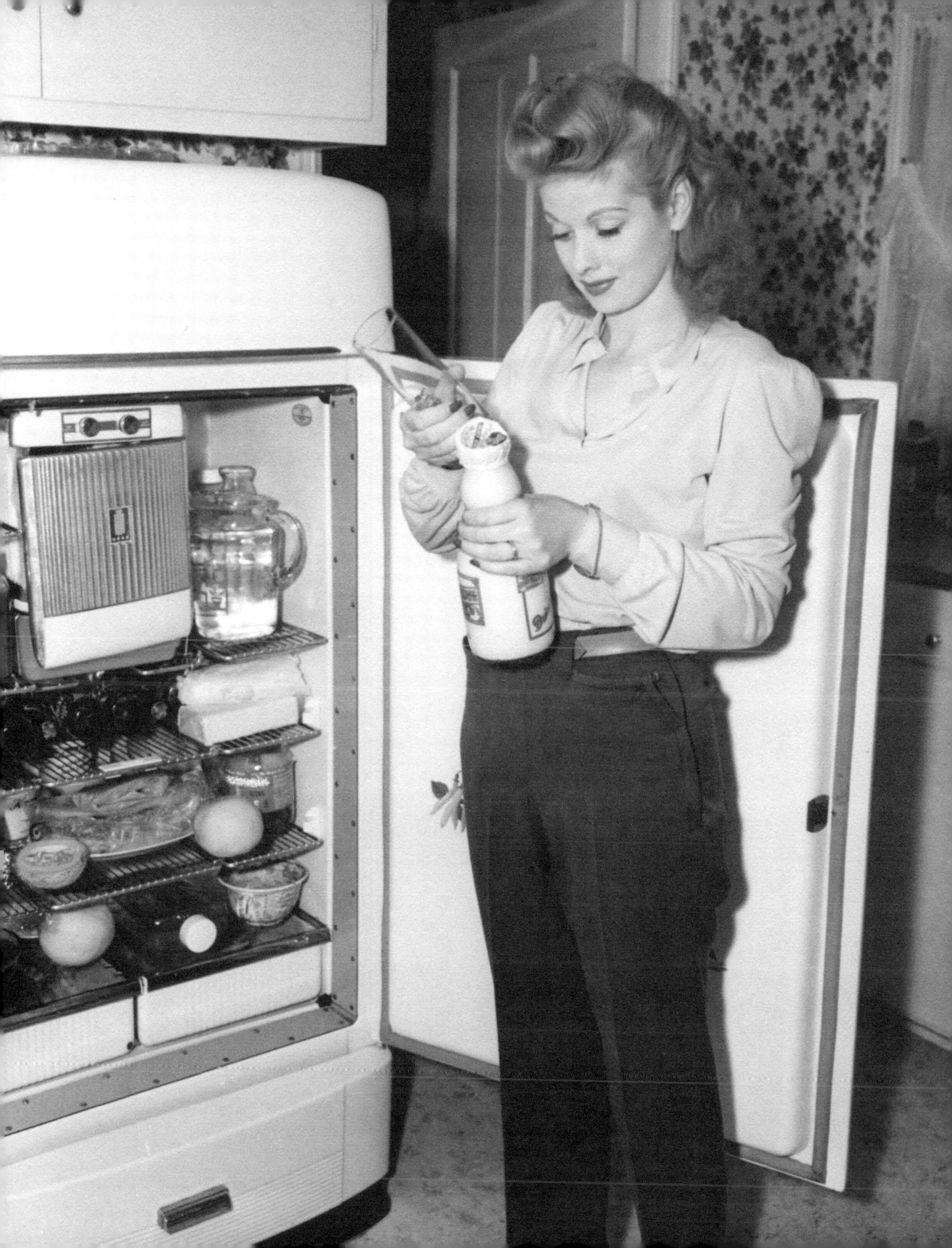

LUCILLE

Am going to send or bring you something, read —

Do you want your o. stationery?

Have you written me I hope so.

How long do you think you'll be in bed?

What's going to happen to San Bernardino?

Life's no fun without you Baby —

Believe me —

And forgive me for letting your Mom get me down — and for telling you about it — but I thought maybe getting it off my chest would make it easier for me to hold my

P.S. Wrote this at the Beauty Parlor — and dropped it on the floor, which was wet — just as I was leaving — Scuse it please —

All my love

Lucy

19700 Devonshire Boulevard
Chatsworth, California

She cried + carried on when she found you were hospitalized—as I knew she would. And made a big thing about getting the hospital on the phone immediately + talking to you—Told her I'd take her down first time I got of course—if I'm still sane.

You hate me when I tell you anything at all about your Mother—but God Desi—when my Mother drives me batty I talk about it to you so I don't know why you think your Mom is perfect—They all of them have their wonderful moments But believe me—when you are not around—Your Mother's disappears. With me anyway.

And of course the way she continues to ignore Des is anything but pleasant—or congenialness provoking.

So much for all that—I'll try to keep her satisfied but believe me it isn't a cinch job—it's a 24 hour duty. She's dissatisfied with everything the painters have done—+ they are her painters so I'm glad of that!

May 26, 1943, Van Nuys postmark

PAGE 69: Mom stands beside the refrigerator of their home in Chatsworth. The "refrigerator story" in this letter reflects the dynamic of her relationship with her mother-in-law during this period.

Called Bill last nite. Was worried about you. He said everything was O.K. Gee hope you call tonite—he told me the visiting hours—will come down first chance I get.

Unless this letter makes you so angry you don't want to see me—if it does—tell me when you call.

Am going to send or bring you something to read—

Do you want your own stationery?

Have you written me? I hope so.

How long do you think you'll be in bed?

What's going to happen to San Bernardino?

Life's no fun without you Baby—

Believe me—and forgive me for letting your Mom get me down—and for telling you about it—but I thought maybe getting it off my chest would make it easier for me to hold my temper with her—

I love you—want to talk to you—

Miss you—

I will see you soon I hope—

Lucille (over)

P.S. Wrote this at the Beauty Parlor—and dropped it on the floor, which was wet—just as I was leaving—S'cuse it please—

All my love
Lucy

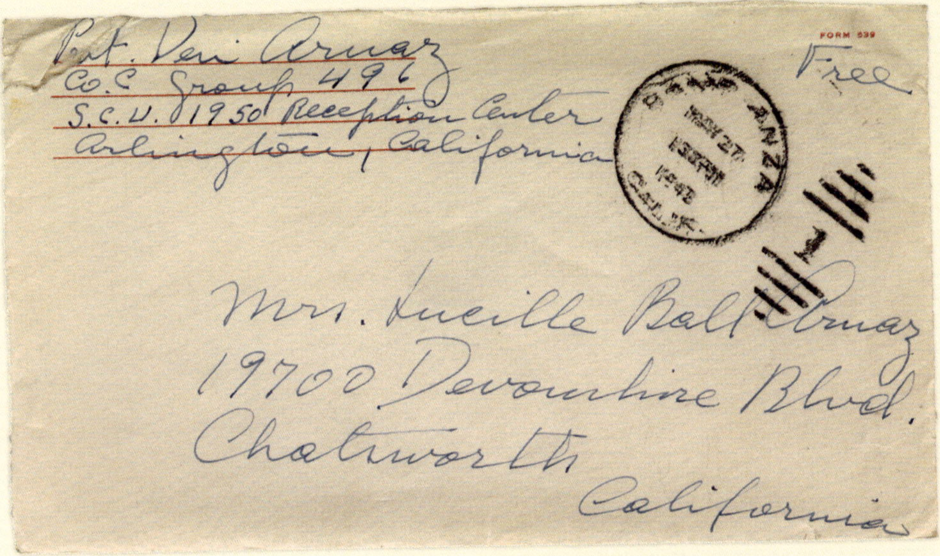
Pvt. Desi Arnaz
Co. C Group 496
S.C.U. 1950 Reception Center
Arlington, California

FORM 539

Free

Mrs. Lucille Ball Arnaz
19700 Devonshire Blvd.
Chatsworth
California

Wed.

Baby darling:

I love you. Yes I love you very much and I miss you so very, very much.

I was so mad I couldn't talk to you today, but I'm still on my back, and I had a fever for the past three days, not today I don't think, but they won't let me out of bed until 24 hours have passed without any temperature at all. Then they'll give me a wheelchair for a few days and then a cane or crutches.

May 27, from Camp Anza, California

Bill came over after talking to you and this is what he told me. Now hold on, it might not be possible. He is going to try to get me a convalescence furlough after ten days or two of being here. Which means I could go home and stay there for a month or until I'm completely well. Wouldn't that be wonderful. You make such a nice nurse and it'll be so wonderful laying by the pool and sitting around or laying in bed or just in any position just as long as it is home, oh God, I hope it comes true. He said it was a pretty good chance of getting.

Please come as soon as you can, I'm dying to see you. Gee, I like to be home and play with the dogs. Bring mother with when you come, tell I haven't written to her because it's awful hard laying on my back. I have to try hard to write to you. You read them to her and give her my love.

Kisses and hugs from your
husband Desi

AMERICAN RED CROSS

Wed.

Baby darling;

I love you.

Yes, I love you very much and I miss you so very, very much.

I was so mad I couldn't talk to you today, but I'm still on my back, and I had fever for the past three days, not today I don't th[illegible]

[illegible] hours have passed without temperature at all. Then they'll give me a wheelchair for a few days and then a cane or crutches.

Bill came over after talking to you and this is what he told me. Now hold on, it [illegible] be sensible.

AMERICAN RED CROSS

there for a month or until I'm com[pletely] well. Wouldn't that be wonderf[ul] you make me[illegible] a nice [illegible] and it'll be so wonderf[ul] laying by the pool a[nd] sitting around or [illegible] in bed or just in a position just as la[zy] as it is home, D[illegible] I hope it comes him[illegible]

He said it was a pretty good chance of getting—

Please come as soon as you can, I'm dying to see you. Gee I like to be home and play with the dogs.

Bring mother with you[illegible] take you home, All I haven't written to her because it's awful hard lying on my back & have to try hard to write to you. You read them to her and give her my love

Kisses and hugs from your husband Dan

UNITED STATES ARMY

Thursday

Honey:

What's the matter
with you? I've bee
here since Sunday ni
and only got the lette
you wrote last wee
You didn't write
Monday or Tuesda
or Wednesday. Toda
is Thursday and
letters only take
one day gettin
here.

I like to see how
you would like it
if you were in
my place, lying here
on my back all
day long the mail
man is the only
excitement and never
a God damn thing from
you. Thank you.
I'm not the begging type
so
la
a

3

UNITED STATES ARMY

I don't feel so much
pain any more
but it's God dam
uncomfortable, I
can even write
as you can se
I don't know
how to write la
down, my ha
writing it's no
good sitting u
either, but the
hell with that

Are you really going
to do me the honor
of coming on Sunday
I would like to see
you to beat the
hell out of you.
Please bring mother
with you, no excuses.
I do love you
though, God damn it
write, or I'll beat
the hell out of you

Your husband
Desiderio

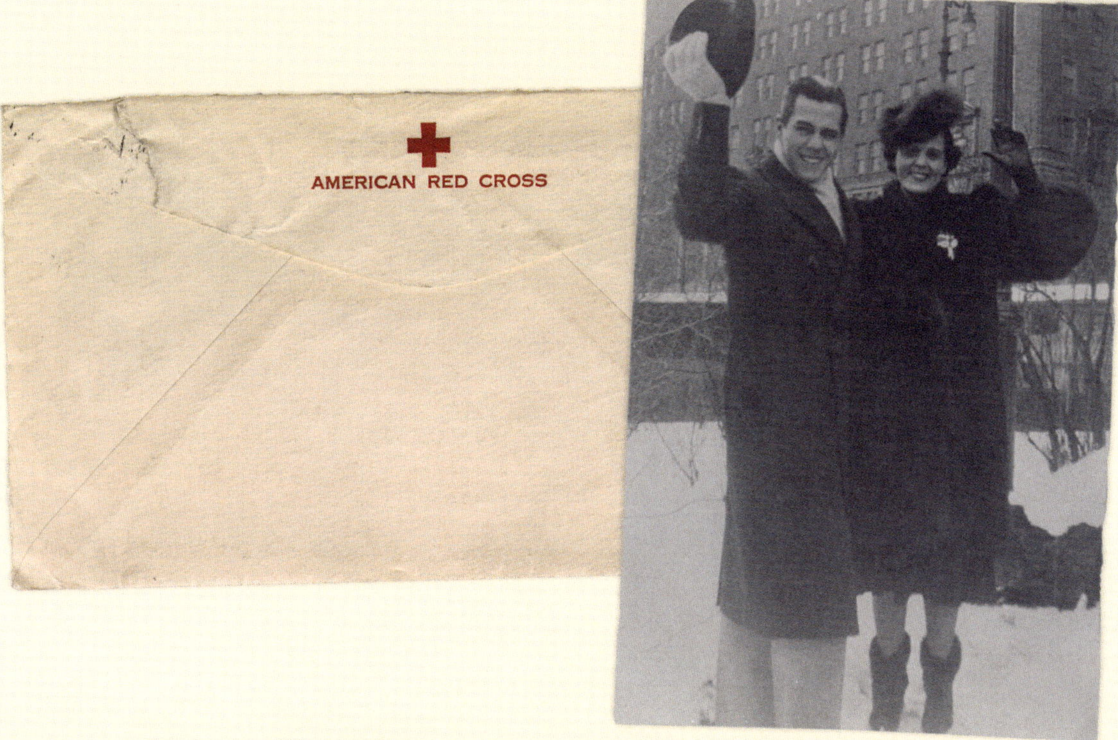

ABOVE: Dad with his mother, Dolores "Lolita" Arnaz, who was his dependent for most of his adult life

Thursday

Honey:

What's the matter with you? I've been here since Sunday night and only got the letter you wrote last week.

You didn't write Monday or Tuesday or Wednesday. Today is Thursday and letters only take one day getting here. I like to see how you would like it if you were in my place, lying here on my back all day long the mail man is the only excitement and never a God damn thing from you thank you.

I'm not the begging type so this is the first and last time I'll say anything, but no more letters from me unless I got one to answer. I don't feel so much pain any more but it's God damn uncomfortable, I can even write as you can see. I don't know how to write laying down, my handwriting it's not so good sitting up either, but the hell with that.

Are you really going to do me the honor of coming on Sunday I would like to see you to bawl the hell out of you. Please bring mother with you, no excuses.

I do love you though, God damn it write, or I'll beat the hell out of you.

Your husband
Desiderio

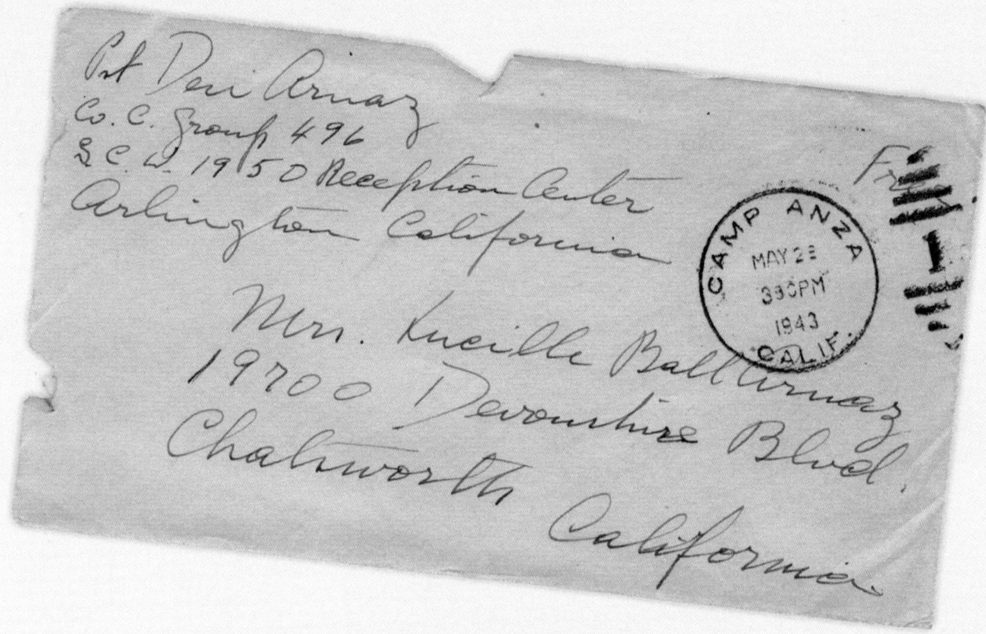

Friday

Dearest:

After bawling you out real good on my letter yesterday I got two letters from you today, Thank God, I couldn't have standed it much longer. You still didn't write Monday though, shame on you.

Your first letter wasn't at all the type of letter I was waiting and dying for. So I won't even mention that one, unfortunately I open that one first. It wasn't pleasant after waiting for so long. It's too bad you and mother don't get along better, she has her faults but so have you. I don't mind you telling me about them I know them I'm only asking you to please try and try hard, now that I'm gone and she has nobody but you and I would like to feel that though it might be a tough job you will like your job and like mother I know she needs you, you don't need her.

So please, darling, feel that it's something, that although it's tough doing you like doing it. I love you so much and I also love mother very much. So if you two would really come to know and love each other it would make things much easier for me and for all of us. Every night I pray for father, for mother and for you from now on I will pray that you two will get along well. You have done well for her, I know, so please darling, don't let it get you down now. Do it for me, please.

May 28, 1943, from Camp Anza, Arlington, California

OPPOSITE: Dad in a rare quiet moment with his cherished pups.

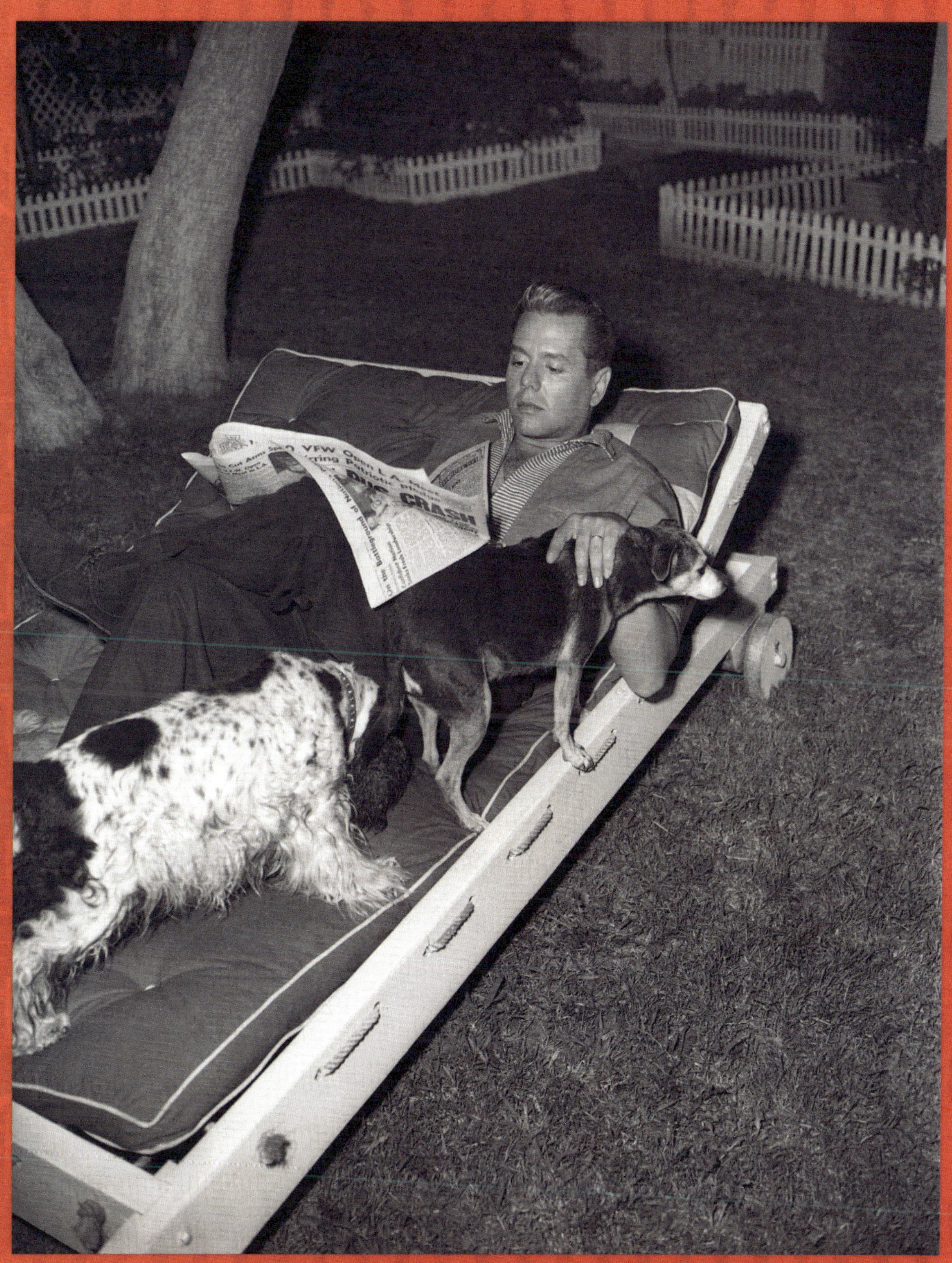
VFW Open L.A.
CRASH

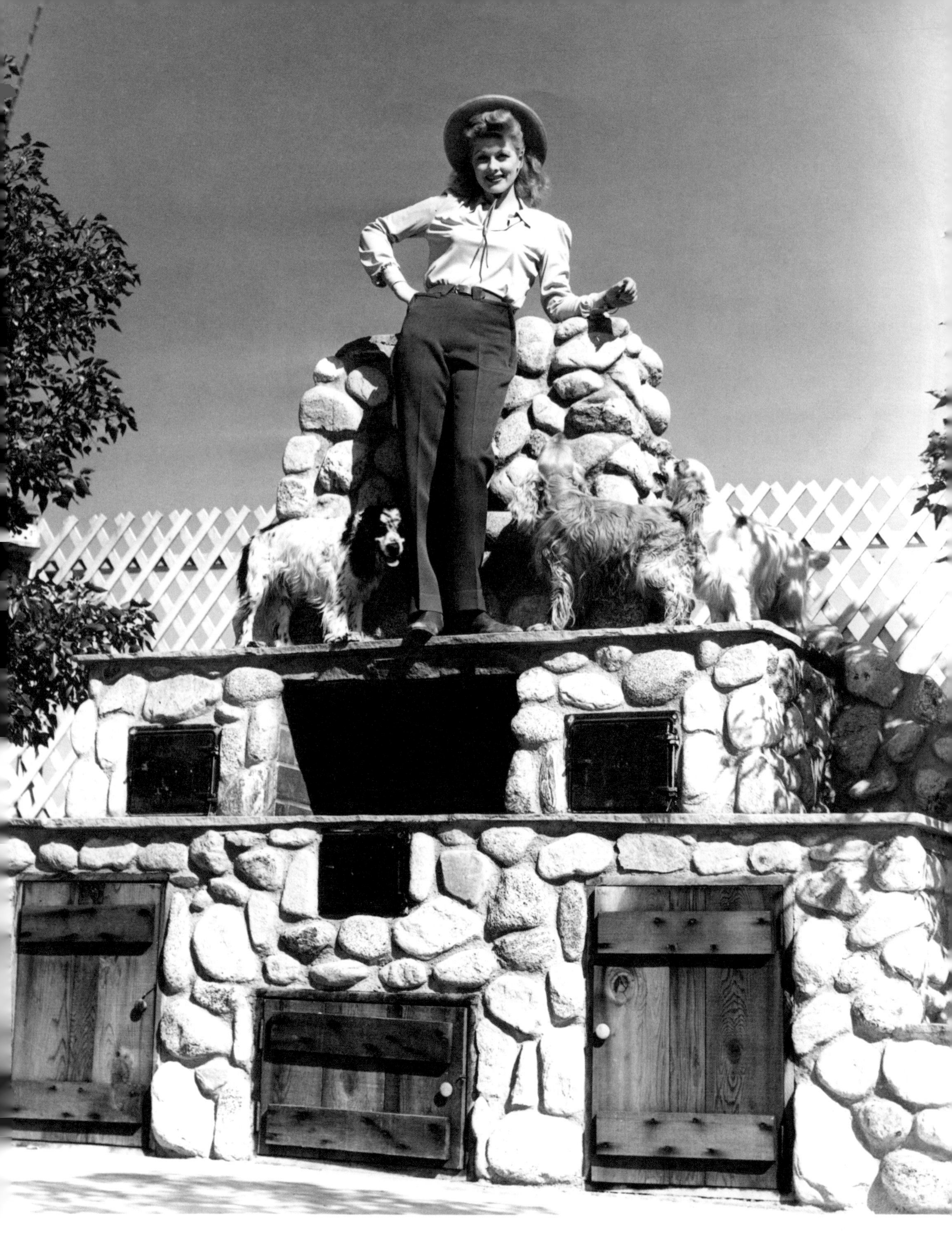

UNITED STATES ARMY

Friday.

Dearest:

After bawling you a[ut] real good on my letter yesterday I got two lette[rs] from you today, Thank God, I couldn't have standed it much longer. You still didn't write Monday though, shame on you.

Your first letter was

after waiting for so long. It's too bad you and mother don't get along better, she has her faults but so have you. I don't mind you telling me about them I know them. I've only ask you to please try and try hard, now that I'm gone she has nobody but you and I would like to feel that though it might be a tough job you will like your job and like

3

UNITED STATES ARMY

doing it. I love you so much and I also love mother very mu[ch] so if you two would rea[lly] come to know and lov[e] each other it would make things much easier for me and f[or] all of us. Every nig[ht] I pray for father, fo[r] mother and for you from now on I will pray that you two will get along well. You have done so m[uch] for her, I know,

please darling, don't let it get you down now. Do it for me, please.

Your second letter was what I was waiting for, what I was hungry for, and I've read it three times already and only got it half an hour ago. Since then I've had lunch, read your letter three times and started to write. Scoop! I'm in a wheelchair today, feel much better and more comfortable.

Ed and Ebba figured
out a way we'll figure
out something, and
I know just what too.
Oh how I miss you here
at nites when they turn
the lights off at nine d...
I just lay there and thin[k]
of you in the shower an[d]
then coming out of the
bathroom with just your
nightie on and laying do[wn]
by my side, so nice and
clean and warm and
beautiful a...
put my arm...
and kiss your...
big eyes, your...
kiss you and...

UNITED STATES ARMY

5

I can't seem to wait until
Sunday comes along so I
can see you, gee it's
lonesome here, so much
worse than at the post.
Just doing nothing all
day, day after day.
... how much
... your bed no
... sick I am.
... saying that
... and about
... an sick lone
... true, Oh God
... so. You'll
...ple husband
... the hell

and I will be thrilled
to hear your voice.
Say hello to the dogs and
cats for me.

Be good my darling
and tell Freddy if he
comes to Arlington
to contact Bill right
away. I hope he's done
something about his
request. Give my love
to Des and Grandpa
and to Ed and Ebba.

Millions and millions
of kisses from your
husband who adores
you and misses you terribly
Den

Your second letter was what I was waiting for, what I was hungry for, and I've read it three times already and only got it half an hour ago. Since then I've had lunch, read your letter three times and wanted to write. Scoop! I'm in a wheelchair today, feel much better and more comfortable. I can't seem to wait until Sunday comes along so I can see you, gee it's lonesome here, so much worse than at the fort. Just doing nothing all day, day after day, you know how much I hate to stay in bed no matter how sick I am.

I'm just praying that what Bill said about going home on sick leave will come true, Oh God how I hope so. You'll have a cripple husband but what the hell

Ed and Ebba figured out a way we'll figure out something, and I know just what too. Oh how I miss you here at nite when they turn the lights off at nine o'clock. I just lay there and think of you in the shower and then coming out of the bathroom with just your nightie on and laying down by my side, so nice and clean and warm and beautiful and then I find my arms around you and kiss your lips, your big eyes, your ears, and kiss you and kiss you and and kiss you, Oh darling how I miss you. I hope you know. I hope you love me very much like you say you do. I hope you are good and think of me all the time.

PAGE 78: Mom was so proud of the craftsman Dad was. He built this barbecue with his own hands. (Not sure how the dogs got up there, though!)

I hope I'll be home soon I just got to that's all I couldn't stay here two month's, it'll drive me nuts.

I don't need anything sweetheart, just my little radio. No stationery, no books. I will listen to you tonite, of course, and I will be thrilled to hear your voice.

Say hello to the dogs and cats for me.

Be good my darling and tell Freddy if he comes to Arlington to contact Bill right away. I hope he's done something about his request. Give my love to Des and Grandpa and to Ed and Ebba.

Millions and millions of kisses from your husband who adores you and misses you terribly.

Desi

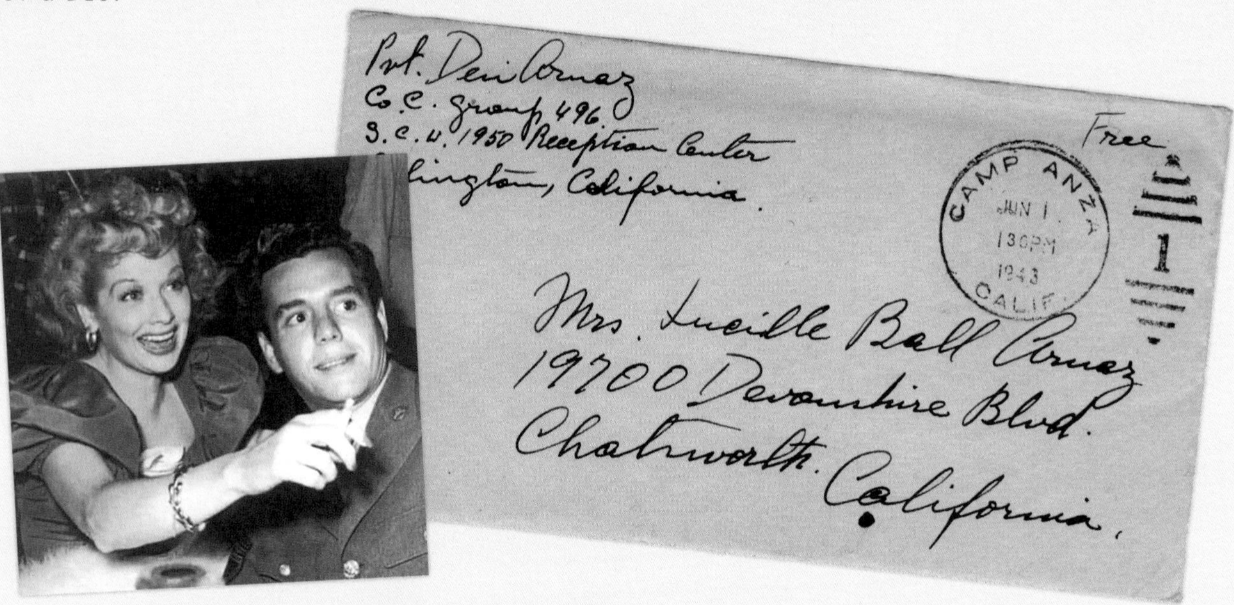

June 1, 1943, from Camp Anza, Arlington, California

ABOVE: A rare night out for Sergeant Arnaz and his wife. The bracelet was rose gold with "I love you. I love you. I love you" engraved on the back.

Monday 7:25 P.M.

Hello Sweetheart:

You've only been gone a little but I already miss you a lot. Gee, it was nice having you here, darling, you have no idea how happy you've made me, really and fully happy. I don't think it'll be so tough this week, what with you on the air tomorrow and Bataan on Wed. and Seven Days Leave on Friday and calling you everyday and being sooo… in love with you, that I know Sat. will come along in a hurry.

You are a wonderful baby and I adore you. I don't mistrust you baby, but I am jealous I can't deny that, and although I know you are o.k. always and all the way, I can't help thinking of those bastards, knowing that I'm away and trying to make passes at you without me being able to be by your side and smash their dirty puss. But I know as you said you don't give them a chance and I know you love me; you could not say it so nicely and so sincerely if you didn't.

Our arguments out here seem so trivial and dogonne silly that they are not even worth mentioning—or apologizing for them.

I think this war it'll make a better man out of me and it'll probably help you a little too. (no sarcasm involved) I had dinner after you left. Hamburger, salad, french fried potatoes, milk and desert. Very nice. I then came back to my little porch and finished reading "The House with a Thousand Candles" and proceeded to write you. I'm going to bed now, I'm kind of tired today, I will listen to the radio for a little while and then to sleep.

So goodnight darling I love you terribly, I'll be thinking of you when I go to sleep, I'd love to kiss your pretty face, God bless you.

Desi

Monday 7:25 P.M.

Hello Sweetheart:

You've only been gone a little but I already miss you a lot. Gee, it was nice having you here, darling, you have no idea how happy you've made me, really and fully happy. I don't think it'll be so tough this week …

…nd calling you every-day and being sooo… in love with you, that I know Sat. will come along in a hurry.

You are a wonderful baby and I adore you. I don't mistrust you baby, but I am jealous I can't deny that, and although I know you are o.k. always and all the way, I can't help thinking of … knowing …

3

smash their dirty pu… But I know as you sa… you don't give them … chance and I know … you love me; you can… not say it so nicely a… so sincerely if you didn't.

Our arguments out… seem so trivial an… dogone silly that … are not even worth… mentioning – or a… gizing for them.

I think this war … make a better man … of me and it'll fin… help you a little … the sarcasm invo…

I had dinner after you left. Hamburger, salad, french fried potatoes, milk and desert. Very nice. I then came back to my little porch and finished reading "The House with a Thousand Candles" and proceeded to write you! I'm going to bed now, I'm kind of tired today, I will listen to the radio for a little while and then to sleep. So Good night darling I love you terribly, I'll be thinking of you when I go to sleep, I'd love to kiss your pretty face,

God bless you

Dei

LUCILLE

11:00 P.M.
Monday Nite

My Baby —

You made me fall in love all over again today. I was dreaming so on the way home I didn't even notice the road.

Felt terribly lonesome for you the <u>minut</u>
you.

And <u>then</u> finding

letters when I got home —

Oh <u>honey</u>! Your second letter nearly <u>threw</u> me — I went over it & over it — and now I'm going to sleep with it under my pillow —

I love you Desi darling — Love you more than anything or anybody in the whole world and I always will — <u>Always</u> — the rest of my life — and we are very lucky Baby — Goodnite Angel —

Your Wife.

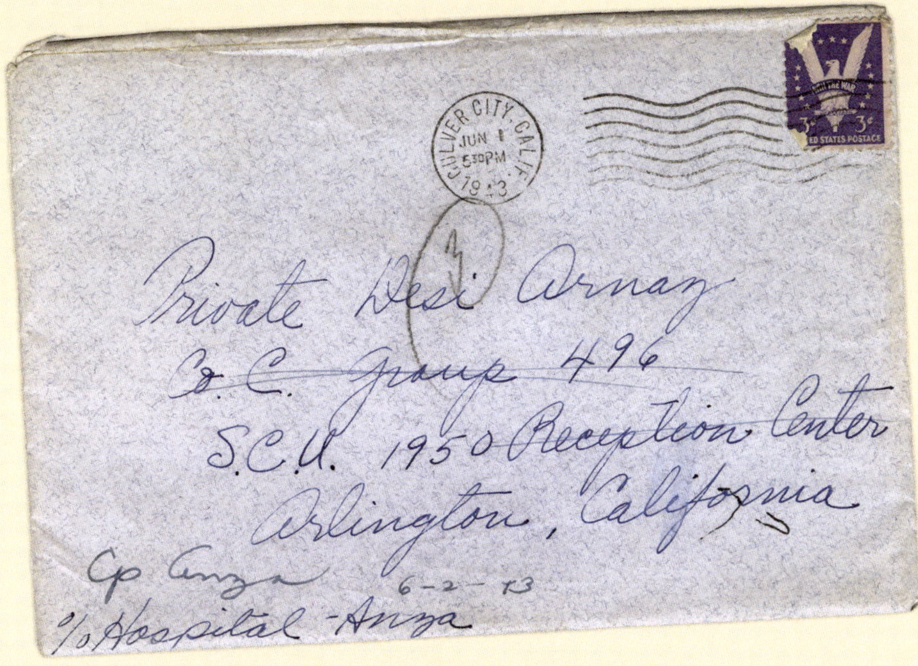

11:00 P.M.
Monday nite

My Baby–

You made me fall in love all over again today. I was dreaming so on the way home I didn't even notice the road.

Felt terribly lonesome for you the minute I left you.

June 1, 1943, Culver City postmark

And then finding these two letters when I got home—oh honey! Your second letter nearly threw me—I went over it + over it—and now I'm going to sleep with it under my pillow—

I love you Desi darling—love you more then anything or anybody in the whole world and I always will—Always—the rest of my life—and we are very lucky Baby—goodnite Angel—your wife.

—¤¤¤—

9:45 A.M.
Tuesday–

Good morning Baby–

Here we go again—back to the old routine—taking care of families—animals + studios—but at least it makes the time pass more quickly—

—¤¤¤—

And right there you called. Gee! it's not going to be half bad this week darling—being able to talk will make the time go much faster—you wait + see. It will make my letters all second hand news probably—but we don't care about that.

Right after you called Mom called.—Daddy fell again this morning. Very bad. Dr coming. Maybe we'll have to take him to the hospital. Will call you, of course, if he gets worse. Although I doubt if they will allow you to leave camp for any reason.

Started trying to trace the dog through City Hall. No luck so far. He gave us a mild tussle when I left him at Lolita's. Wanted to stay with me. Seemed alright this A.M. though.

Please don't forget to call your Mom—often. It's not hard for you now and she will just love it. She'll be home a lot now too.

Damn it—wish to God our letters arrived in 12 hours as they certainly should!

Studio called already this morning—+ said unofficially that we start shooting Thursday. Hope not. Hate to go over there today + get in the middle of that discussion—

Let's see—it ten minutes to 11:00 now—rehearsal is at 3:00 for that lousy Jolson show—guess I better get going to the studio for fittings—

No sun here again today—

Jim + John working like beavers outside—

Mom a nervous wreck downtown with Daddy—guess I better get my hat + pants on—get going.

LUCILLE

9:45 A.M.
Tuesday -

Good Morning Baby -

Here we go again - b
to the old routine -
taking care of families
animals & studios - bu
at least it makes the ti
pass more quickly -

~~~~~~~~

And right there yo

darling - being able to
talk will make the time
go much faster - you
wait & see. It Will make
my letters all second hand
news probably - but we
don't care about that.

Right after you called
Mom called - Daddy
fell again this morning.
Very bad. Dr coming.
Maybe will have to take
him to the hospital.

LUCILLE

if he gets worse.
Although I doubt if
they will allow you to
leave camp for any reason

Started trying to trac
the dog through City Ha
No luck so far. He gav
us a mild tussle wh
I left him at Lolita's.
Wanted to stay with
Seemed alright this
though.

Please don't forget to
call your Mom - often.
It's not hard for you
now and she will just
love it. She'll be home
a lot now too.

Damn it - wish to god
our letters arrived in
12 hours as they certainly
should!

Studio called already
this morning - & said
~~~~~~~~

LUCILLE

unofficially that we start shooting Thursday. Hope not. Hate to go over there today & get in the middle of that discussion —

Let's see – it ten minutes to 11:00 now – rehearsal is at 3:00 for that lousy Jolson show — guess I better get going to th

studio for fittings —

No sun here again today —

Jim & John working like beavers outside —

Mom a nervous wreck downtown with Daddy —

Guess I better get my hat & pants on & get going.

Dogs terrific — jumped all ... last nite ...

LUCILLE

you – & I told them everything. Cats climbing all over the back fence & up the walls & springing at you from every place. Will soon be time to give Lolita her two. Hope someone else will want the others too. Will just leave our Mamma kitty with her little favorite which is a female – and then

Mother & sons won['t] be mating around ... or brothers & sisters

Siegl took the Pigg[y] Thank God! And gee s[he] sure was pretty & fa[t] But glad she's gon[e] We all hate to kill t[he] chickens but will giv[e] you a report later. Will see that your Mo[m] gets lotsa stuff from

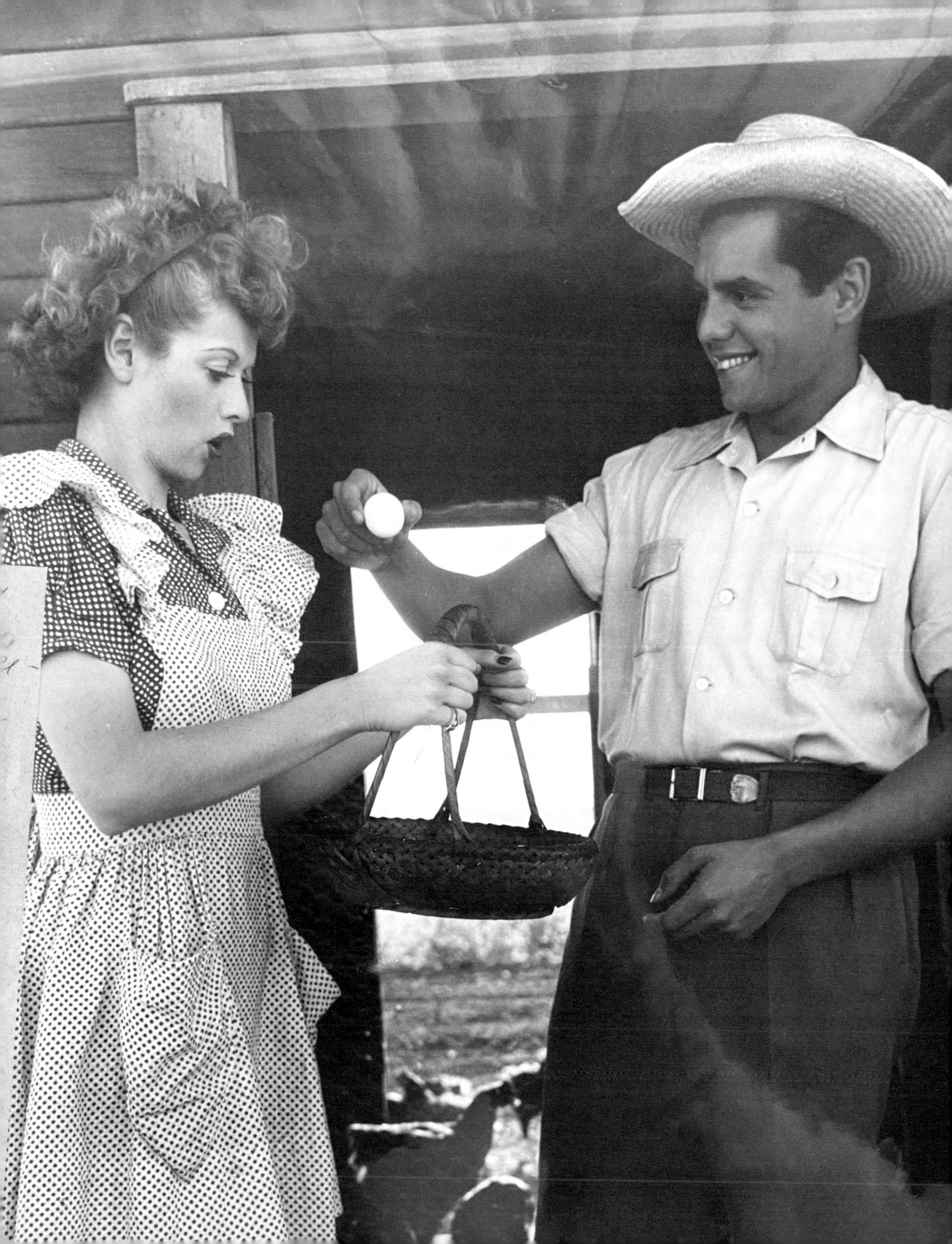

Dogs terrific—jumped all over me last nite and asked all about you—+ I told them everything. Cats climbing all over the back fence + up the walks + springing at you from every place. Will soon be time to give Lolita her two. Hope someone else will want the others too. Will just leave our Mamma kitty with her little favorite which is a female—and then mother + son won't be mating around here—or brothers and sisters—

Seigel took the Piggy, Thank God! And gee she sure was pretty + fat. But glad she's gone. We all hate to kill the chickens but will give you a report later.

Will see that your Mom gets lottsa stuff from the garden this week. In fact right now so I can take it in town with me—

Guess I'll try to get Arthur Freed on the show now + see what he says about a starting date—leading man etc—

PAGE 89: They actually created a real, working farm with chickens, a cow, a pig, vegetable gardens, and orchards, which they reveled in.

—¤¤¤—

later—by 20 minutes—Freed says Picture starts maybe Friday—but still nothing deffinite. Still trying to get Bob Young.

Gotta go in studio now for fittings.

Called again + found address of dog. Almost fell over—dog belongs to Phillipino who used to work for me—+ stupid wife sounded very disappointed we had found it so will probably make a deal with them tonite to keep it. I dun'no—

Anyway—gotta go now—love my one + only husband very much today—miss him more every minute—and will see him Sunday anyway—if not before—

All my love
Lucy

P.S. I said "I gotta go" about 14 times in this letter—guess you have the idea by now—when "I gotta go"—"I gotta go"—

Bye—

In fact right now so—
can take it in town
with me—

Guess I'll try to get ~~Fred~~ Arthur
on the 'phone now & see
what he says about a
starting date—leading
man etc—

Later—by 90 minutes—
Fred says Picture starts

maybe Friday—but
...ll nothing deffinite.
...ll trying to get Bob
...ng.

...otta go in studio now
... fittings.

...led again & found
...ress of dog. Almost
...over—Dog belongs
...hillipino who used
...work for me—

LUCILLE

had found it so
will probably make a
deal with them tonite
to keep it. I dunno
Anyway—Gotta go now
love my one & only husba...
very much today—mis...
him more every minute
and will see him
Sunday anyway—if
not before—
all my lov...
Lucy

LUCILLE

P.S.

I said "I gotta go"
about 14 times in this
letter—guess you
have the idea by
now—when "I
gotta go"—"I gotta
go"—

Bye—

E PLURIBUS UNUM

UNITED STATES ARMY

Tuesday.

Hello baby:

I haven't received
a letter from you today
yet, it's after five P.M.,
so I don't think I ...ill
but I just fell li...
hello to you any...
You are such a ...
pretty baby with ...
big blue eyes th...
just can't help ...
you more and ...
That's all.

It was nice t...
you this mo...

I got my little radio
with me, and I will
just love you hearing
you tonight before I go
to bed, it'll be the last
thing I'll do before going
to bed. Wish you were
coming along. But that's
neither here nor there,
or is it? Yes, I think it
is, I think it's still
here; got it? no, of course
you don't, I do, don't I?
Yes, I just checked, It is
here.

Love you, love you, love you
yes mam, just that,
good night, so long
pretty baby Dei.

Pvt. Desi Arnaz.
C.C. Group 496
S.C.U. 1950 Reception Center
Arlington, California

Free

Mrs. Lucille Ball Arnaz
19700 Devonshire Blvd.
Chatsworth California.

Tuesday

Hello baby:

I haven't received a letter from you today yet, it's after five P.M. so I don't think I will, but I just fell like saying hello to you anyway. You are such a nice pretty baby with such big blue eyes that I just can't help loving you more and more, that's all.

It was nice talking to you this morning I got my little radio with me, and I will just love you hearing you tonight before I go to bed, it'll be the last thing I'll do before going to bed. Wish you were coming along. But that's neither here nor there, or is it? Yes, I think it is, I think it's still here, got it? No, of course you don't I do, don't I? Yes, I just checked. It is here.

Love you, love you, love you, yes mean, just that, good night, so long pretty baby.

Desi

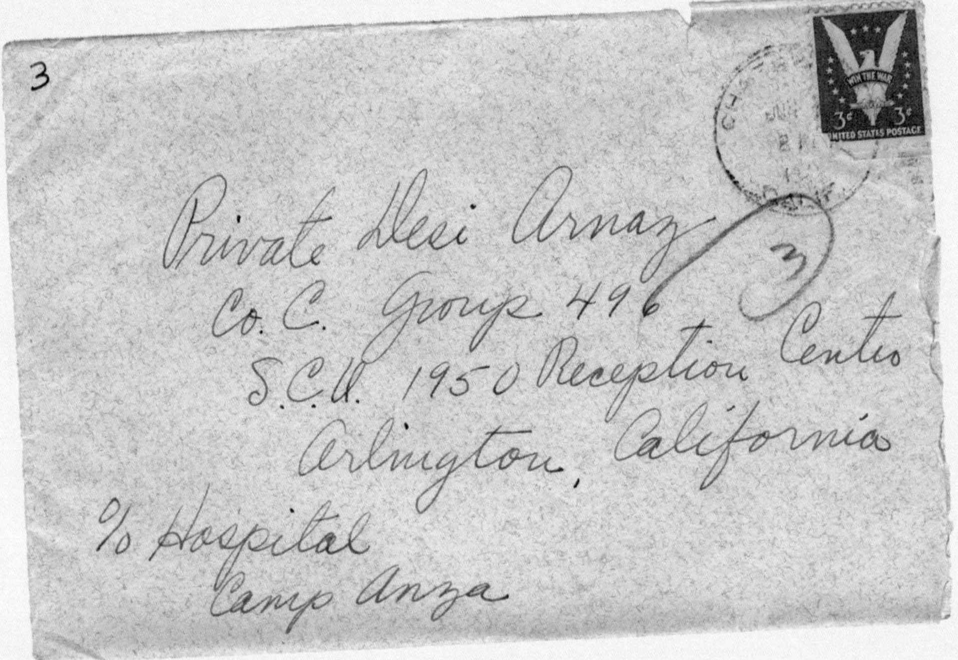

June 1943, Chatsworth postmark

Wednesday
9:10 P.M.

Hello Lovebug—

Going to bed with you tonite—in fact a little ahead of you—but I want to write to my wonderful husband and bed is the place to do it—write I mean—of course—

Wish this thing could be mailed tonite. That's what takes so long—getting to a mailbox.

Oh! Desi darling! The letter I received this noon was so wonderful! Have read it about 8 times. Wish I had you here right now to show you how much I love you for writing it. Gee! It was beautiful. I'm so glad I could spend that much time with you—I loved it. But I couldn't keep my mind off the sex dept. I must admit—the whole time I was with you!

I just wanted to eat you up! Smother you with kisses first—squeeze the breath out of you + bite you—then eat you! You're so damned cute!

Well—I'll get you home again one of these days and now I'd better stop thinking + writing those things or I won't be able to get the humdrum everyday things down on paper—

Guess I'll call Ed + Ebba + get back down to earth—wait a minute

—¤¤¤—

LUCILLE

Wednesday
9:10 P.M.

Hello Lovebug—

Going to bed with you tonite—in fact a little ahead of you—but I want to write to my wonderful husband and bed is the place to do it—write I mean—of course—

Wish this ... mailed tonite ... takes so long ... mailbox.

Oh! Desi darling! The letter I received this noon was so wonderful! Have read it about 8 times. Wish I had you here right now to show you how much I love you for ... ! It was ... I'm so glad I ... that much ... —I loved ... couldn't keep ... the sex dept. ... —the whole ... with you!

LUCILLE

I just wanted to eat you up! Smother you with kisses first—squeeze the breath out of you & bite you & then eat you! You're so damned cute!

Well—I'll get you home again one of these days—and now I'd better stop thinking & writing those things or I won't be able to get the humdrum

everyday things down
on paper —

Guess I'll call Ed + Ebba &
get back down to earth —
Wait a minute ~~~~

5 minutes later

Talked with Ed & Ebba both.
Got my laugh for the
evening — which I layed
the groundwork for this
afternoon — took all
four do[...]
the stude[...]
was wea[...]

LUCILLE

for a wedding color s[...]
Put the top down & le[...]
them climb all over me
I loved it. Had some
fittings with "Irene" - so
[...] office door
[...]all four boy[...]
[...]nctuary for
[...] hour — just
[...] & left him
[...]hey went all
[...]ce & jumped
[...] — and —

well you can just hear
him can't you? So I had
a swell laugh tonite
letting him bawl me
out.

Did you receive a letter
from Ebba? She wrote.

Your Mom has the dog
until Sat. now. No verdict
as yet. Guess they want
it back — don't know for
sure.

Finally got into the back

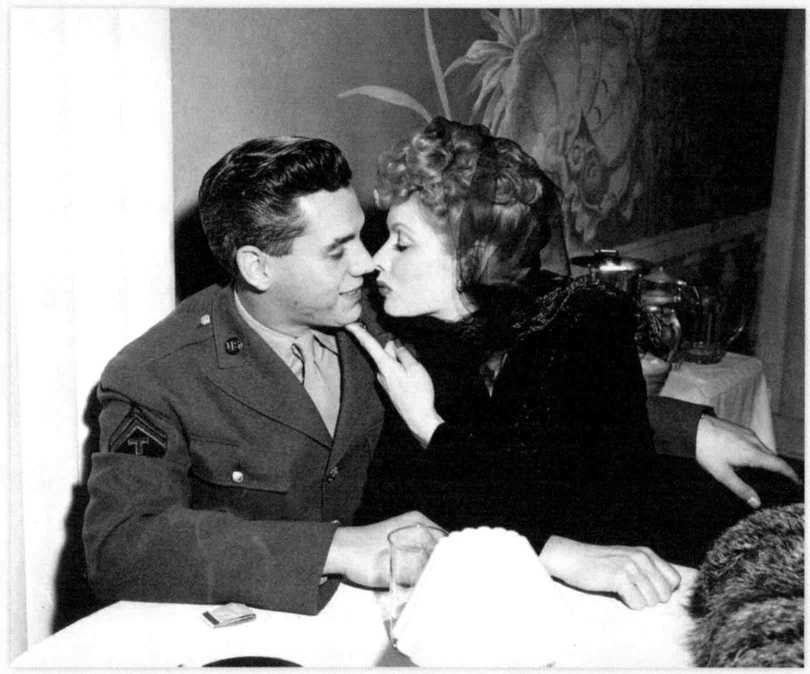

ABOVE: My mother told me that she "couldn't be around him without wanting to touch him."

5 minutes later

Talked with Ed + Ebba both. Got my laugh for the evening—which I layed the groundwork for this afternoon—took all four dogs with me to the studio today—as I was wearing my dungarees for a welding color shot. Put the top down + let them climb all over me + I loved it. Had some fittings with "Irene"—so opened Ed's office door + tossed all four boys into his sanctuary for almost an hour—just ran away + left him yelling + they wet all over his office + jumped all over him—and—well you can just hear him can't you? So I had a swell laugh tonite letting him bawl me out.

Did you receive a letter from Ebba? She wrote.

Your Mom has the dog until Sat. now. No verdict as yet. Guess they want it back—don't know for sure.

Finally got into the back yard today—first time in ages. We have gardenias. Three out + dozens of buds. Cut some roses + shasta daisies—took a walk around looking over some of the weeding John + Jim have done + are doing. John has been swell + Jim wants him next week also so I said alright.

Put in the order to have the bamboo room weather-stripped—all the windows + door + floorboards—also front door. We'll lose our windy comedy wail I guess but thought I might as well have it done while the guy was at it. They'll do it in about a month. Now if I can get the sewer fixed I'll be happy.

LUCILLE

yard today—first time in ages. We have gardenias. Three out & dozens of buds. Cut some roses & shasta daisies—took a walk around looking over some of the weeding John & Jim have done & are doing. John has been swell & Jim wants him next week also so I said alright.

Put in the order to have

the bamboo room weather-stripped—all the windows door & floorboards—also front door. Well be our windy comedy ... I guess but thought ... might as well have it ... while the guy was ... it. They'll do it in about a month. Now ... if I can get the sewer ... ppy.

... ns to

LUCILLE

like her house a lot. Very tired every nite from pushing furniture around & getting everything settled—but she's doing fine. Got her stove & refrigerator delivered & turned on. Please call her desi darling. Hate to tell her you've called me—without you calling her—please do honey &

Bill Smith called me at the studio today. Told me about trying to hurry you to San B. But I already knew the answer — and even if they did — you might *not* be able to come home and you'd just be farther away from me & in a strange ... least we ... es a bit at ... ston

LUCILLE

that. Baby, I just want to tell you how m... like to have you ... in my arms ton... right *now* — I ... keep my mind off ... big wonderful na... body of yours lo... enough to write ... anything else — E... with *clothes* on I'd ... to have you here ... Gosh honey — we m...

never, *never* waste time fighting again — when we could be just buried in each other — Just think all the nites we've thrown away —

If I had you here now I'd start at your eyes & forhead & ears & mouth & work my way down until I'd covered every inch of your beautiful brown body —

Your Mom seems to like her house a lot. Very tired every nite from pushing furniture around + getting everything settled—but she's doing fine. Got her stove and refrigerator delivered and turned on. Please call her Desi darling. Hate to tell her you've called me—without you calling her—please do honey—She would just love it—any time.

Bill Smith called me at the studio today. Told me about trying to hurry you to San B. But I already knew the answer—and even if they did—you might not be able to come home and you'd just be farther away from me + in a strange place—at least we know the ropes a bit at Anza + Arlington.

Oh the hell with all that. Baby I just want to tell you how much I'd like to have you here in my arms tonite—right now—I can't keep my mind off that big wonderful naked body of yours long enough to write about anything else—Even with clothes on I'd like to have you here—Gosh honey—we must never, never waste time fighting again—when we could be just buried in each other—Just think all the nites we've thrown away—

If I had you here now I'd start at your eyes + forehead + ears + mouth + work my way down until I'd covered every inch of your beautiful brown body—

We wouldn't need scotch + plain water + plenty of ice but that wouldn't hurt any either—

And it won't be long before I can do that Angel Baby—and we have so much to be thankful for—you're so near—only two hours away—I can see you every Sunday anyway—can talk to you every day—without it costing anything—(if you were 3000 miles away we'd talk too but we'd be broke for the duration)———

And even when you leave Arlington you'll still be close—and let's hope your work won't have you hopping about the country—

Going to make some candy for you Sat—Hope you gave your chocolate to the boys.

Looks like we shoot Fri! Will leave early Sunday. Be there by noon.

Love you with all my heart—thank you for finally saying you trust me—you don't know how I've hoped you'd write it—

All my love Always—
Your wife

It's 10:15 goodnite Desi

LUCILLE

We wouldn't need scotch + plain water + plenty of ice but that wouldn't hurt any either —

And it won't [illegible] before I can do [illegible] Baby — and we [illegible] much to be than[illegible] for — you're so [illegible] only [illegible] I can [illegible] anyway [illegible]

you every day — without it costing anything — (if you were 3000 miles away we'de talk too but we'de be broke for the [illegible]

[illegible]hen you [illegible] you'll still [illegible] let's hope [illegible] won't have [illegible] about the [illegible]

[illegible]ake some

LUCILLE

candy for you Sat — Hope you gave your chocolates to the boys.

Looks like we shoot Mi. Will leave early Sunday. Be there by noon.

Love you with all my heart — thank you for finally saying you trust me — you don't know how I've hoped you'de write it — All my love Always your Wife

It's 10:15 Goodnite dear.

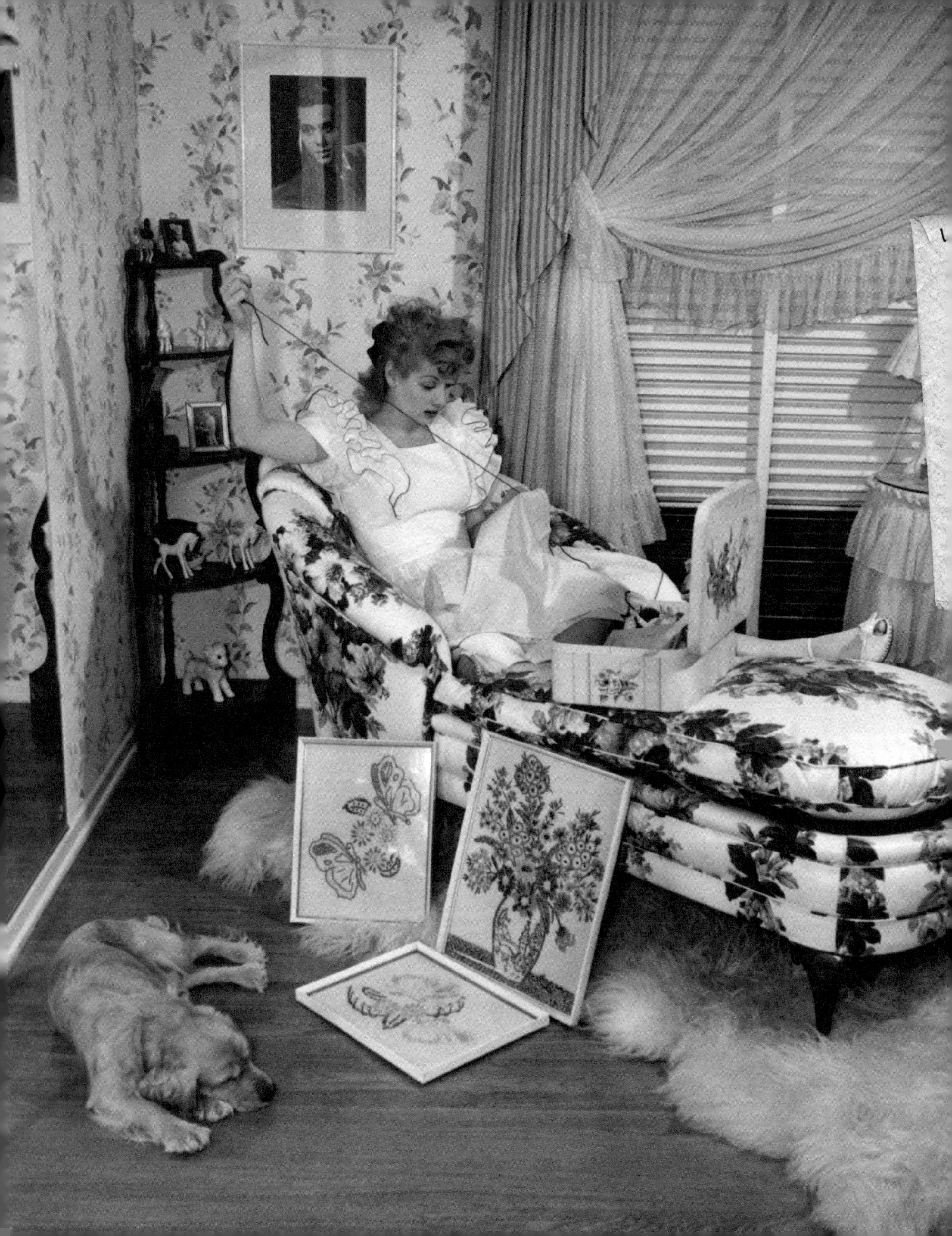

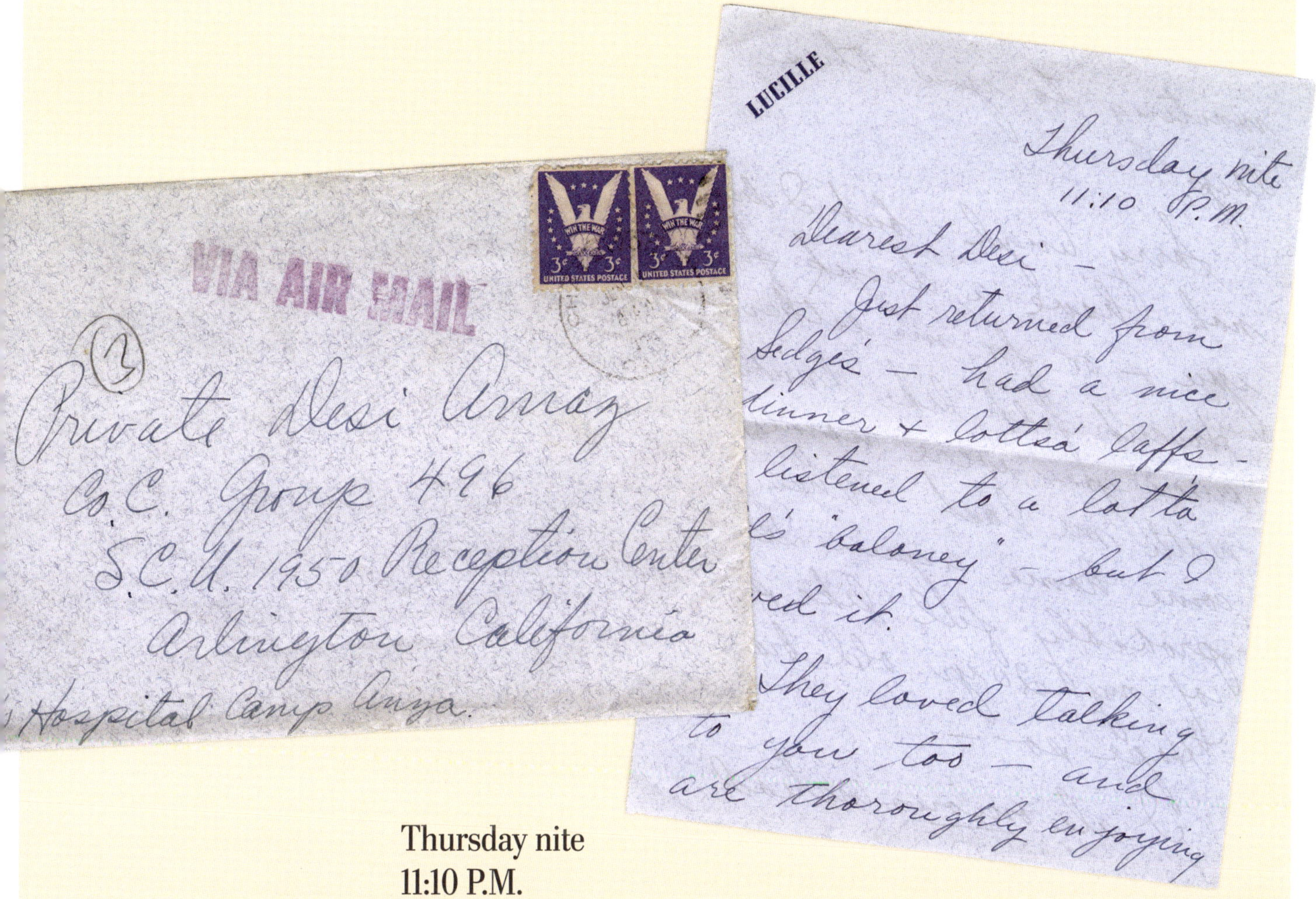

Thursday nite
11:10 P.M.

Dearest Desi–

June 1943, Chatsworth postmark

OPPOSITE: I know this is a posed studio shot, trying to pump up Mom's "homemaker" image, but she did love to pass the time crocheting, knitting, or anything that kept her mind off how much she missed my father.

Just returned from Sedge's—had a nice dinner + lottsa' laffs—+ listened to a lotta Ed's "baloney"—but I loved it.

They loved talking to you too—and are thoroughly enjoying writing to you these days.

Sorry Angel but I did not have a drink for you—or for me either—Haven't felt like drinking since you were home with me last. When you come home again I'll probably feel like some of my 20 yr. old brandy—Hope so—

I ate onions instead—and they are really knocking me out!

I'm kinda tired tonite too so I guess I'll go to sleep and write again in the morning.

Hope I dream about you. Darn it—I very seldom do though—always having nitemares about snakes etc instead—

Do you ever dream about me?—wouldn't it be swell if we could actually meet in our dreams at nite? Gee—wouldn't that be sompon'? No matter where you were—how far away—all we had to do was go to sleep simultaneously and—meet and enjoy ourselves all nite!

Let's work on it.

Love you
Lucy

—¤¤¤—

Friday
11:00 A.M.

Good Morning "Lovebug"–

Well, feel a little more chipper today than I did last nite. Haven't gotten out of bed yet though—maybe I'll just stay here today—no—I know I won't do that—too many things I should get done—because that picture's starting. Such as my suit fitting—+ some shopping—etc etc—"girl stuff."

Gee! forgot to ask you if you were going to call tonite—guess you won't though. You're going to the movie.

So far I have no call for the pic. Hope it starts Monday. If I get a deffinite call for Mon. I'll be out of here early tomorrow A.M. And you won't even get this letter until I'm down there and home again!

Went to the ration board yesterday. Mr. Slane's private little sanctuary. And is he pompous now! But was very nice to me—I am now the possessor of a C ticket + book. I don't know how long it's s'posed to last me—4 years I guess. But anyway—I got it cuz he couldn't say no—it's the law now—so—I also started my "pitch" for new tires—

I'm getting the station wagon all fixed up. That is if I can get some new tires—It'll take me about a month. I'm afraid to drive that station wagon—those tires are so bad. I'm getting more gas for it also—but not until I get it fixed up—and then it'll last me longer—

Mr. Freed said I could bring both pictures down—oh I said that last nite didn't I—? Yes! Anyway—guess I'll call him right now + see what he says about the prints + my starting date (which is much more important to me right now!) Wait a minute—

—¤¤¤—

ting to you were

ery angel -
have a d
- or for me
ut felt lik
you were
me last.
home ag
ably feel
ny 20 yr.
e so -
ate onions

LUCILLE

and they are real
knocking me out! -

I'm kinda tired tonite
so guess I'll go to sleep
write again in the
morning.

Hope I dream abou
Darn it - I very seld
do though - alway
nitemares about bua
etc instead -

Do you ever dream

about me? - wouldn
it be swell if we could
actually meet in our
dreams at nite? Gee -
wouldn't that be sompou
No matter where you
were - how far away -
All we had to do was
go to sleep simultaneously
and - meet and enjoy
ourselves all nite.
Let's work on it. Love you
Lucy

LUCILLE

Friday
11:00 A.M.

"Good Morning Lovebug" -

Well, feel a little
more chipper today than
I did last nite. Haven't
gotten out of bed yet
though - maybe I'll
just stay here today -
No - I know I won't do
that - too many things
I should get done -

because that picture's
starting. Such as my
suit fitting - & some
shopping - etc etc -
"girl stuff."

Gee, forgot to ask you if
you were going to call
tonite - Guess you won't
though. You're going to
the movie.

So far I have no call
for the pic. Hope it
starts Monday. If I get

LUCILLE

a definite call for [illegible]
I'll be out of here ea[illegible]
tomorrow AM. And yo[illegible]
won't even get this l[illegible]
til I'm down there an[illegible]
me again!

Went to the ration boa[illegible]
yesterday. Mr Slane's [illegible]
the sanctuary. And [illegible]
mpous now! Bu[illegible]
very nice to me

I am now the possessor of a C ticket + book. I don't know how long it's s'posed to last me — 4 years I guess. But anyway — I got it anyway he couldn't say no — it's the law now — so I also started my "pitch" for new tires — I'm getting the station wagon all fixed up.

LUCILLE

That is — i[illegible]
some new tir[illegible]
take me abo[illegible]
I'm afraid to [illegible]
station wagon
tires are so b[illegible]
more gas for
but not unt[illegible]
fixed up —
it'll last m[illegible]

Mr Freed sa[illegible]

bring both pictures down — oh I said that last nite didn't I —? Yes! Anyway — guess I'll call him right now + see what he says about the prints + my starting date (which is much more important to me right now!) wait a minute ~~~~~~

Wheeeee!

No prints until maybe

LUCILLE

next week — but — I don't start until Mon. so I'm practically on my way! to see my Baby!!

Called those stale ornery characters that own that police dog — + told them if they were going to pick him up

Wheeeeee!

No prints until maybe next week—but—I don't start until Mon. so I'm practically on my way! to see my Baby!!

Called those stale ornery characters that own that police dog—+ told them if they were going to pick him up to get the hell up here tonite—instead of Sat. nite. Because I had to leave town. So they finally condescended to arrive at 7:00 P.M. at my Mom's. So I'll be there—want to see how the dog reacts to them—how happy he is to see them + if he prefers to go home with them. And if they don't ask too much money. They know my name so they'll probably stick the price up. But I won't pay them a cent as much as I love the dog. Lolita wants to I know—and if it isn't too high a price will get it I'm sure—but I don't know how smart we are trying to keep it.

It almost tore down Lolita's screen door when it met my 4 pooches the other day. I believe they would have killed each other! He will never be able to even visit the ranch—but he is a perfect dog for you in the army—but I wonder how soon you would be able to take him?—about four mo's. I figure. In the meantime—if these stupid people don't want him tonite—we'll be dragging him back + forth because Lolita can't leave him any place—alone—although—I think this week—if he belongs to Lolita for good I will suggest he go into the hospital for a bath etc—good time for it. There! I certainly went on + on about "Rinboy" didn't I? Yes—"Rin Boy."

Guess I'll call your Mom—Wait—

—¤¤¤—

5 min later—had a long talk—gee she sure was happy to talk to you. Besure + call her often honey. She's hoping they don't want the dog. Says he is very happy down there now. Plays with his ball and eats well + loves his backyard.

My God this whole letter is about "Rin Boy" Latest development on "Meet the Jerks"—Dick Carlson leading man—if they can't get Bob Young—I'd rather have Bob. Gee I certainly have plenty of qualms about this picture—plenty. Mr. Freed just said they were in there right now trying to inject some fun + business for me + a number or something. Sounds like trying to make a "silk purse out of a sow's ear"—to coin a phrase. Anyway—I'm stuck so I'm just going to plow into it + keep my head about me—My clothes are sensational "Irene" of course. And my hair goes a swell soft blonde shade in black + white and the camera man is very good. And the director likes me very much.

...xt the hell up here
...te – instead of Sat.
... Because I had
leave town. So
... finally condescended
arrive at 7:00 P.M.
my Mom's. So I'll
there – want to see
... the dog reacts to
...hem – how happy he
to see them & if h...
...refers to go home

LUCILLE

with them. And if
they don't ...
money. ...
name so ...
stick the ...
I won't ...
be much ...
dog. Lolit...
know – an...
too high ...
it I'm ...

know how smart we are
trying to keep it.
It almost tore down
Lolita's screen door when
it met my 4 pooches
the other day. I believe
they would have killed
each other! He will
never be able to even
visit the ranch – but he
is a perfect dog for you

LUCILLE

I wonder how soon you
would be able to take
him? – about four mo's.
I figure. In the
meantime – if these
stupid people don't
want him tonite – we'll
be dragging him back
& forth because Lolita
can't leave him anyplace
alone – although I
think this week – if

he belongs to Lolita for
good I will suggest
he go into the hospital
for a bath etc –
good time for it. There!
I certainly went on &
on about "Rinboy"
didn't I? Yes – "Rin Boy".
Guess I'll call your Mom –
Wait ——
5 min later – had a long
talk – gee she sure was

LUCILLE

happy to talk to you.
Be sure & call her often
honey. She's hoping
they don't want the do[g]
Says he is very happy
down there now. Plays
with his ball and eats
well & loves his backya[rd]

My god this whole
letter is about "Rin Bo

Latest development on
"Meet the Jerks" — Dick Carlson
leading man - if they can't
get Bob Young - I'd rather
have Bob. Gee I certainly
have plenty of qualms
about this picture —
plenty. Mr Freed just
said they were in
there right now trying
to inject some fun
& business for me &

LUCILLE

a number or something
Sounds like trying to
make a "silk purse out
of a sow's ear" — to
coin a phrase. Anyway -
I'm stuck - so I'm just
going to plow into it
& keep my head about
me — My clothes are
sensational "Irene" of
course. And my hair

goes a swell soft blonde
shade in black & white
and the camera man is
very good. And the
director likes me very
much.

They settled on Ginny
Simms for the lead in
that technicolor "Broadway"
so if Ginny Simms can
do it — I don't want
it any way — I know

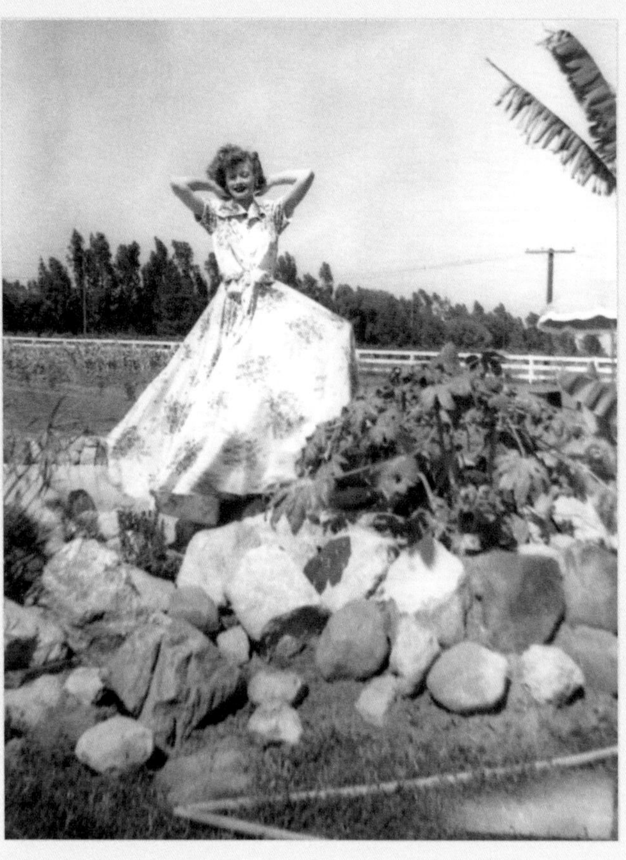

They settled on Ginny Simms for the lead in that technicolor "Broadway" so if Ginny Simms can do it—I don't want it anyway—I know you think she's wonderful but I think she stinks!

Wish they'd hurry up + finish my suit at Dunkirk shop. Honestly—it takes months to get anything made. Course I'm not too good about coming for fittings.

Have been pestered to pieces about the Hollywood Canteen—Ida Koverman Is making—getting L. Ball to the canteen—her life's work I think—So far I've held out—but I'm running out of excuses. Except for Sundays—I don't need any better excuse than my Baby—but I guess one nite a week—on the early shift—6 to 9—I'm going to have to do something.

ABOVE: What they created together, in Chatsworth, was their dream come true.

Daddy is better this week. Dr says there is a possibility that this slight elevation 1100 ft—but here is what makes Daddy worse every time he comes to the ranch—could be you know—it's not enough for us to notice but for his poor old overworked heart it might be. In fact the Dr has almost forbidden him to come out here—if he has more of those "spells" out here—he can't come any more—

Gee it's 12:25 Gotta hurry this up to the mailbox—

I love you
Lucy

LUCILLE

you think she's wonder[ful]
but I think she stinks

Wish they'de hurry u[p]
& finish my suit at
Dunkirk shop. Honestly
it takes months to get
anything made. Course
I'm not too good abou[t]
coming for fittings.

Have been pestered
to peices about the
Hollywood Canteen —

Ida Koverman is
making — getting L. Ball
to the canteen — her
life's work I think — So
far I've held out — but
I'm running out of excuses.
Except for Sunday —
I don't need any better
excuse than my Baby —
but I guess one nite
a week — on the early
shift — 6 to 9 — I'm

LUCILLE

going to have to do
something.

Daddy is better this
week. Dr says there
is a possibility that
this slight elevation
1100 ft — but here is
what makes daddy worse
every time he comes
to the ranch — could b[e]
you know — it's not
enough for us to

notice but for his
poor old overworked
heart it might be. In
fact the Dr has almost
forbidden him to come
out here — if he has
more of those "spells" —
out here — he can't come
any more —

Gee it's 12:25 Gotta
hurry this up to the
mail box —
I love you
Lucy —

Pvt. Desi Arnaz
Co. C. Group 496
S.C.U. 1950 - Reception Center
Arlington, California

Free

CAMP ANZA JUN 4 1 30 PM 1943 CALIF.

Mrs. Lucille Ball Arnaz
19700 Devonshire Blvd
Chatsworth
California

UNITED STATES ARMY

Thursday.

My dear Miss Ball:

I have seen yo[ur] pictures, I have heard yo[u on] the air, I have met you [I] have gone out with you [I] have liked you, I have [loved] you. I have marry you [I] have slept with you, [and] I am in love with yo[u]. May I have an autog[raphed] picture of yourself.

Just a fa[n]

Hello sweetheart:

I'm just w[aiting] until six thirty or seven o'c[lock] to start trying to get y[ou]

on the phone.

I got a very nice letter from Emily ~~today~~ today and I've already answered it.

I also got two nice, wonderful lovely, pretty letters from you angel, and I've read them and read them, over and over again. Baby, when am I going to have you again all to myself in a nice candle lit bedroom? Gosh darling, I miss you something awful, I don't want to wait too much longer, it doesn't agree with me.

Last nite I went to see Bataan and everybody seemed to enjoy it very much and I got all kinds of compliments, in fact, this morning I was given a price, it might not be an Oscar

Thursday

My dear Miss Ball:

I have seen you in pictures, I have heard you on the air, I have met you, I have gone out with you, I have liked you, I have loved you, I have marry you, I have slept with you, oh boy!!! I am in love with you, may I have an autographed picture of yourself.

Just a fan.

—¤¤¤—

Hello sweetheart:

I am just waiting until six thirty or seven o'clock to start trying to get you on the phone.

I got a very nice letter from Emily today and I've already answered it.

I also got two nice, wonderful lovely, pretty letters from you angel, and I've read them and read them over and over again. Baby, when am I going to have you again all to myself in a nice candle lit bedroom? Gosh darling, I miss you something awful, I don't want to wait too much longer, it doesn't agree with me.

PAGE 114: Mom and Dad huddle with fellow RKO contract player Jackie Cooper.

Last nite I went to see Bataan and everybody seemed to enjoy it very much and I got all kinds of compliments, in fact, this morning I was given a price, it might not be an Oscar but it's an Army price namely: "LATRINE DUTY," like I wrote Emily, I guess I'm on my way to stardom now.

I've talked to mother this noon and she seemed to be very happy with her house and everything, she just loves that kitchen, I guess you've done a nice job, as I knew you would, you pretty angel. Mother said you weren't coming until Sunday morning, gee, that's too bad, what's the matter work? Well I guess I'll know when I talk to you tonite

I got some Cuban papers from Dad and a note saying he was sending some cigars and a nice long letter and to take care of my knee.

I miss the Ranch so much, it must be just out of this world.

Take care of yourself baby, good care, you are going to need every ounce of strength you have when you come face to face with me again in that candle lit room. I am going to e-a-t y-o-u u-p. If you think your hair is red, wait 'till I get through with you, you are going to be burning all over.

I got to stop this somehow, it doesn't get me anywhere fast.

Bye. Desi

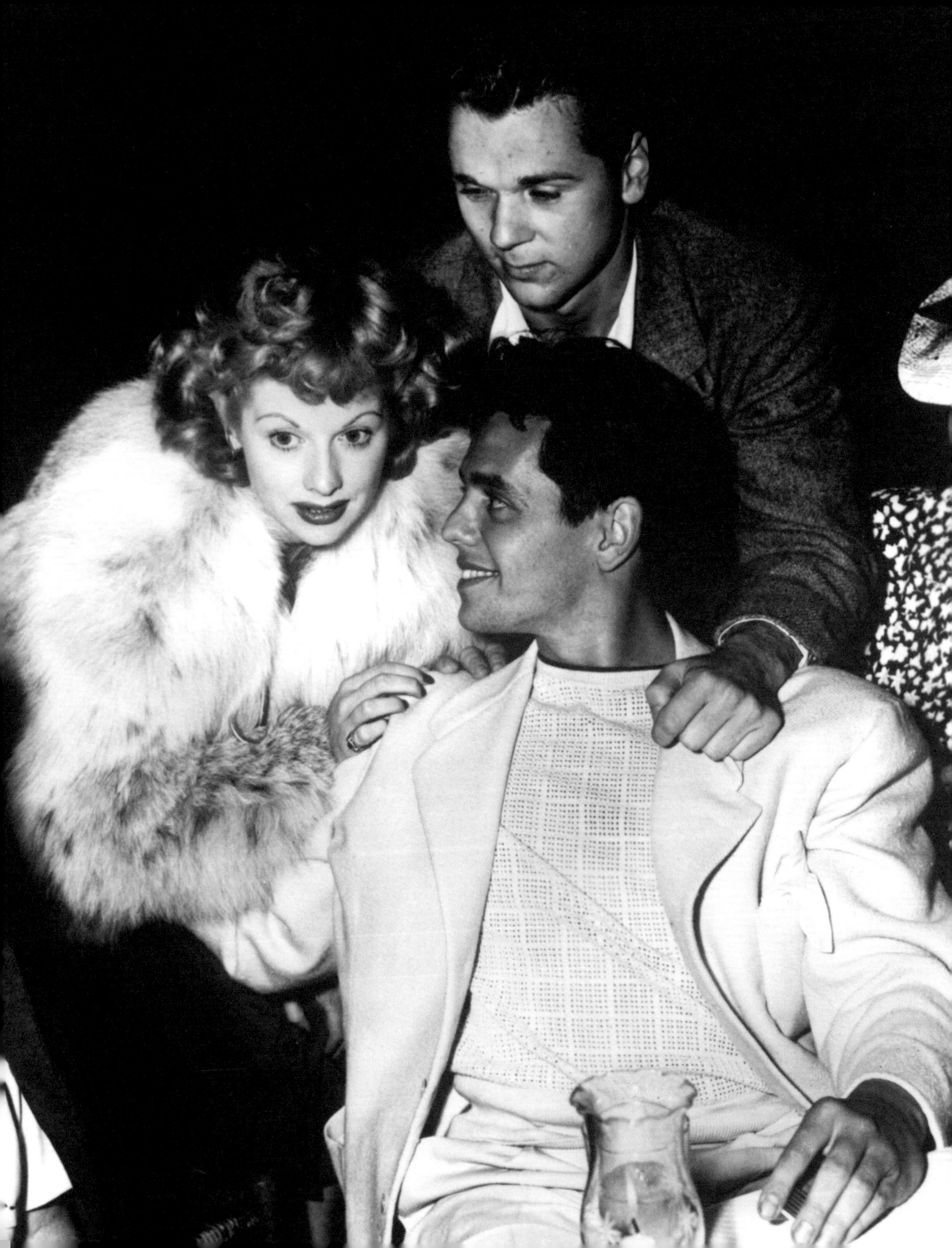

3

UNITED STATES ARMY

but it's an Army price.
namely: "LATRINE DUTY"
like I wrote Emily, I guess
I'm on my way to stardom
now.

I've talked to mother th[illegible]
noon and she [illegible]
be very happy [illegible]
and everything [illegible]
that kitchen, I g[illegible]
done a nice j[illegible]
you would, you [illegible]
mother said you [illegible]
coming until S[illegible]
morning, Gee, tha[illegible]
what's the matte[illegible]
Well I guess I'll [illegible]
when I talk to y[illegible]

I got some Cuban papers
from dad and a note
saying he was sending some
cigars and a nice long
letter and to take care of
my knee.

I miss the Ranch so much,
it must be just out of this
world.

Take care of yourself baby,
good care, you are going
to need every ounce of
strength you have when
you come face to face
with me again in that
candle lit room. I am
going to e-a-t y-o-u u-p.

If you think your hair is
red, wait till I get through
with you, you are going
to be burning all over.

I got to stop this somehow, it
doesn't get anywhere fast Bye Den.

Friday 3:00 P.M.

Dearest Desi,

Just mailed a long rambling—probably way boring letter to you—but have just been outside working for a couple of hours and hate to tear myself away—get dressed + go into town for my fittings and 7:00 o'clock appointment for dog—but guess I gotta. Course I'll be very late as usual. It's 3:00 now and I haven't even started to dress—and am waiting for Auntie to prepare some freshly killed chickens I'm taking in for Mom to fix tonite—for me to take to you tomorrow—or at least take with us tomorrow cuz I'll probably eat most of them. Anyway we are "taking our picnic lunch" with us.

June 4, 1943, Los Angeles postmark

OPPOSITE: Young, fresh faced, and as in love as they'd ever be.

Jim is very pleased with John + showed me all he had accomplished. The kid really works like a beaver. I'm so glad I thought of hiring him. We never would have found anyone who would do this weeding.

So—

Thousands of people ask about you at the studio yesterday. I didn't even know their names, let alone remember them. But you certainly have not been forgotten—and there have been a couple of stories in the paper about you this week so everyone is well "up" on your activities.

I'll save clippings when I get them—I didn't happen to buy those papers the day they ran.

I love you today so much darling and have been thinking of you every minute this A.M. Thought maybe you'd call today early as you are going to the movie tonite—

But I did talk to you so late last nite—I s'pose it's best to save it now until I see you.

Bye darling
Your Esposa
???
Is that right
???

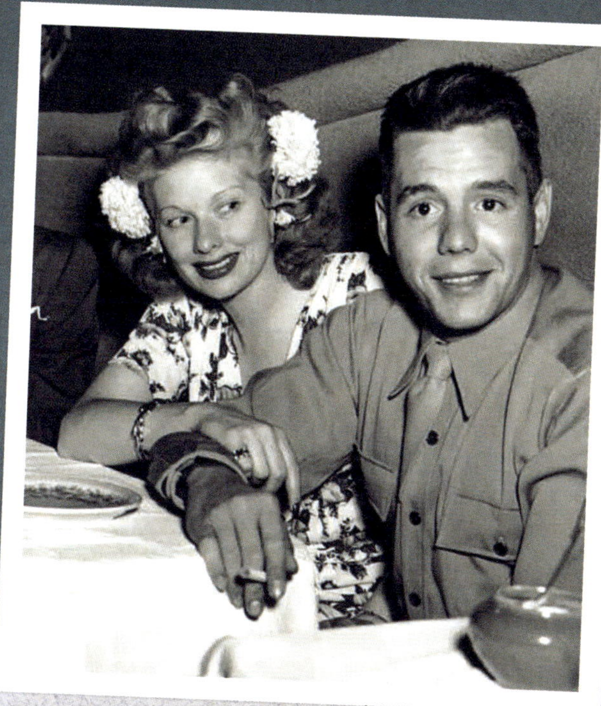

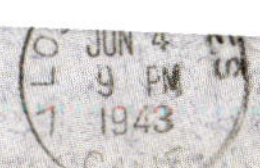

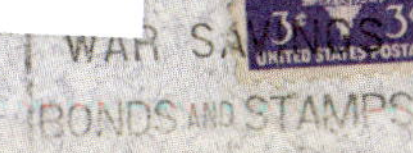

Private Desi Arnaz
Co C Group 496
S.C.U. 1950 Reception Center
Arlington, California
c/o Hospital Camp Anza

LUCILLE

Friday

Dearest Deei, 3:00 P.M.

Just mailed a long rambling - probably ve[illegible] boring letter to you - [illegible] but have just been outside working for a coup[le] of hours and hate to tear myself away - ge[t] & go into town fo[r] fittings & 7:00 o'cloc[k] for dog - but g[illegible]

gotta. Course I'll be very late as usual. It's 3:00 now and I haven't even started to dress - and am waiting for Auntie to prepare some freshly killed chickens I'm taking in for Mom to fix tonite - for me to take to you [illegible] least [illegible] [tom]orrow [illegible] eat [illegible] [an]yway

LUCILLE

we are taking our picnic lunch" with us.

Jim is very pleased with John & showed me all he had accomplished. The kid really works like a beaver. I'm so glad I thought of hiring him. We never would have found anyone who would do this weeding. So ——

Thousands of people ask about you at the studio yesterday. I didn't even know their names, let alone remember them. ... you certainly have ... been forgotten — ... there have been a cou... stories in the paper about you this wee... so ever... "up" on...

LUCILLE

I'll save clippings when I get them — I didn't happen to buy those papers the day they ...

...ow today so ...ling and have ...king of you ...date this A.M. ... maybe you'd ...y early as ...going to the

movie tonite —

But I did talk to you so late last nite — I s'pose it's best to "save it" now until I see you —

Bye darling

Your Esposa

???

Is that right

???

LUCILLE

Monday A.M.
10:20
In the Bamba
Room –

My Baby –
Auntie, John & Jim
haven't arrived yet –
so have the peacefulln

You know which those
are? I have several
all around – but out
in front especially. Guess
they'll still be good when
you get here.

And everything goes
ahead now until you
arrive to stay for a
month. I mean – everything
will be planned for

LUCILLE

"When Desi g
that" – or
Anyway – I
ed work ou
Had my doub
But now whe
the cast is com
24th – I'm sure
home –

Thought m

call me at the ranc
last nite. Even thou
I did just leave yo
I stopped in at Carl
& left word at M
where I was. But
call. S'pose it wa
silly to expect
so soon but I w
love to have talke
you last nite.

Stayed at the

LUCILLE

much too late. W
talked & talked &
didn't get home
almost 11:00. F
spaghetti – (Is th
the way to spell it
I still don't like the
she cooks it – but
like to eat in thei
kitchen on Sunday
nites. But I fou

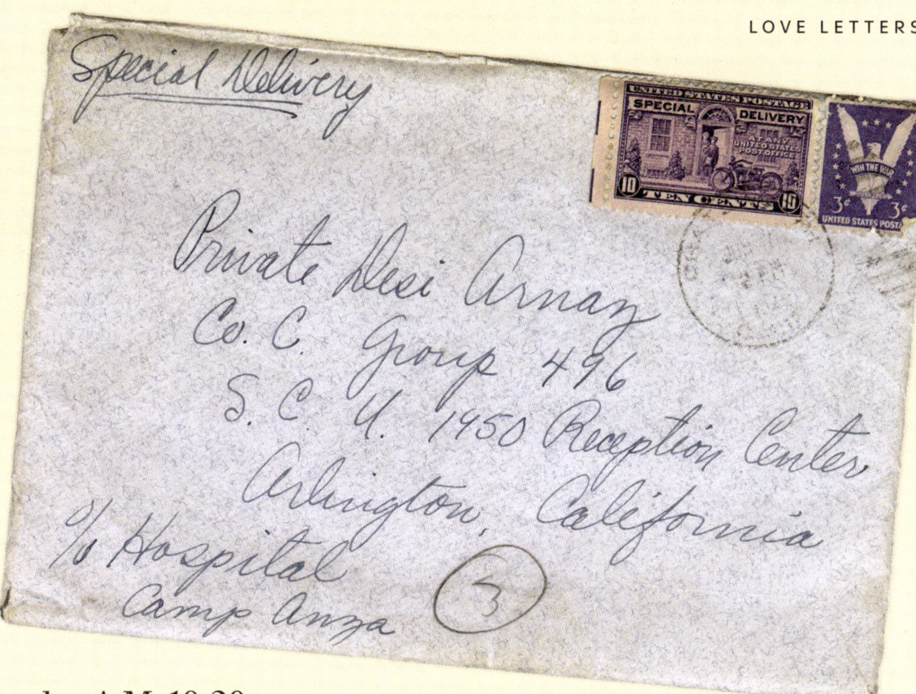

Monday A.M. 10:20
In the Bamboo Room–

My Baby–

Auntie, John + Jim haven't arrived yet—so have the peacefulness of the whole ranch around me—It is so beautiful here this morning—Wish you could see the big hydrangeas. You know which those are? I have several all around—but out in front especially. Guess they'll still be good when you get here.

And everything goes ahead now until you arrive to stay for a month. I mean—everything will be planned for that—all statements will be prefaced with "When Desi gets here we'll do that"—or this—

June 7, 1943, Chatsworth postmark

Anyway—I'm sure it'll all work out this time. Had my doubts last week. But now when I know the cast is coming off the 24th—I'm sure you'll get home—

Thought maybe you'd call me at the ranch last nite. Even though I did just leave you—I stopped in at Carlsons + left word at Mom's where I was. But no call. S'pose it was silly to expect one so soon but I would love to have talked with you last nite.

Stayed at the Carlson's much too late. We talked + talked + I didn't get home until almost 11:00. Had spaghetti—(Is that the way to spell it?)—I still don't like the way she cooks it—but I like to eat in their kitchen on Sunday nites. But I found out one thing—it is one of the things that makes me miss you more than anything else. Isn't that funny—That's just the kind of an evening when I get kinda blue + crybaby—when I'm having a quiet Sunday nite supper in their kitchen seems as though you've just gotta be there! Same thing when I go to Ebba's + Ed's. Those two places remind me constantly of you. The other places are numerous of course but topping the list is the bedroom + pool.

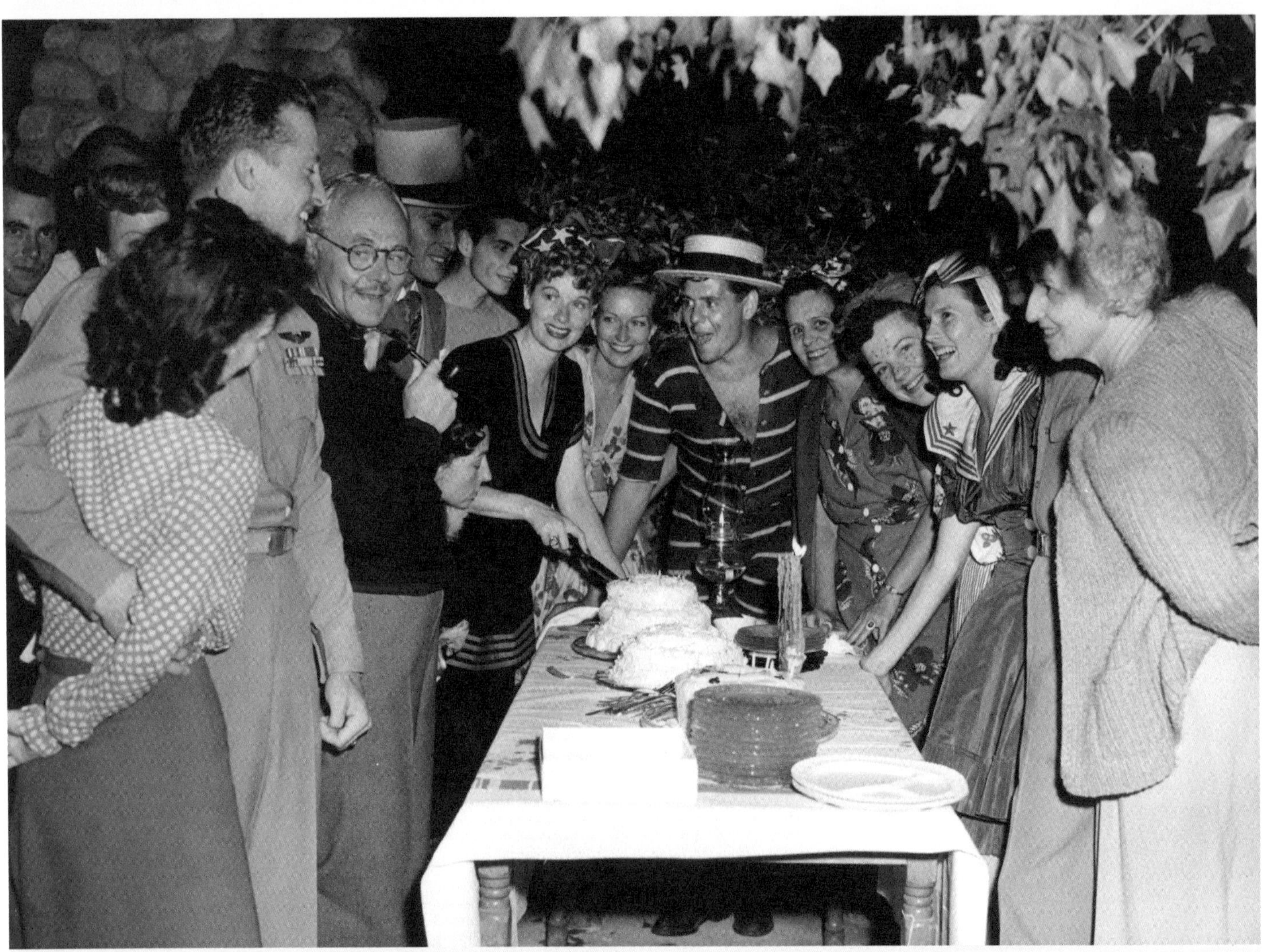

ABOVE: Many Hollywood pals were Chatsworth neighbors and they all loved the Desilu Ranch costume picnics. That's actor Charlie Ruggles in the glasses and to his left, peeking out between him and my mother, is Agnes Moorehead.

Couldn't find the Sedge's last night when I got in town. Ebba was probably busy at that North Hollywood plane crash—I don'no.

Mom + Aunt Helen left the house spotless + made me several new crotcheted—now how do you spell that!—doilies—anyway you know what I mean—table centerpieces—chair things like the ones on your chair. They really are beautiful + the sort of thing I hope I may keep for years + years + and hand down to our children.

No call from studio yet this morning.

Arthur Lyons office called—Botsford wanted your address as the Cecil B. De Mille office was trying to locate you—why I don't know as yet—nor did they. You'll get a letter probably.

Got a cute letter from you when I got home last nite. Was nice to have just before I went to sleep. And incidentally—Boy! Did I sleep! Bet you did too. Hope you had no ill effects from your sexy weekend. And be very careful this week—especially walking out of doors—those nasty ruts are the menace.

out one thin
is one of the
that makes
you more th
else. Don't th
That's just
an evening
get kinda
crybaby —
having a gr
nite supper

LUCILLE

there! &
when I go
& Ed's. Th
remind m
of you. Th
are numerou
but topping
is the bed
Couldn't f
last night

probably busy at that
North Hollywood plane
crash — I donno.

Mom & Aunt Helen left
the house spotless &
made us several new
crotcheted — now how
do you spell that! —
doilies — anyway you
know what I mean

LUCILLE

ones on your chair. The
really are beautiful &
the sort of thing I
hope I may keep for
years & years & hand
down to our children

No call from studio y
this morning.

Arthur Lyons Office
called — Botsford wa

your address as the
Cecil B. de Mille Office
was trying to locate
you — why I don't
know as yet — nor
did they. You'll get
a letter probably.

Got a cute letter from you
when I got home last
nite. Was nice to have
just before I went
to sleep. And incidentally —

LUCILLE

Boy! Did I sle

Bet you did too.

you had no ill

from your sexy

And be very caref

week - especially

out-of-doors - th

ruts are the me

I had a wond

we

an

bu

not find anything to

be unhappy about - for

a couple of days at

a time

Listen,

special

very m

Besure a

if I do

answer

before

LUCILLE

instruction with Father

English tonite or tomorrow -

whenever he can make it.

And so please as a very

nice gesture - and in

keeping with what I'm

doing - will you

for two weeks - that

ill - just two weeks -

Please Desi - don't get

mad at me for pi

two weeks. Please do

have any disbelief a

me at all. Just t

everything out of y

mind that bothers

you and wash

nice & clean - Just

give me a clean

slate for a couple o

weeks anyway - and

then if you want,

LUCILLE

go back to mistrusting

me after that - you

may. But while

I'm working with Father

English - let that be

your contribution.

Please? I have to

have a thorough &

direct answer on this

right away Desi. And

now don't think

you can do
for 2 weeks t
start with
English. So
know.

The deadline for
combination
from last S
better have e
ready for yo
e

LUCILLE

is Jim can have John—
Sounds like
example does.

Auntie want
all about you
They all arrive
an hour ago
now – I've bee
for about an
in between. t

+ coffee –

I'm very happy this
Dear darling – and ve
anxious to talk to yo
tonite. Isn't that silly
We talked & talked –
I can hardly wait to h
your voice – Wish the
would hurry up and te
me what goes today. M

LUCILLE

I'm going to get so
cooking done toda
maybe. So I get
nourishment this
for a change.

Phyllis has called
times – About star
with me on this
I really don't wan
because she for
damned many thi
but I dunno

haven't called her yet.
I need someone & I hate
to go through that
dinge dept. again –
Wish to heavens Harriett
would come back!

Hope you love me today –
hope the weekend wasn't
a dis(s)appointment to you
in *any* way – (not counting
that fifth try –) darn you
Wish you could receive my
letters quicker – Bye

Lucy

I had a wonderful weekend Desi baby—and I know you did too but I wish you would not find anything to be unhappy about—for a couple of days at a time anyway.

Listen, I have a very special and, to me, very important request. Besure and answer this if I don't get your answer over the phone before your letter arrives.

I am starting 2 weeks instruction with Father English tonite or tomorrow—whenever he can make it. And so please as a very nice gesture—and in keeping with that I'm doing—will you for two weeks—that's all—just two weeks—erase all superstition from your mind?

Please Desi—don't get mad at me for just two weeks. Please don't have any disbeliefs about me at all. Just take everything out of your mind that bothers you and wash it nice + clean—Just give me a clean slate for a couple of weeks anyway—and then if you want to go back to mistrusting me after that—you may. But while I'm working with Father English—let that be your contribution. Please? I have to have a thorough + direct answer on this right away Desi. And if you don't think you can do it—easily for 2 weeks then I can't start with Father English. So let me know.

OPPOSITE: At their home, in Chatsworth, making a wish after their second wedding, this time in the Catholic Church, 1949.

The deadline for the Jim + John combination is two weeks from last Sat. They better have everything ready for your eager eyes by then or else! Anyway that's as long as Jim can have John—Sounds like an algebra example doesn't it?

Auntie wants to know all about you this morning. They all arrived about an hour ago. It's 11:23 now—I've been writing for about an hour—in between telephone calls—dog fights—+ coffee—

I'm very happy this A.M. Desi darling—and very anxious to talk to you tonite. Isn't that silly? We talked + talked—yet I can hardly wait to hear your voice—Wish the studio would hurry up and tell me what goes today. Maybe I won't have to go in at all—it's 11:30 now! If I was going to work after lunch I should have left here at 10:00. Goody!

I'm going to get some cooking done today maybe. So I get some nourishment this week for a change.

Phyllis has called many times—about starting with me on this picture—I don't really want her because she forgets so damned many things—but I dun'no—I haven't called her yet. I need someone + I hate to go through that dinge dept. again—Wish to heavens Harriett would come back!

Hope you love me today—hope the weekend wasn't a disappointment to you in any way—(not counting that fifth try—) darn you. Wish you could receive my letters quicker—Bye

Lucy

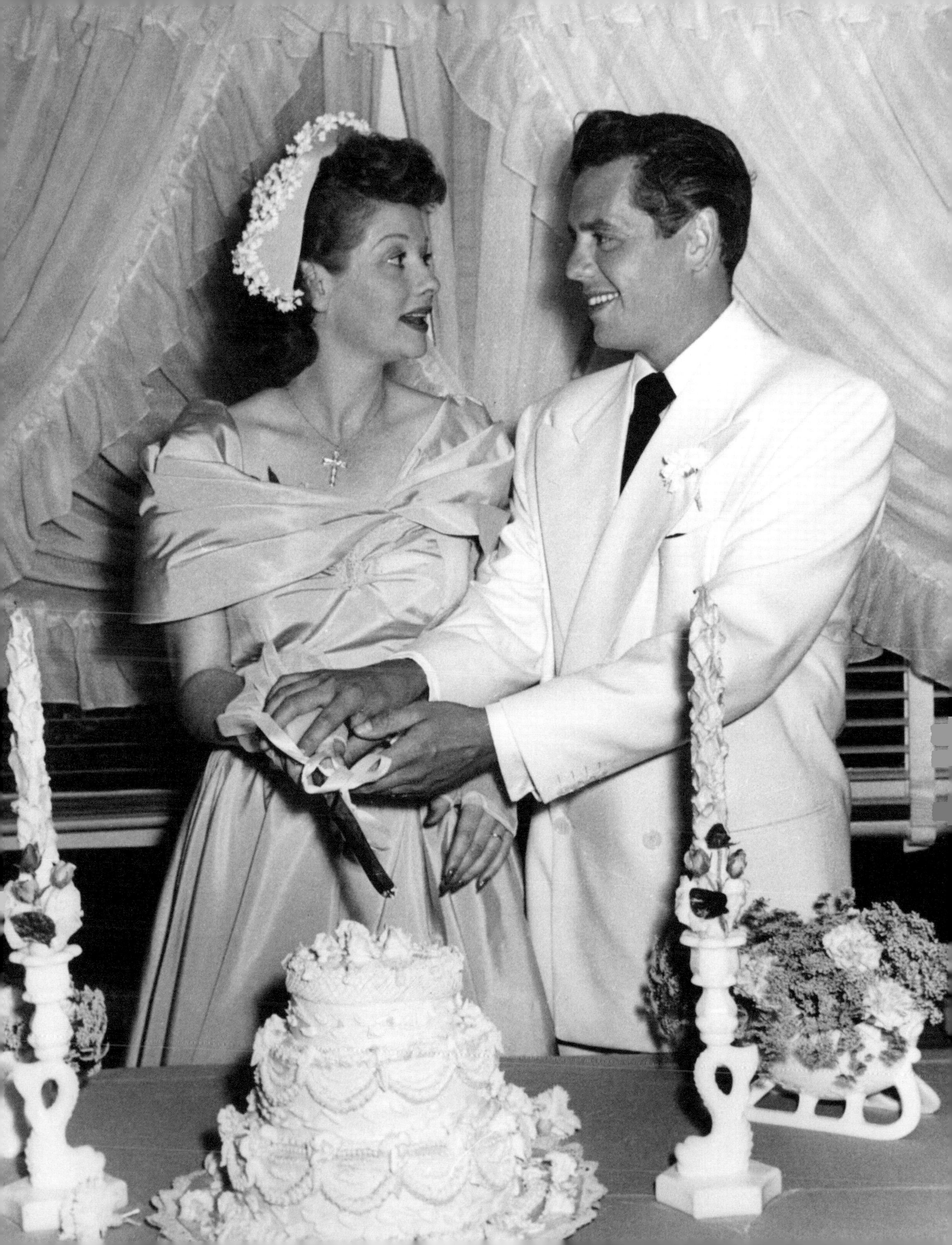

DESI

Monday 5:30 P.M.

Hello pretty baby!

How are
got two letters from yo
after we talked, one of
from Thursday night a
other from Friday n
the one you've talked a
your other letter that
Sunday. A nice long let
you, for writing so
all

the cast I mean, so I supposed he'll change it tomorrow.
Well, Monday is almost gone
that's one day less tha
have to wait to kiss you
after you left yesterday
to supper and came b
smoke a couple of c
read a little, but now
ded that the best thin
was to go to bed and
your wonderful lette
talk !!! I
how you
Then I thought of o
day together, from t
I saw the red car
down the road, I
outside watching for

DESI 3

Then I rushed to the front
door to meet you and you
had come to the back, I
started rushing back trying
to get there before the nurse
would tell you about my
getting a pass, I saw you coming
through the corridor and I
was soooooooooo happy
I had something inside of
me going up and down, like
just before going on the stage
sometimes, and then chan-
ging clothes and getting
out of here driving with
you and mother towards
"liberty". Oh honey.

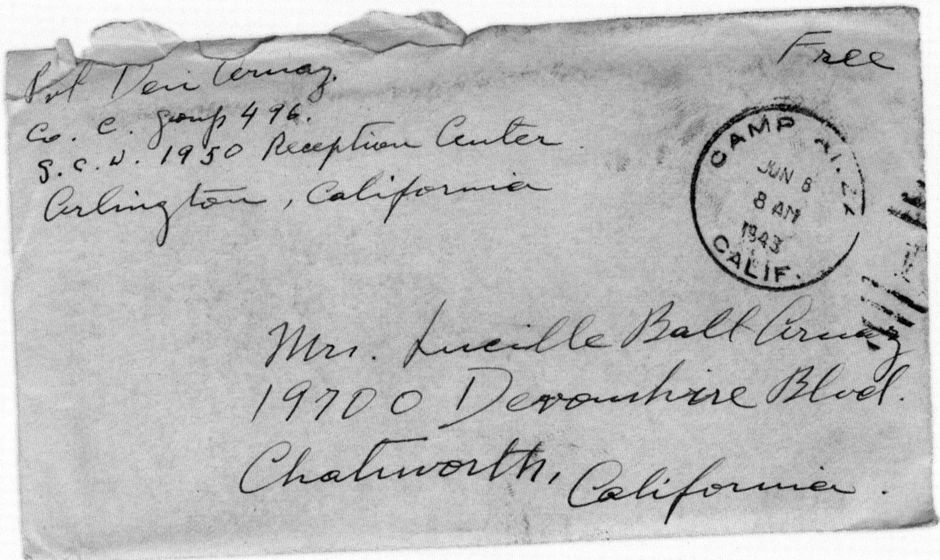

Monday 5:30 P.M.

Hello pretty baby!

How are you? I got two letters from you today after we talked, one of them from Thursday night and the other from Friday morning, the one you've talked about in your other letter that I got Sunday. A nice long letter. Thank you for writing so wonderfully all last week, I love you more and more for it, if that is possible. I was so glad to find you home, really hated to hang up. He hasn't change my cast yet, but it's cutting in right above my ankle, the cast I mean, so I suppose he'll change it tomorrow. Well, Monday is almost gone, that's one day less that I'll have to wait to kiss you again.

June 8, 1943, from Camp Anza

OPPOSITE AND PAGE 130: Dad's gifts: an aquamarine cross and matching jumbo-sized aquamarine ring.

After you left yesterday, I went to supper and came back smoke a couple of cigarettes read a little, but soon decided that the last thing to do was to go to bed and read your wonderful letter, honey!! how you talk!!! I love it.

Then I thought of our whole day together, from the moment I saw the red car coming down the road, I was sitting outside watching for it. Then I rushed to the front door to meet you and you had come to the back. I started rushing back trying to get there before the nurse would tell you about my getting a pass, I saw you coming through the corridor and I was sooooooooooo happy I had something inside of me going up and down, like just before going on the stage sometimes, and then changing clothes and getting out of here driving with you and mother toward "liberty." Oh honey you don't know how good I felt, really wonderful, the green grass, and the trees and everything looked so beautiful; then getting that nite at the Hotel, and the Scotch, and

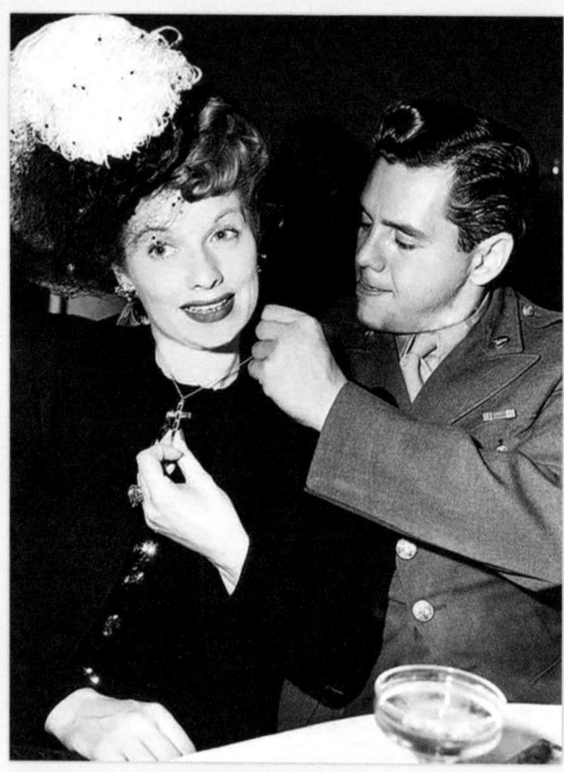

mother wanting to go to the movies, and then, then darling, there you were, so beautiful, so loving, so close to me, so alone with me, to be able to kiss your sexy lips as long as I wanted as hard and sexy as I wanted, to be able to hold you as I wanted, to touch you where I wanted, to know that it wasn't going to be just that, but that I could have you, all of you, and there is some much of you to have, like I first said when I saw you first: "there is a hunk of woman," just darling you are that all of that a hunk of beautiful, gorgeous, sexy, loving woman, and I love you.

Those twenty four hours were of the very best we've spent and in my memory they'll go right along with Florida, Lou Maxon's, the Pierre, and your apt. in Laurel, and all the other wonder-hours we've had. And by God we'll have them again, just as many times that many and more much more, wouldn't we honey? You are darn right we will.

I love you darling, hurry up and work with Father English, so we can make it legal with God, he's been darn good to us. Say hello to the family, kiss the dogs and kittens for me and salute the chickens.

Be good (I don't have to say that, do I?) and take care of yourself,

All my love
Desi

I felt, really wonderful, the
green grass, and the trees
and everything looked so
beautiful; then getting
that wire at the Hotel
and the Scotch
mother was ...
to the moves, an...
then darling, th...
were, so beautifu...
loving ...
so alo...
be able ...
as long ...
and se...
be able ...
wanted ...

5

DESI

I wanted, to know that it wasn't
going to be just that, but that
I could have you, all of you,
and there is some much of you
to have, like I first said when
... first: "there is a hunk
... darling you are
... a hunk of
... you, sexy,
... and I love you
... four hours
... ry best we've
... y memory,
... along with
... masons, the
... apt. in Laurel,
... other wonder-

hours we had. And by God we'll have them again, just as many times that many and more much more, wouldn't we honey? You are darn right we will.

I love you darling, hurry up and work with Father English, so we can make it legal with God, he's been darn good to us. Say hello to the family, kiss the dogs and kittens for me and salute the duchess.

~~Be good~~ and take care of yourself, All my love Desi

(I don't have to say that, do I?)

Pvt. Desi Arnaz
Co. C. Group 496
S.C.U. 1950 Reception Center
Arlington, California

Free

CAMP ANZA
JUN 9
1:30PM
1943
CALIF.

Mrs. Lucille Ball Arn
19700 Devo
Chatsworth,
Ca

DESI

Tuesday:

Hello my darling:

I need you so very mu
today, right now, just to s
with me and ho
only that, it would
derful.

Well I'm back
e took the cast of
nd we found the
nd of big and ca
end any too mu
t scared, it's n
ecause I can ben
nd he says it'l
n a couple of
t's pretty clear

cartilage it's not healed
and maybe not even in
where it was supposed t
be. You feel so darn
helpless here without you
own doctors that can t
you what it is and wh
you know and trust.
I expected it to find it pre
good, but there you are
he says it's as bad as
started. Oh
y, you
ry to
ngs, b
some
nebo
t's pre
s I
it's

DESI

just that I expected it to be
so much better when he
took the cast off, and
when I couldn't almost
move it and started
thinking about what Ed
had told you about taking
that stuff out of there
might cause a stiff
leg, I got pretty scared
but he assured me that
it was not stiff, that the
cartilage was probably not
in place, having slipped
out or maybe having never
been in place, but he wouldn't
put another cast on until
he sees how much mo

Tuesday:

Hello my darling:

I need you very much today, right now, just to sit with me and hold my hand if only that, it would be wonderful.

Well I'm back in bed. He took the cast off today and we found the knee still kind of big and cannot bend any too much, didn't get scared, it's not stiff because I can bend it some, and he says it'll be better in a couple of days, but it's pretty clear that the cartilage it's not healed and maybe not even back where it was supposed be. You feel so darn helpless here without your own doctors that can tell you what it is and whom you know and trust; I expected it to find it pretty good, but there you are he says it's as bad as when we started, oh God I feel so lousy, just lying here, I'm sorry to write all these things, but I've got to talk to somebody and that somebody it's only you. It's probably not as bad as I made it sound, it's just that I expected to be so much better when he took the cast off, and when I couldn't almost move it and started thinking what Ed had told you about taking that stuff out of there might cause a stiff leg, I get pretty scared but he assured me that it was not stiff, that the cartilage was probably not in place, having slipped out or maybe never having been in place, but he wouldn't put another cast on until he sees how much movement I can get out of it in a couple of days and how much he can reduce it. I hope it doesn't spoil our weekend, but gee I guess it might honey, oh God I wish I was home. Sorry.

June 9, 1943, from Camp Anza

Well baby, I might not be able to get to a phone again for a while just walking without the cast. And I don't know yet if he is going to put on another one or not.

Please write, write every day I hate it so in bed, without talking to you. By the way my going out last weekend had something to do with this. It probably wasn't right when he first fixed it.

Love you, Desi

P.S. Oh I just don't want to stop writing to you. I've read those first two pages over and I guess I seemed pretty low, but please don't worry, I'm sure it'll be all right in a couple of days, anyway it's not stiff he says.

I love you darling, I miss you so much. All I do is think of you and home. Well everything has an ending so I'll be up and around again before long and we won't even think of these awful days here.

I'll always remember that wonderful weekend though, one of the nicest we've ever had, I think. Honey I think I'll say so long until tomorrow don't worry, probably everything it'll look better by the time this reaches you in case I can't call you tomorrow which it's very probable I will wire you so you won't worry.

So long darling sleep well, gee I love you

Desi

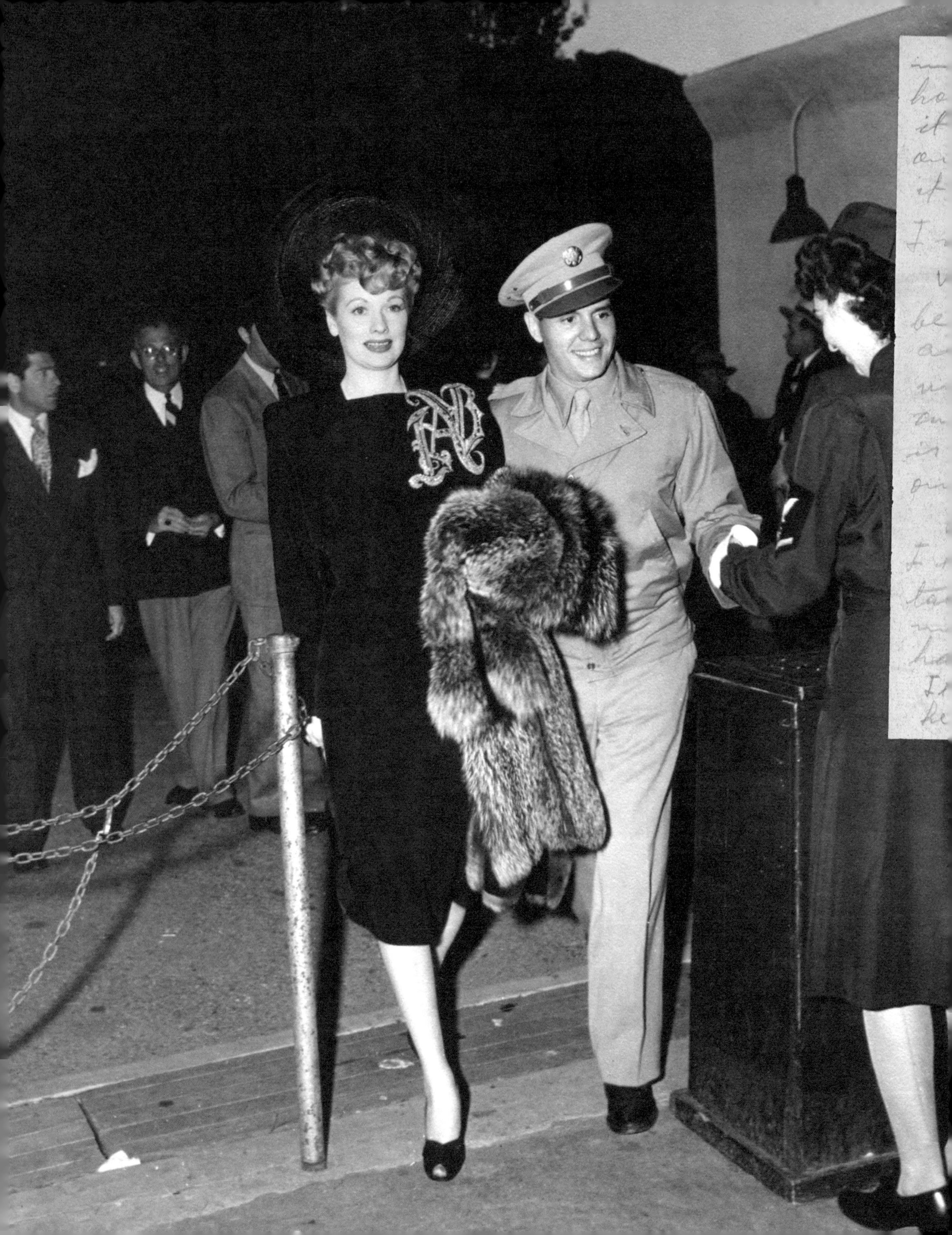

a couple of days and
… much he can realize
I hope it doesn't spoil
weekend, but gee I guess
night honey, Oh God
… ish I was home. Sor…
… ll baby I might …
… ble to get to a phon…
… me for a while, …
… hime without the car…
… I don't know yet if …
… oing to put on anoth…
or not.
… ease write, wr…
… te it so in be…
… ing to you. …
… going out la…
… nothing to d…
… robably won't …
… irst fixed it. Lov…

5

DESI

P.S. Oh I just don't want
to stop writing to you.
I've read those first
two pages over and I guess
I sound pretty low, but
… I'm
… ight
… ys, any-
… e says.
… I miss
… I do
… d home.
… an
… and
… re hang
… think
… here.
… mber

that wonderful weekend
though, one of the nicest
we've ever had, I think.
Honey I think I'll say
so long until tomorrow
don't worry, probably everything it'll look better
by the time this reaches you and
in case I can't call you
tomorrow which it is very
probable I will wire you
so you won't worry.

So long, darling, sleep
well, gee I love you

Desi

DESI

Wednesday.
1:45 P.M.

Hello my baby darling:

Well I'm still laying in bed, no cast, the knee still swollen and not knowing what the hell is going o[n] ... stiff, thank ... bend even m... day, but he s... have to wait a... days to know... to put on and... just let me b... BO... wi... I ... I'm...

but probably won't get it. This will probably mean no outside week end, I guess it was too good to be true. Gosh darling I need you and miss you so terribly. I just lay here ... think of you all day ... until I fall ... thing will work ... well, let's ... get a heat ... so I'll finish

4:45 P.M.

... knee is landing ... and he says

3

DESI

its coming along well. God Am I relief!! Whoopee!!!!!

He gave me an exercise to let it hang over the bed sitting by the side of the bed and I straighten the leg up and then let it down easy and it started bending a little and a little more, far from complete movement yet but it does move.

And to top everything I told him you were waiting by the phone for my call

Pvt Desi Arnaz.
Co. C. Group 496.
S.C.U. 1950 Reception Center
Arlington, California.

Free

CAMP ANZA, CALIF.
JUN 10
1:30 PM
1943

Mrs. Lucille Ball Arnaz.
19700 Devonshire Blvd.
Chatsworth, California.

Wednesday.
1:45 P.M.

Hello my baby darling:

June 10, 1943, from Camp Anza

Well, I'm still laying in bed, no cast, the knee still swollen and not knowing what the hell is going on. It's not stiff, thank God, I can bend it even more than yesterday, but he says that he'll have to wait a couple or more days to know if he'll have to put on another cast or just let me lay here like Bob and the other boys with the heat treatment. I wish I could go home. I'm going to try and try but probably won't get it.

This will probably mean no outside week, and I guess it was too good to be true. Gosh darling I need you and miss you so terribly. I just lay here and think of you all day and night long until I fall asleep.

I hope everything will work out soon and well, let's pray for it.

I am going to get a heat treatment now so I'll finish this later.

—¤¤¤—

4:45 P.M.

Honey!!! my knee is bending much better and he says it's coming along well. God am I relief!! Whoopee!!!!

He gave me an exercise to let it hang over the bed sitting by the side of the bed and I straighten the leg up and then let it down easy and it started bending a little and a little more, far from complete movement yet but it does move.

And to top everything I told him you were waiting by the phone for my call tonight and to please let me go down there in the wheelchair and he said O.K. Oh I haven't been sooo happy since last week-end, yesterday and today until just now I feel almost like crying. I still doubt it very much about Sat. and Sunday, but I'm certainly going to do everything he tell's me to make it better. Let me see, I got all night tonight, Thursday, Friday and part of Saturday.

It's three days, with God's help it might be good enough to be able to spend the night in the Hotel with you. Oh honey, I feel so much better, you don't know. It's so horrible to think that one might be a cripple. But let's not talk about it. I CAN TALK TO YOU and that keeps me going. I got a nice long letter from Deke. I'll keep it so you can read it Saturday, I hope it's Sat. You'll try, won't you honey?

Gosh I love you, your pretty face. I thank God for you and mother all the time and also for father, only I wish so much he was with us. Wouldn't it be perfect then. Well, everything happens for the best, they say.

So long baby, I'll call you in a little while.

All my love sweetheart
Desi

tonight and to please let
me go down there in
the wheelchair and he
said O.K. Oh I haven't
been sooo happy since
last week-end, …
and today until …
now I felt almost …
crying. I still don't …
very much about …
and Sunday, but …
certain …
thing …
it bette…
got a …
There…
part…

DESI 5

Its three days, with
God's help it might be
good enough to be able
to spend the night
in the Hotel with you.
Oh … I feel so much
… don't know
…le to think
…ght be a
… let's not
… I CAN
…u and
…e going.
…e long
Duke. I'll

keep it so you can read it
Saturday, I hope it's Sat.
You'll try, won't you honey?
Gosh I love you, you
pretty face. I thank
God for you and mother
all the time and also
for father, only I wish
so much he was with us.
Wouldn't it be perfect then.
Well everything happens
for the best, they say.
So long baby I'll call
you in a little while.
All my love sweetheart
Desi

LUCILLE

Thursday
10:00 A.M.

Good Morning Darling —

Been awake since 8:30. Had so many nitemares last nite it looked like [illegible] convention in my su[illegible] conscious. And at [illegible] moment cant rememb[illegible] what any of them [illegible] about. All I know [illegible] Dr Evert is sending [illegible] a comp[illegible] vitami[illegible]

been discovered to have a deficiency of sugar in my system that is frightening. So am doin[g] something about it. Ed [illegible] & Ebba were truly alarm[ed] [illegible] nite at Charlie[s] [illegible] literally dive [illegible] andies from [illegible] us — Pralines [illegible] w I never [illegible] of any kind [illegible] s — I didnt

LUCILLE

I sure as hell have recently.

No call from studio for work. But three calls about fitting. Just checked again and I have to go in.

No sun again today! More of these dull days. I don't mind them. Wish we'd not have heat all summer.

Hope I get a letter from

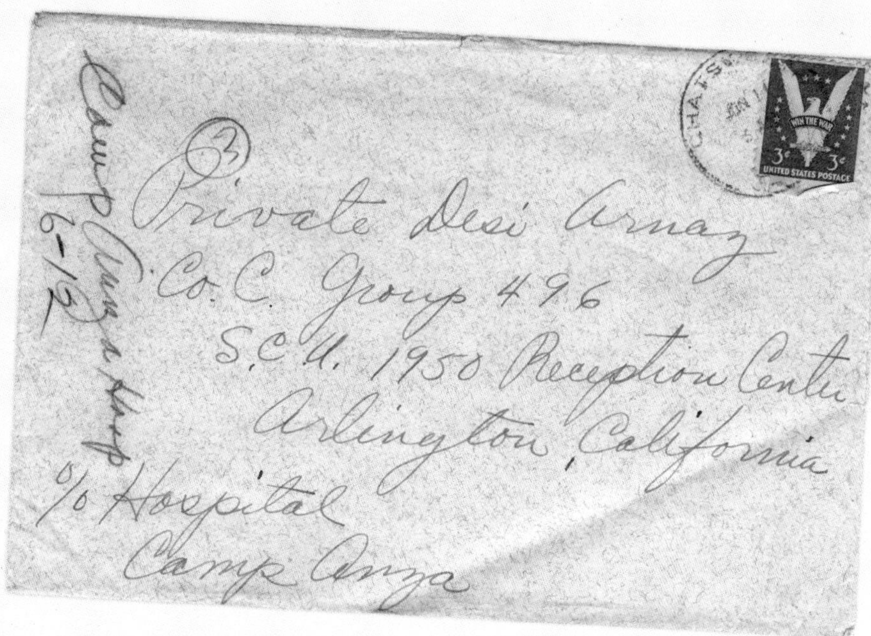

Private Desi Arnaz
Co. C. Group 496
S.C.U. 1950 Reception Center
Arlington, California
c/o Hospital
Camp Anza

Camp Anza Hosp
6-12

Thursday
10:00 A.M.

Good morning, Darling–

Been awake since 8:30. Had so many nitemares last nite it looked like a convention in my subconscious. And at this moment can't remember what any of them were about. All I know—Dr. Evert is sending me a complete change in vitamins. It seems I've been discovered to have a deficiency of sugar in my system that is frightening. So am doing something about it. Ed + Ebba were truly alarmed the other nite at Charlies to see me literally dive into some candies from New Orleans Pralines—you know I never eat sweets of any kind—that is—I didn't. I sure as hell have recently.

No call from studio for work. But three calls about fittings. Just checked again and I have to go in.

No sun again today! More of these dull days. I don't mind them. Wish we'd not have heat all summer.

Hope I get a letter from you today.

Gee all this laying off during the week—and probably on Sat. I'll be busy as hell. Oh Well! And don't you worry if you can't get a pass for this weekend—it's much more important that you get really O.K. as soon as possible. That you know.

PAGE 142: One of my favorite photos of Mom posing for a photog during a glamorous night on the town at the iconic El Morocco on East 54th Street in New York City.

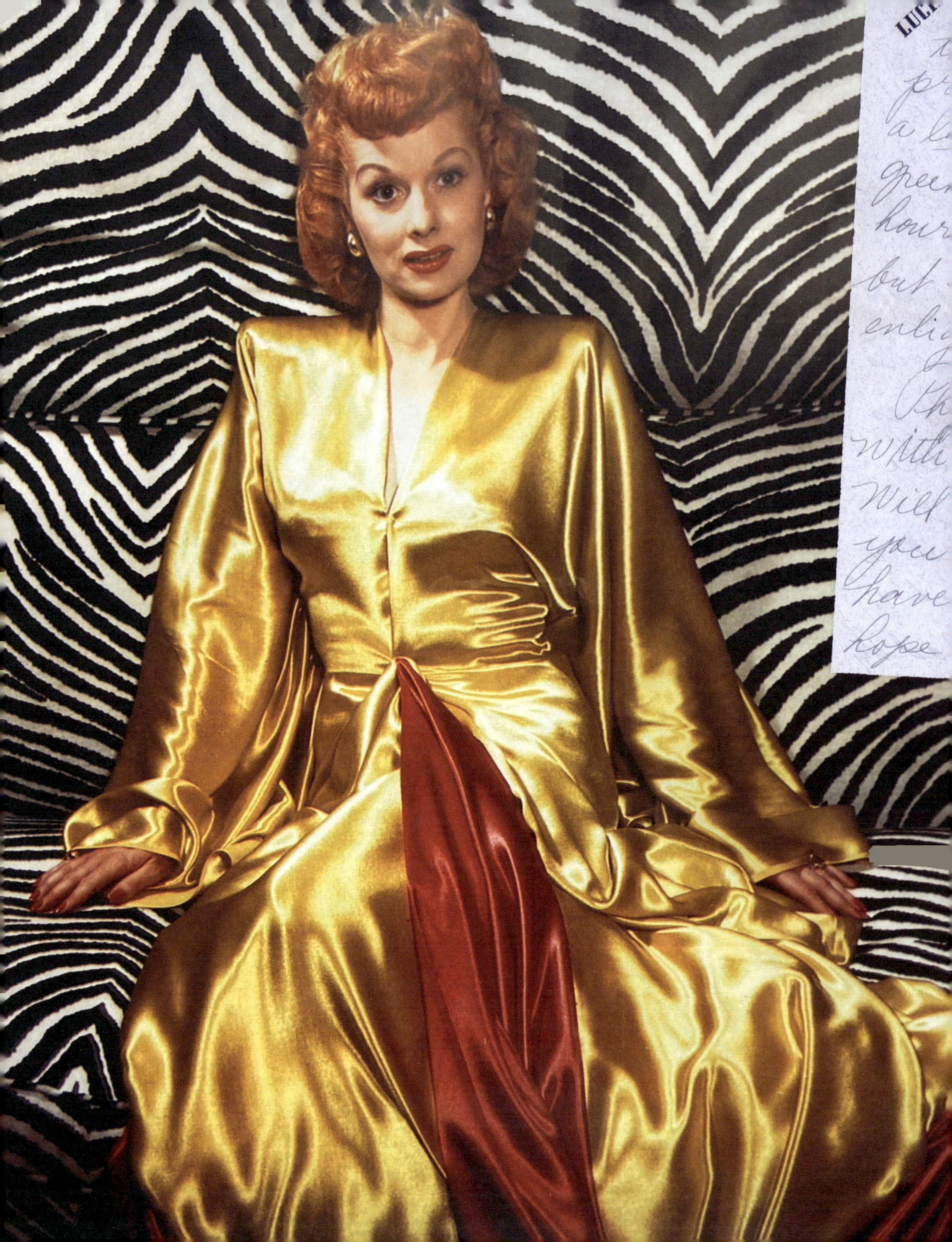
but
with
Will
you
have
hope

s A.M. Understand things
ty well so far. Learned
t last nite. It was all
to me before that
with Father English
gave me many very
tening fundamentals
llis is coming back
ne this afternoon.
e back here in case
can
h be
you'l

me anyway.
You received another
big batch of fan mail
which I shall take to
the studio.

answer
pronto.
you been
Lou Maxon's
He really is
the middle
! Even
er carried a
Couldn't
my daddy

LUCILLE

hasn't read it yet.
Will enclose that story.
Talked with your Mom
last nite. She understood.
Gosh I hate to get out
of bed this morning. It's
cool & damp outside and
a wonderful day for
staying in bed. But
it's 10:40 now & I have
to cook a chuck roast
before I leave here -
Will have my fittings

at Irene's and then my
two in Beverly. My suit
at Beal's – my hat at
Hopkin's – my suit a
Dunkirk – that incidenta
is such a mess I may
not accept it unless
there has been a great
improveme
material
I really d
to do. Th
a botche
it. Didn
the mate

LUCILLE

plaid you kno
the one at Bea
swell – hope yo
it.

Got some more
ake Pool man
damn
sent o
week!
O.S. to
nny for
Stock
3 de
– Woe

Gotta get up now and
do my cooking –
tonite will be back home
early sewing on baby
clothes & studying my
catechism. Gee aren't
I sensational these days!

So long honey for
now –

I love you Desi
Your Wife

Have been reading my catechism book with all the explanations, already this A.M. Understand things pretty well so far. Learned a lot last nite. It was all Greek to me before that hour with Father English but he gave me many very enlightening fundamentals.

Phyllis is coming back with me this afternoon. Will be back here in case you can call—if you haven't been able to—hope you'll be loving me anyway.

You received another big batch of fan mail which I shall take to the studio.

Hope you answer Deke's letter pronto.

Gee! Have you been following Lou Maxon's big battle? He really is right in the middle of a tempest! Even Daddy's paper carried a big thing. Couldn't cut it out cuz Daddy hasn't read it yet.

Will enclose that story.

Talked with your Mom last nite. She understood.

Gosh I hate to get out of bed this morning. It's cool + damp outside and a wonderful day for staying in bed. But it's 10:40 now + I have to cook a chuck roast before I leave here—

Will have my fittings at Irene's and then my two in Beverly. My suit at Beale's—my hat at Hopkin's—my suit at Dunkirk—that incidentally is such a mess I may not accept it unless there has been a great improvement today. My material too you know—I really don't know what to do. They made such a botched up mess of it. Didn't even match the material—and it's plaid you know. But the one at Beale's is swell—hope you like it.

Got some more calls to make. Pool man quit—and that damned firm hasn't even sent someone else for a week! Had to send an S.O.S. to Bullocks this morning for a girdle! Have no stockings left and just 3 decent pr of shoes—Woe is me.

Gotta get up now and do my cooking—

tonite will be back home early sewing on baby clothes + studying my catechism. Gee aren't I sensational these days!

So long honey for now—

I love you Desi
Your Wife

Thursday
6:45 P.M.

Hello my darling:

June 11, 1943, from Camp Anza

I'm just waiting in bed for seven or seven fifteen when I'll go and place my call. I want to give you time in case you went to the studio today.

I got a letter from you today and another from mother.

Today I sat in the wheelchair all morning then came back to bed for lunch and stayed in bed the rest of the time I wasn't taking any chances on getting to call you tonite.

We had a girl and her husband who is in the Army come in the ward this afternoon and play guitar and sing and then they made me do a couple of my numbers too. It was kind of fun.

The leg it's more or less the same, the Doc doesn't say anything yet, It bends this much: If I sit on the a chair it bends all the way down to the floor, not more. He says he can't tell yet. If nothing comes tomorrow to enlighten him, I'm going to have a heart to heart talk with him and try to find out what the hell is going on. We'll see. I'm dying to see you and talk to you. Hurry, Hurry, pretty please?

I'm very proud of you for starting on your instructions with Father English, as soon as you are ready we'll get marry. Would you marry me again sweetheart, I love you now more than the first time, and I'm also proud of you and I'm in love with you and I'm sure we'll have at least a couple of kids, and there is nothing that I would like better.

I like very much to get out of here, but I'm not as low as I was two days ago.

So long baby, God bless you

Love, Desi

Pvt. Desi Arnaz,
Co. C. Group 496.
S.C.U. 1950 Reception
Arlington, Calif.

CAMP ANZA CALIF. JUN 11 1943

Free

Desi Arnaz.
Devonshire Blvd.
...worth.
California.

DESI

Thursday.
6:45 P.M.

Hello my darling:

I'm just waiting in bed for seven or seven fifteen when I'll go and place my call. I want to give you time in case you went to the studio today. ...

... chance ...

... and ...

... play guitar and sing and then they made me do a couple of numbers too. It was kind of fun. The leg it's more or less the same, the Doc ...

DESI

3

He says he can't tell ... If nothing comes tomorrow to enlighten him, I'm going to have a heart to heart talk with him and try to find out what the hell is going on. We'll see. I'm dying to see you and talk to you. Hurry, Hurry, pretty please.

I'm very proud of you for starting on your instructions with Father English, as soon as

---

you are ready we'll get marry. Would you marry me again sweetheart, I love you now more than the first time, and I'm also proud of you and I'm in love with you and I'm sure we'll have at least a couple of kids, and there is nothing that I would like better.

I like very much to get out of here, but I'm not as low as I was two days ago.

So long baby, God bless you

Love Desi.

LUCILLE

Friday - 10:00 AM
In Bed -

And do you realize I could have practically spent the whole week with you! The darned uncertainty of this p[illegible] business!

Good Morning Darling[illegible]
Another grey dull da[illegible]

call from the studio just as I leave here - But nevertheless - I'm going into town to take some material to Thirza - so I can have a new dress made for me - for our big moment when [illegible]

LUCILLE

this morning. Bet I know more of them t[illegible] you do - someday maybe -

The cement commandos cleared out last even[illegible] did a very good job. W[illegible] we get the road & dr[illegible] all filled in & packed d[illegible] it's going to be swell. And won't all dribble away now every time [it] rains. Hope you like it

Have been trying to line up some furniture for Lolita. Stuff we spoke about last week. But every time I get a line on what she wants - she decides to wait until she talks with you again. So I dunno -

Phyllis & I spent a very quiet evening last nite. Read & spanked the dogs and listened to the radio - and spanked the dogs and finally gave up &

Friday–10:00 A.M.
In Bed–

And do you realize I could have practically spent the whole week with you! The darned uncertainty of this pic. business!

Good Morning Darling—

Another grey dull day. In fact it's drizzeling. I'll probably get a hurry call from the studio just as I leave here—But nevertheless—I'm going into town to take some material to Thirza—*so* I can have a new dress made for me—for our big moment when you arrive for our wedding. It's gotta be *just* right! And very pretty. For you.

Have studied my prayers this morning. Bet I'll know more of them than you do—someday—maybe—

June 12, 1943, Los Angeles postmark

The cement commandos all cleared out last evening. Did a very good job. When we get the road + driveway all filled in + packed down it's going to be swell! And won't all dribble away now every time it rains. Hope you like it.

Have been trying to line up some furniture for Lolita. Stuff we spoke about last week. But every time I get a line on what she wants—she decides to wait until she talks with you again. So I don'no—

Phyllis and I spent a very quiet evening last nite. Read + spanked the dogs and listened to the radio—and spanked the dogs and finally gave up + went to bed.

Ordered the *Examiner* sent here in the morning.

Our rugs for the bedroom are finally coming through! *But now*—the *factory* wants $25.00 more to complete the large one! The factory not Sloans! Oh Brother after this war I hope some of these people get what they deserve.

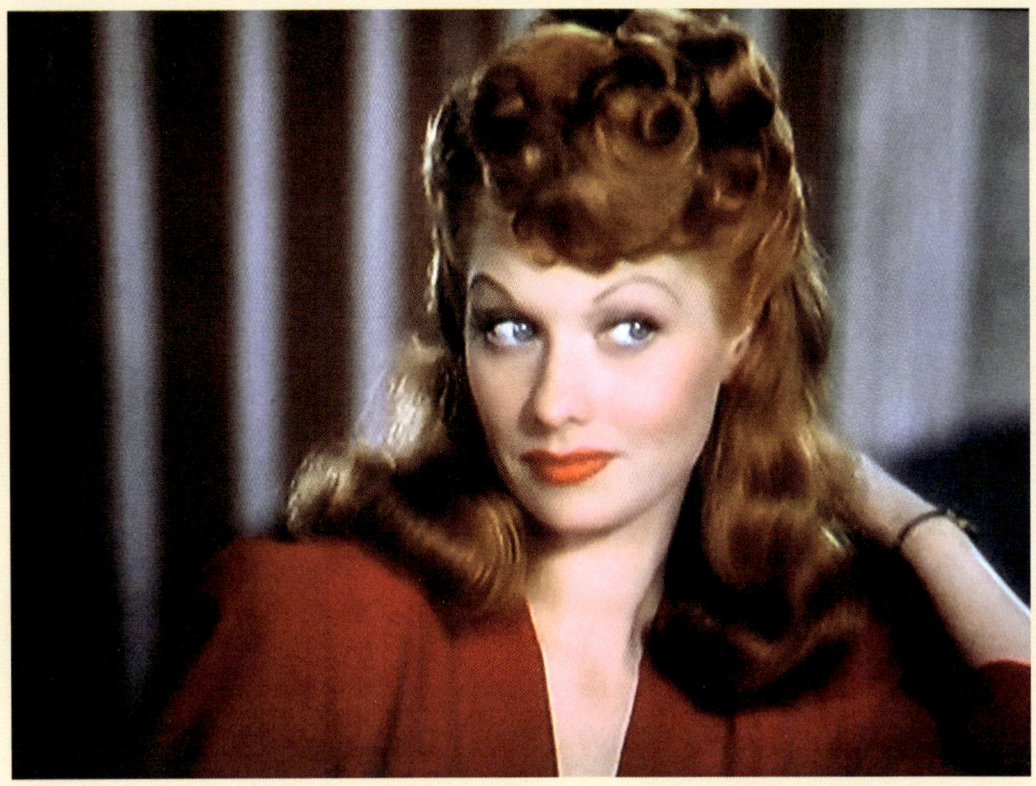

What do you hear from your Daddy? Please write him often now that you have the time Desi. At <u>least</u> once a week.

We haven't heard a <u>word</u> from Cleo and Kenny in <u>weeks</u>! Hope they are having a wonderful vacation. They had 10 days—Seems as though we should have heard before now.

Found these clippings or editorials rather in Newsweek.

Don't have many clippings for you because you have the papers every day—and <u>I</u> bring you the Reporters.

Had a very nice dream about you last nite—hard to explain—no sex—but just nice—woke up loving you—<u>so</u> much!

Gotta go now. Gon'na do some shopping + check with the studio every hour + get home for your call this evening.

You probably won't get this until after I've seen you—but anyway hope you aren't sad about Sat nite. Not good for you to be sad—

I love you Baby—

Always
Your wife

ABOVE: Mom with her newly hot red hair color.

LUCILLE

went to bed.

Ordered the Examin[er]
sent here this mor[ning]

Our rugs for the
room are finally com[ing]
through! But now
the factory wants ...
more to complete ...
large one! The fact[ory]
not Sloans! Oh B...
after this war I hop[e]
? these people get ...
they deserve

What do you hear from
your Daddy? Please
write him often now that
you have the time. Ples!
At least once a week.

We haven't heard a word
from Cleo & Kenny in
weeks! Hope they are
having a wonderful vacation.
They had 10 days —
Seems as though we
should have heard
... now.

LUCILLE

Found these clippings or
editorials rather in Newsweek

Don't have many clippin[gs]
for you because you hav[e]
the papers every day —
and I bring you the
Reporters.

Had a very nice dre[am]
about you last nite —
hard to explain — n[ot]
sex — but just nice
Woke up loving yo[u]
so much!

Gotta go now. Gonna do
some shopping & check
with the studio every hour
& get home for your
call this evening.

You probably won't
get this until after I've
seen you — but anyway
hope you aren't sad about
Sat nite. Not good for
you to be sad!

I love you Baby —
Always
Your Wife

DESI

Friday.

Hello baby darling:

I'm go
call you in a lit
so all of this let
won't be news, but
to write to you now
tell you all my litt
and then you'll have
in writing.

nevertheless it might be a
possibility of what they call
a "locked knee" and if
that is the case he will
have to operate. Now this
is by no means definite, I
have improved. I do bend
my knee to about a ninety
gree angle. and Tuesday
could only bend it to a

3

DESI

and if I do bend it that
far he won't touch it.
So don't get all worry
about it, please darling, but
I had to tell you, as much
as I hated to do so, because
I know you won't be able
to help worrying. I only ask
you not to worry too much
and I had to tell you,
because I want you to call
Marc, and ask him if he knows
about knees, if not he'll probably refer you to a knee

specialist; I want to
find out, in case they
do have to operate, what
kind of an operation tha
is, what the results ma
be, and what the chances
are of being successful or
not, and I must have
your word that you
must tell me the truth
and the whole truth,
because I think, I'm not
sure, that I have the
right to refuse anybody
cutting into me. So
please find out and do it

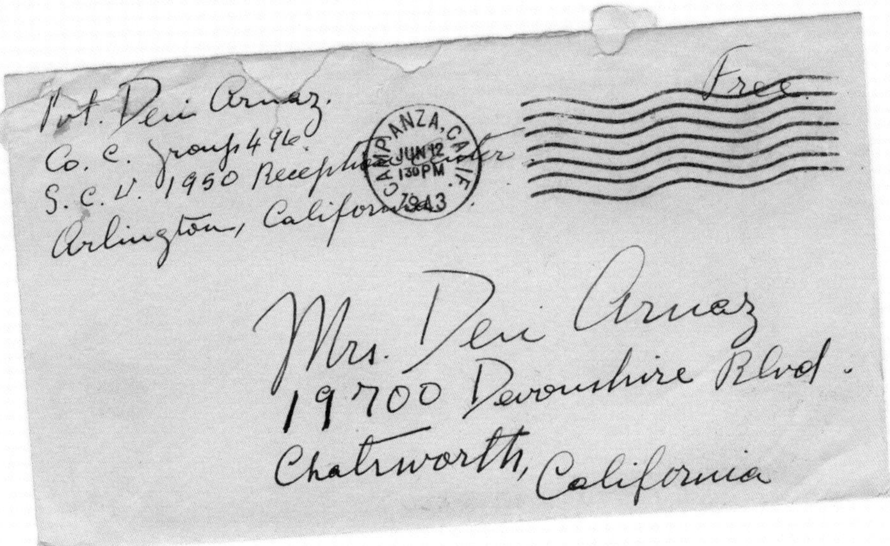
Pvt. Desi Arnaz.
Co. C. Group 496.
S.C.U. 1950 Reception Center.
Arlington, California

CAMP ANZA, CALIF.
JUN 12 1:30 PM
1943

Free

Mrs. Desi Arnaz
19700 Devonshire Blvd.
Chatsworth, California

Friday.

Hello baby darling:

I'm going to call you in a little while so all of this letter won't be news, but I want to write to you now and tell you all my little news and then you'll have them in writing.

I had a talk today with the doctor and he said that although there is an improvement which I can see and feel myself, that nevertheless it might be a possibility of what they call a "locked knee" and if that is the case he will have to operate. Now this is by no means definite, I have improved, I do bend my knee to about a ninety degree angle, and Tuesday I could only bend it to a twenty degree, so there's a definite improvement, but I won't be able to bend it as back as my left knee bends anyway, remember the left is no good either, and if I do bend it that far he won't touch it.

June 12, 1943, from Camp Anza

So don't get all worry about it, please darling, but I had to tell you, as much as I hated to do so, because I know you won't be able to help worrying. I only ask you not to worry too much and I had to tell you, because I want you to call Marc, and ask him if he knows about knees, if not he'll probably refer you to a knee specialist; I want to find out, in case they do have to operate, what kind of an operation that is, what the results may be, and what the chances are of being successful or not, and I must have your word that you must tell me the truth and the whole truth, because I think, I'm not sure, that I have the right to refuse anybody cutting into me. So please find out and do it without getting yourself all worry about it, do it just in case. You are and I'm proud of it, a beautiful hunk of woman so behave like one. Please.

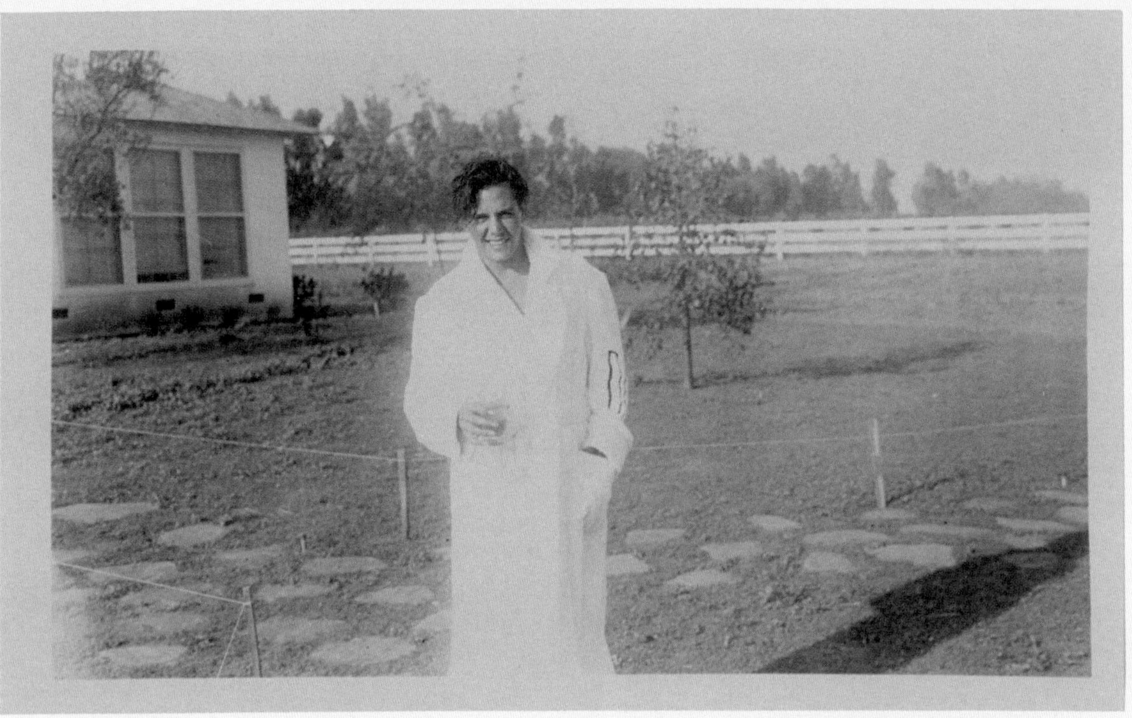

ABOVE: Dad greeting the morning on their newly purchased Chatsworth property, before design and landscaping made it beautiful.

I would not tell you this if I didn't know you so well, and knew that you want to be with me wheter it's good or bad.

Remember I am improving so don't think that the operation is definite.

I'm so terribly unhappy about not being able to leave here Saturday night, but I knew when he told me that today that it would be impossible. Anyway, you'll be here, I wish so much you could be here more, but I know it's impossible; when I feel too bad, I think of those poor bastards in Attu and Africa and India and China and the South Pacific, and I realize that we are definitely, very, very lucky, no matter how bad my knee is. That is what I want you to think anytime, that you feel lonesome, or sad, or worry about me, think darling how much worse it could be and you'll see, you won't mind it so much. And think also, that one way or the other it'll be all right; I'm sure, and wether it's a week more or three weeks more I will be home and we will get marry in the church and have a wonderful time.

I do love you so very much and I don't like to think of your pretty face with a worried look.

Hurry darling I'm waiting for you

Desi

DESI 5

without getting yourself
all worry about
just in case. To
and I'm proud
beautiful punk a
so behave like a

I would not te
this if I didn't

I'm so terribly unhappy
about not being able
to leave here Saturday
night, but I knew when
he told me that today
that it would be impossible
you'll be here, I
much you could
more, but I know
possible when I

DESI 7

I realize that we are
definitely, very
lucky, no mat
bad my knee i
is what I want
to think anythin
you feel lonesom
sad, or worry a
me, think dar
how much wor
could be and you
see, you won't
it so much. An
also, that one w

or the other it'll be
all right, I'm sure, and
wether it's a week more
or three weeks more
I will be home and
we will get marry in
the church and have
a wonderful time.

I do love you so
very much and I
don't like to think
of your pretty face
with a worried look.

Hurry darling I'm
waiting for you
Desi

Friday nite

Desi My Darling–

It's 11:00 but I can't sleep so want to write to you—

You made me cry a little tonite. I know you don't want me to be sad but I am so worried about your leg. You sounded so cute and sweet too I just couldn't help it! Wanted so much to take you into my arms and hug you very tightly and kiss your handsome wonderful head and face—just kiss your eyes + ears and neck and rock you back and forth.

Too bad I have to work tomorrow. But I'll see you before you get this.

Picked up tonites paper and read my "Wishing Well"—my number is 3—same as yours is it not? Well anyway—mine says—A BAD BREAK HEALS—How do you like that!? Will enclose it—also a poem from Darling's column I liked.

June 12, 1943, Culver City postmark

Got you some new books today. Hope you like them. Also checked on your Portuguese things. They are waiting for the grammar to come in.

Nice story about us in Movieland. Will bring it.

Joie sent Phyllis a star sapphire with baguette diamonds! Their 5th anniversary today. She called me to tell me how thrilled she was. He also called from Lacoma, Wash. Gee he sure is going to be away a long time.

Aunt Helen is making more of those cookies—certainly hope you get some this time—Will give them all to you + let you distribute them—I should have done that before—

We're bringing more chicken also. Don'no when you'll eat it—but I want Lolita to fix it her way—and I don'no why I'm writing all this because it'll just be an old dead letter when you get it. We'll already be down + back and the chickens will be eaten!

Guess I better turn out the light and try to sleep. Maybe I better go make some Ovaltine.

Goodnite Darling

My love
Lucy

—¤¤¤—

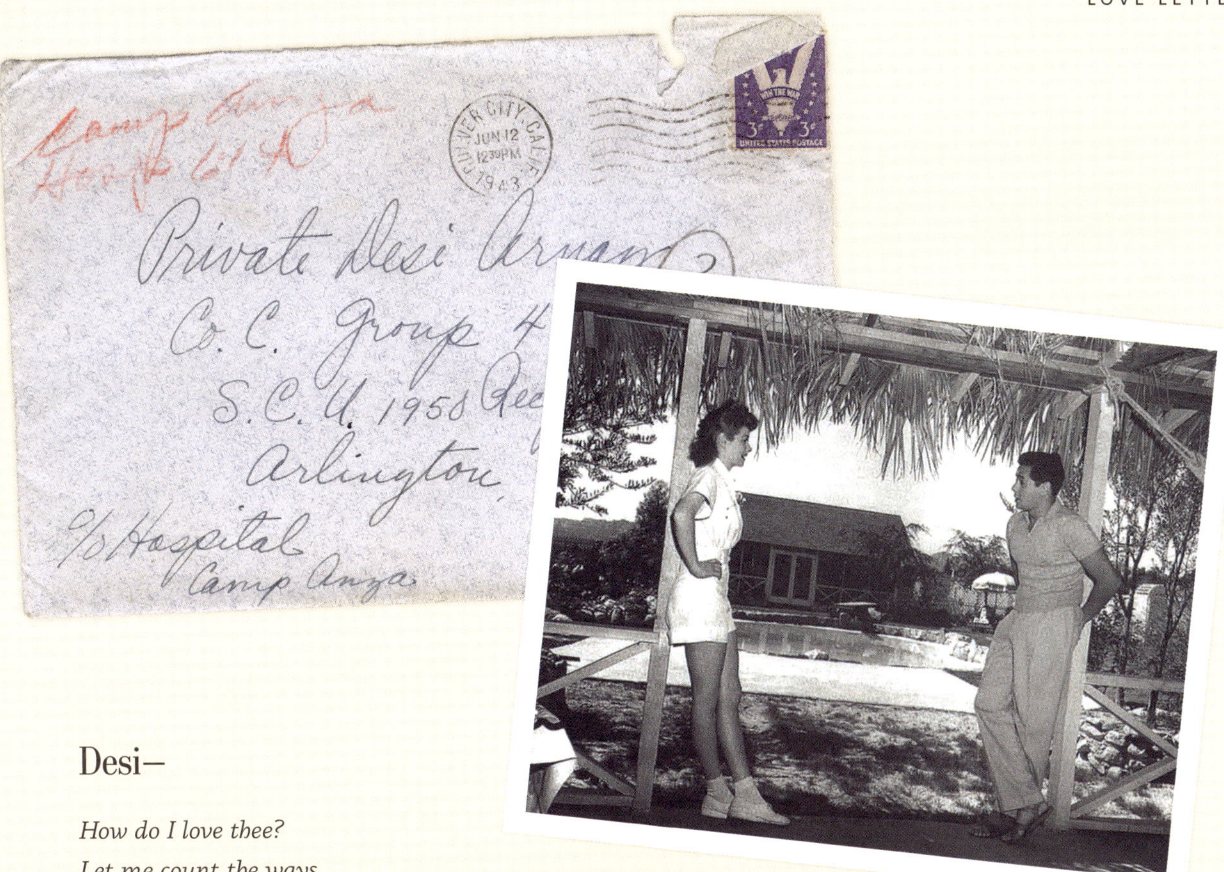

Desi–

How do I love thee?
Let me count the ways.
I love thee to the depths and breadth and height
My soul can reach, when feeling out of sight.
For the ends of Being and ideal Grace.
I love thee to the level of everyday's
Most quiet need, by sun and candlelight.
I love thee freely, as men strive for Right;
I love thee purely, as they turn from Praise.
I love thee with the passion put to use
In my old griefs, and with my childhood's faith
I love thee with a love I seemed to lose
With my lost saints,—I love thee with the breath,
Smiles, tear, of all my life!—
and, if God choose,
I shall love thee better after death.—

Elizabeth Barrett Browning

That's the way I feel about you.
Isn't it beautiful?

Goodnite.

LUCILLE

Friday Nite

Dear My Darling—

It's 11:00 but I can't sleep so want to write to you—

You made me cry a little tonite. I know you don't want me to be sad but I am so worried about your leg. You sounded so cute and sweet too I just couldn't help it! Wanted so much to take

into my arms and
ow very tightly and
handsome

LUCILLE

is it not? Well anyway—Mine says—
—A BAD BREAK HEALS—
How do you like that!?
Will enclose it—Also
poem from darlings'
umm I liked

I'm writing all this because it'll just be an old dead letter when you get it. Will already be down & back and the chicken will be eaten!

Guess I better turn out the light and try to sleep. Maybe I better go make some ovaltine.

Goodnite Darling
My Love
Lucy

LUCILLE

Aunt Helen is ma
more of those cook
certainly hope you
some this time—
give them all to y
let you distribute
I should have do
before—

We're bringing
also. Donno w
eat it—but
[illegible] to fix it

LUCILLE

Desi —

How do I love thee?

Let me count the w[...]

I love thee to the [...]

and breadth and hei[...]

My soul can reach[...]

feeling out of sight [...]

LUCILLE

I love thee freely, as

men strive for Right;

I love thee purely, as

they turn from Praise.

I love thee with the

passion put to use

In my old griefs, and

with my childh[...]

I lo[...]

I seeme[...]

With [...]

I love [...]

Smiles, [...]

and, if [...]

LUCILLE

I shall love thee better

after death.

Elizabeth Barrett

Browning —

That's the way I feel

about you.

Isn't it beautiful?

Goodnite.

RMS 351

AND EXPRESS —Largest [...]

WISHING WELL

Registered U. S. Patent Office.

2 M	6 A	3 A	7 R	2 U	8 R	4 S	3 S	7 B	2 O	6 N	8 I
4 E	3 A	5 T	2 H	6 E	4 C	3 D	7 M	2 M	8 E	6 W
2 O	6 Z	4 R	7 N	8 I	2 N	5 S	6 E	4 E	3 R
6 S	3 E	5 C	4 T	2 Y	7 I	6 T	4 I	3 A	2 I
8 P	2 N	6 I	7 C	4 E	3 H	5 M	2 S	6 N	7 U
6 L	4 N	5 I	3 A	7 R	2 G	6 I	4 E	5 N	8 W
2 H	6 F	7 G	5 G	4 S	3 S	8 R	6 E	2 T	7 E

[...]ant little game that will give you a message [...] is a numerical puzzle designed to spell out [...] the letters in your first name. If the number [...]re, subtract 4. If the number is less than 6, [...] your key number. Start at the upper left-[...]ectangle and check every one of your key [...]. Then read the message the letters under [...]e you.

[...]m J. Miller, Distributed by King Features, Inc. 6-11

Pvt. Desi Arnaz
Co. C. Group 496
S.C.U. 1950 Reception Ctr.
Arlington, California

CAMP ANZA CALIF JUN 14 1:30 PM

Free

Mrs. Desi Arnaz
19700 Devonshire Blvd.

DESI

Saturday
5:30 P.M.

My darling sweetheart:

Remember last Saturday at this time? I can't get it off my mind, I waited and waited all week, hoping and praying for the same
knee ...
loo...
stil...
whe...
pos...
but ...
cou...
you...

---

how wonderful it was. The knee, am sorry to say, it's about the same, doesn't seem to want to go any farther back, no matter how much I try and ... girl, they say it takes ...

DESI

tonite and I'll be
waiting for tomorr...
just waiting to see
baby and hold you
and kiss you dar...
and look and loo...
Never get tired of
that. If I could ...
out of here with y...
why think of that

Next week we ...
know one way or ...
what goes with ...
little knee. I ho...

I guess this is not a very nice letter darling but sometimes I just would blow up if I didn't let it out. Sorry.

I'll be thinking of you all night tonite, I always do and when I pray at bed time I pray for you too. Pretty soon you'll be doing your own praying, won't you? I think it's wonderful the way you want to come in the Church and get marry, I love you all the more for it. God bless you

Desi

Saturday
5:30 P.M.

My darling sweetheart:

Remember last Saturday at this time? I can't get it off my mind, I waited and waited all week, hoping and praying for the same kind of a week-end and look at what I got, am still sitting in this Goddamn wheel-chair in the Goddamn porch, Nuts!!! Am sorry but I had a long day, couldn't help thinking of you and last week and how wonderful it was.

The knee, am very sorry to say, it's about the same, doesn't seem to want to go any farther back, no matter how much I try and exercise, they say it takes time, but what the hell do they call three whole weeks?

Thank God you called me this noon, it certainly helped a lot, also Charlie's letter was so funny I couldn't help but laugh a little bit anyway.

June 14, 1943, from Camp Anza

I'm going to call you tonite and I'll be just waiting for tomorrow, just waiting to see my darling baby and hold your hands and kiss you and look and look and look at you. Never get tired of doing that. If I could only get out of here with you,... but why think of that.

Next week we should know one way or the other what goes with my darling little knee. I hope.

I guess this is not a very nice letter darling but somedays I just would blow up if I didn't let it out. Sorry.

I'll be thinking of you all night tonite, I always do and when I pray at bed time I pray for you too. Pretty soon you'll be doing your own praying, won't you? I think it's wonderful they way you want to come in the Church and get marry, I love you all the more for it.

God bless you
Desi

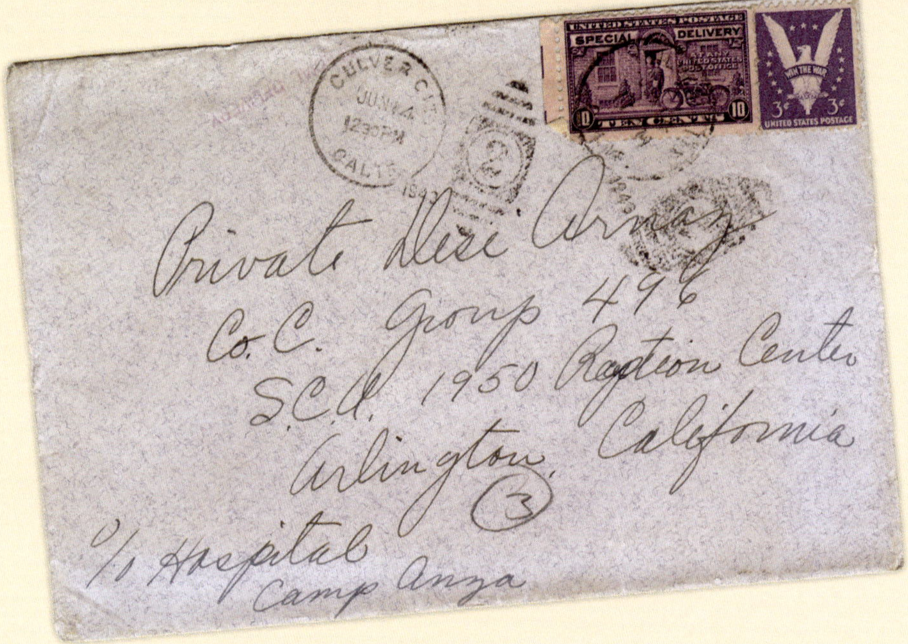

June 14, 1943, Culver City postmark

Monday A.M.
On the Set
10:30

Good morning Desi Darling–

It's a beautiful morning for a pleasant change and I was thinking of you as I pranced about the kitchen and gazed upon our lovely "estate" this early A.M.

Was, as usual, late getting to work. Been laying off too much I guess.

We had a nice ride home—no casualties after our ingenious start—plowing through 2 by 4's—

We were both glad to be home however—quite a few screwy + nasty drivers out that didn't make driving any nicer. Got home at 10:00—that is—to your Mom's—stopped by my Mothers for a second then went over Laurel—bought the papers + went by Ed's house + quietly laid your old dead leg across their threshold and got away into the moonlight without even a dog yelping. I must have looked mighty suspicious + damned gruesome carrying that bit of torso and creeping around in the bright moonlight. Expected to get a shot in the fanny any minute. You must admit I'm a mighty brave character to dare go near Ed's like that—with all that ammunition he harbors. Anyway—I dood it!—(Forgive me—) (Imagine me saying I dood it!)—and I haven't as yet heard any reverberations. And—say I just thought of this—I'll bet money his way of acknowledging my practical joke—is with complete

On the Set
10:30

Good Morning Desi Darling
It's a beautiful morning for a pleasant change and I was thinking of you as I pranced about the kitchen and gazed upon our lovely "estate" this early A.M.
Was as usual, lat...

getting to work. Been laying off too much I guess.

We had a nice ride home – no casualties after our ingenious start – plowing through 2 by 4's –

We were both glad to home, howev... quite ... didn't

LUCILLE

make driving any nicer.
Got home at 10... that is to your M... Stopped by my M... for a second then ... over Laurel-bought ... papers & went b... house & quietly lay... your old Head l... across their thresh... and got away in t... moonlight witho...

even a dog yelping. I must have looked mighty suspicious & damned gruesome carrying that bit of torso and creeping around in the bright moonlight. Expected to get a shot in the fanny any minute. You must admit I'm a mighty brave character to dare go near Ed's like that – with all that ammunition he

LUCILLE

harbors. Anyway —
dood it! — (Forgive m
(Imagine me saying
dood it!) — And I ha
as yet heard any revera
And — say I just
of this — I'll bet mo
his way of acknowledge
my practical joke — b
with complete silence

found it — just to
annoy me — I'll kill
them if they do that —
But I'll be damned if
I'll mention it first!
Will just have to wait.
Sorry I didn't write
Sat. Will make a gap
in this week now won't
it — but gee it would
be just old dead news
really shouldn't

LUCILLE

Gotta get dresse
darling —
Love you very
this morning —
Glad you impr
so much yesterday
were quit depress
because of the
found you when
first arrived —
you certainly perke
Thank God!

Write you tonite
Angel —
Kiss Kiss
Lucy

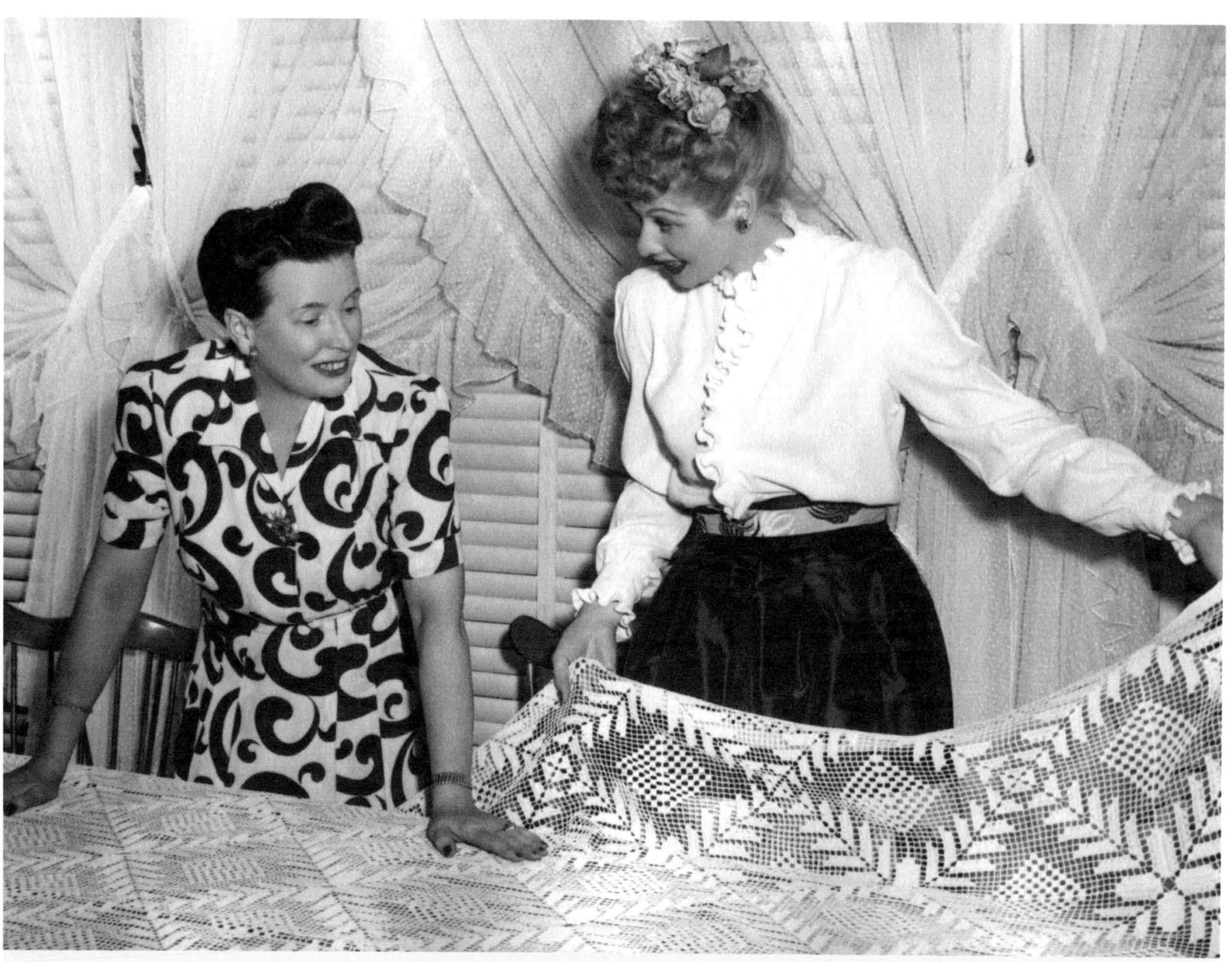

ABOVE: Mom ready to surprise Dad with Grandmother DeDe's handmade, crocheted tablecloth.

silence! Not letting on they found it—just to annoy me—I'll kill them if they do that—But I'll be damned if I'll mention it first! We'll just have to wait.

Sorry I didn't write Sat. Will make a gap in this week now won't it—but gee it would be just old dead news you really shouldn't mind too much.

Gotta get dressed now Darling—

Love you very much this morning—

Glad you improved so much yesterday. We were quite depressed because of the way we found you when we first arrived—but you certainly perked up Thank God!

Write you tonite angel—

Kiss Kiss
Lucy

Monday night

Hello my baby:

I just finished talking to you and I feel very good, the best I felt in several days, you can do wonders to me, precious, I love you. I actually believe that you fixed my knee just by looking at it, yesterday with those beautiful big blue eyes of yours, the light that shines from them seems to be much better than the one that shines from the "portable baker".

I believe that if it keeps getting better we might be able to work something out by the end of the week. Anyway I got my second wind now and I can stand it a little longer if I have to.

I'm sorry I felt bad and had to tell you about it but the thought of being a cripple is not a nice one.

June 15, 1943, from Camp Anza

As I told you tonite McArthur send me a wire thanking father for the cigars, it reads: "I have just received the magnificent box of cigars you so graciously sent me this but adds another link to the long chain of friendship which binds me to your country. I shall smoke the cigar with greatest satisfaction and always with thoughts of the delightful spirit of comradeship which animated you in sending them. =MACARTHUR=

It was a cable from Brisbane Queensland "Via Imperial "Government."

To father as the representative of the "Comisión Nacional de defensa y propaganda del tabaco Habano" which means "National commission of defense and propagand of the Havana cigars."

I might make a good story, tell it to Emily and show her the copy of the wire.

Father's letter was very nice and I'll save it for when I see you again. It's close to nine o'clock and I want to take a tub before going to sleep.

I love you very much and I want to hold you very tight right now and squeeze you and kiss you and love you all night until you can't take it anymore. Ha ha!!! I can brag, can't I?

Oh baby, let's pray that I'll get home this week for a while, what fun we'll have

Oh Boy!!!

Desi

Pvt. Desi Arnaz
Co. C. Group 496
S.C.U. 1950 Recep. Center
Arlington, California

CAMP HAAN CALIF. JUN 15 1:30 PM 1943

Free

Mrs. Desi Arnaz
19700 Devonshire Blvd.
Chatsworth, California

DESI

Monday night

Hello my baby:

I just finished talking to you and I feel very good, the best I felt in several days, you can do wonders to me, precious, I love you. I actually believe that you fixed my knee just by looking at it yesterday with those beautiful big blue eyes of yours, the light that shines from them seems to be much

better than the one
that shines from the
"portable baker".
I believe that if it
keeps getting better we
might be able to work
something out by the
end of the week. Anyway
I got my second wind
now and I can stand
it a little longer if I
have to.
I'm sorry I ...
had to tell ...
but the tho...
a cripple ...

DESI 3

As I told yo...
Mc Arthur ...
thanking fa...
cigars, it ...
"I have just received the
magnificent box of cigars
you so graciously sent me
this but adds another link
to the long chain of
friendship which binds
me to your country. I
shall smoke the cigar
with greatest satisfaction
and always with thoughts
of the delightful spirit
of comradeship which
animated you in send
them.

= MACARTHUR =

It was a cable from Bri
Queensland "Via Imperial
"Government".
To father as the represen
tative of the "Comision
Nacional de defensa y
propaganda del tabaco
Habano" which means:
"National commission
of defense and propagand
of the Havana cigars".

DESI

I might make a goo[d]
story tell it to Emily
and shows her the co[py]
of the wire.

Father's letter was ver[y]
nice and I'll save it
for when I see you aga[in]

It's close to nine o'cloc[k]
and I want to take a
tub before going to
sleep.

I love you very much
and I want to hold

DESI

you very tight right
now and squeeze you
and kiss you and love
you all night until
you can't take it
anymore. Ha ha!!!
I can brag, can't I?

Oh baby, let's pray
that I'll get home this
week for a while,
what fun we'll have
Oh Boy!!!

Desi

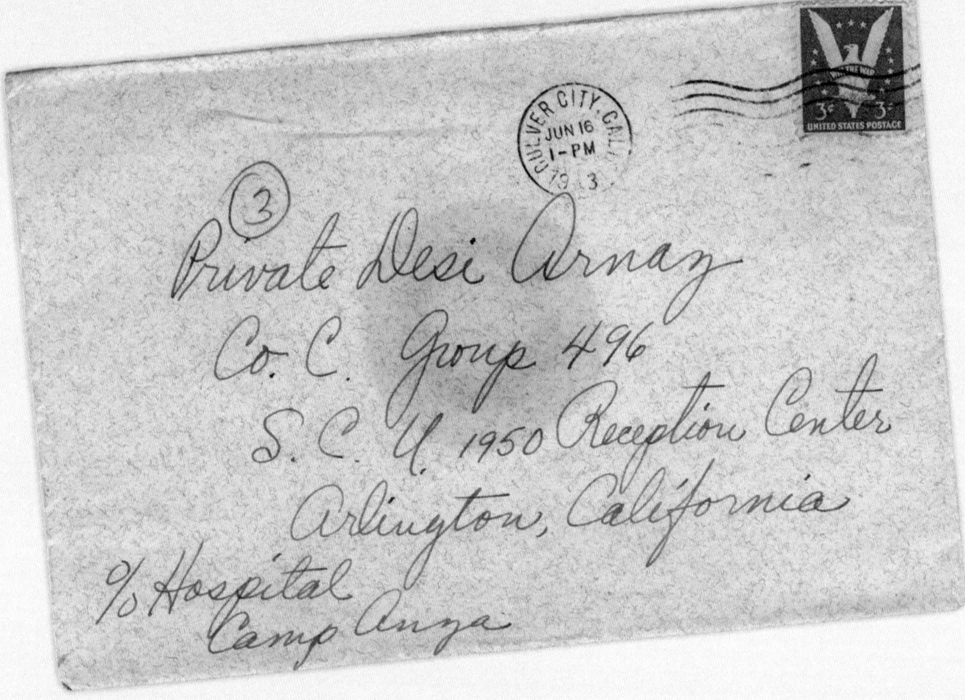
CULVER CITY, CALIF.
JUN 16
1-PM
1943

UNITED STATES POSTAGE 3¢

(3)
Private Desi Arnaz
Co. C. Group 496
S. C. U. 1950 Reception Center
Arlington, California
% Hospital
Camp Anza

Tuesday Nite
9:00 P.M.

Dearest–

June 16, 1943, Culver City postmark

After talking with you—had dinner and took Erma for a walk around our beautiful ranch. Been wanting to write you all day but couldn't hold a pen in my hand.

Since talking to you at 7:30 I have a sinus attack on it's merry merry way.

So that little nerve session I put in today has taken it's toll alright. Hope it's not one of those sneezing red eye affairs cuz I just started this picture and I haven't the time to fool around being ill.

Anyway—I'm sorry I sounded so icky when you called tonite but I've wanted to be just with you all day + no one else—and I've been so sick all day—and tonite I feel awful—and I want you here to hold me in your arms and make a fuss over me.

Gee I'm so glad you've really improved honey—and there doesn't seem to be any doubt of that today from what you said. Wonder if you'll get any kind of convalescence furlough at all? Hope you can swing that.

I'm still shaky and my writing looks it doesn't it?—or does it always look this badly?

LUCILLE

Tuesday Nite
9:00 P.M.

Dearest -

After talking with you - had dinner and Erma for a walk ... our beautiful ranch ... wanting to write y... day but couldn't ... few ...

S... 7:30 ... on it...

So that little nerve sessio[n] I put in today has take[n] its toll alright. Hope not one of those sneezy red eye affairs ... this pictur[e] ... the tim[e] ... being il[l] ... I'm sorry I ... ky when yo[u] ... but I'm ... just with ... no one else

LUCILLE

and I've been so sick all day - and tonite I feel awful - And I want you here to hold me in your arms and make a fuss over me.

Gee I'm so glad you've really improved honey - and there doesn't seem to be any doubt of that today from what you said. Wonder if you'll get any kind of convalescence (?) furlough at all? Hope you can swing that.

I'm still shaky and my writing looks it doesn't it? — or does it always look this badly?

Was going t[o] last nite but [...] badly by t[...] home from [...] couldn't — [...] get mailed [...] A.M. — [...]

LUCILLE

forgive me I know [...] try to call your [...] least one mornin[g] [...] week honey. Try [...] I think it's hard [...] to understand why [you] never call her yet you can call me. Please try.

Maybe I can bring you home next weekend — gee hope I'm not still feeling lousy — Please forgive me darling I don't seem

to be able t[o] [...] except how [...]

Tomorrow I [...] be O.K. G[...] sleep now — [...]

Please love [...] and I'm sorr[y] [...] Today — bu[t] [...] mixed up & [...] you here whe[n] [...] feel well

I love you [...]

L[...]

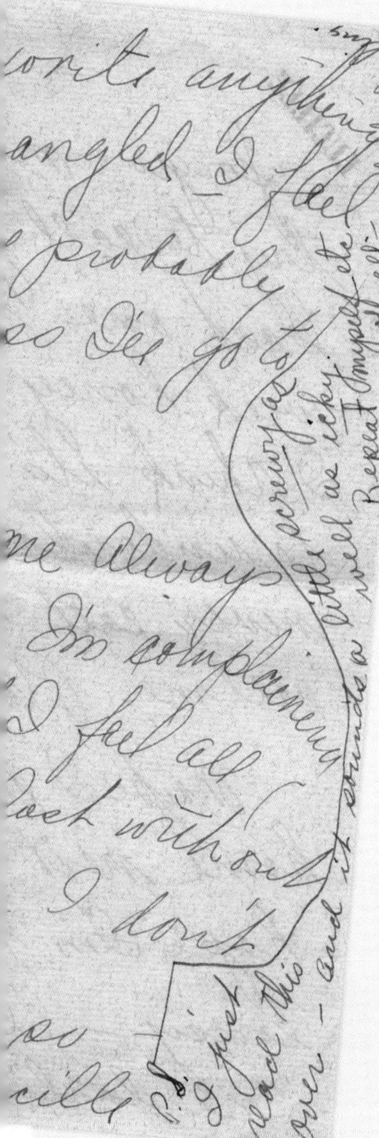

write anything
angled – I feel
probably
ss I'll go to
me always
I'm complaining
I feel all
lost without
I don't
so
cille

P.S. I just read this over – and it sounds a little screwy as well as icky. Repeat myself etc. oh well – good nite

Was going to write you again last nite but was feeling so badly by the time I arrived home from Sedgwicks I couldn't—and this won't get mailed until tomorrow A.M.—but—you'll forgive me I know. Do try to call your Mom at least one morning this week honey. Try very hard. I think it's hard for her to understand why you never call her yet you can call me. Please try.

Maybe I can bring you home next weekend—gee hope I'm not still feeling lousy—Please forgive me darling I don't seem to be able to write anything except how mangled I feel.

Tomorrow I'll probably be O.K. Guess I'll go to sleep now—

Please love me always and I'm sorry I'm complaining today—but I feel all mixed up + lost without you here when I don't feel well

I love you so—

Lucille

P.S. I just read this over—and it sounds a little screwy as well as icky. Repeat myself etc. oh well—good nite Darling.

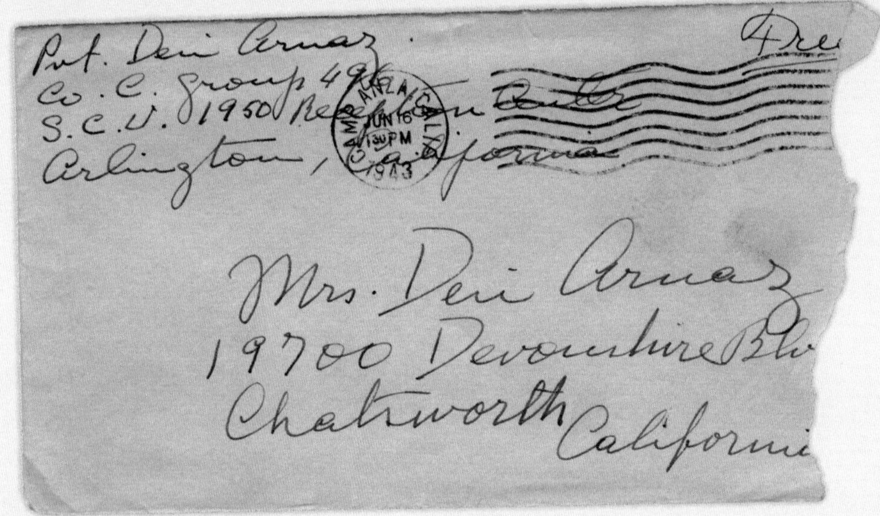

Tuesday nite

My darling baby:

June 16, 1943, from Camp Anza

I just talked to you and you were sick, sweetheart and you cried, my poor little darling, I wish I could have hold you in my arms and kiss your eyes and stop your tears, baby I don't like to think of you crying, I feel so helpless here, not being able to be with you and hold you and then you can cry on me on my shoulders, all you want because I know that I'm there with you and no matter what your troubles may be at that time I can help you with them, but here, so close and yet so far. So please baby take care of yourself, of your health and don't cry, sweetheart, I'll be home soon. I'm trying everyday I'm trying doing exactly what I'm told, not taking even the ghost of a chance. So don't worry, I think the worst is over, and soon it'll be wonderful, you and me and the ranch, I'm just dying to have you take care of me, and help me with my bath and my exercises and go swimming with me and just act good and spoiled. Have you cook for me, those wonderful deserts, and steaks???? and goulash. Oh Boy!!

I know it'll be soon. We'll try it again this week and see what happens if it keeps getting better I don't see why he shouldn't let me go.

You have been writing wonderfully honey, everyday I get a letter from you, may be just a couple of exceptions, but you have been sweell (I never know how to spell that).

The people with the movie are here got go and get in my wheelchair and get a good place.

Bye now darling I love you more and more all the time

A million kisses
Your husband,

DESI

Tuesday [illegible]

My darling baby:

I just [illegible] to you and you were [illegible] sweetheart and you cried [illegible] my poor little darling, [illegible] wish I could had hold [illegible] you in my arms and [illegible] kiss your eyes and stop y[illegible] tears, baby I don't like [illegible] think of you crying, I fee[illegible] [illegible]

because I know that I'm there with you and no matter what your troubles may be at that time I can help you with them, but here, so alone and get so far. So please baby take care of yourself, of your health and don't cry, sweetheart, I'll be home soon. I'm trying every day I'm trying doing exactly what I'm told, not taking even the short of a chance. So don't [illegible]

DESI

3

and the ranch, I'm just dying to have you take care of me, and help me with my bath and my exercises and go swimming with me and just act good and spoiled. Have you cook for me, those wonderful deserts, and steaks ???? and goulash. Oh Boy!! I know it'll be soon. We'll try it again this week and see what happens if it keeps getting better I don't see why he shouldn't let me go.

You have been writing

wonderfully honey, every-day I get a letter from you, may be just a couple of exceptions, but you have been sweetle (I never know how to spell that).

The people with the movie are here got go and get in my wheelchair and get a good place.

By now darling

I love you more and more all the time

A million kisses

Your husband,

LUCILLE

Wednesday

My darling -
Am in our nice
landing field we ca
bed - it's 10:44 P.M.
returned from Fath
English" S'pose I
have written you b
I went but my day
been so uneventful
wanted to wait un
I went to bed - I

writing you in bed anyway.
As I already told you
on the phone I stayed
at Mom's last nite. And
spent a quiet day at her
house sewing on baby clothes.
Went to hairdressers at
4:15 and came home &
waited for your call.
Glad you were over
being frightened and
able about your leg. I'm
re you have nothing

LUCILLE

make sure you do
thing the Dr. tells yo
Don't be blue darling
really are very lucky
we know it - and yo
health is fine otherw
so that's a big help.
Bought a magazine to
that had a story in it
about us - as part of
lot of other stories abo
"homelife of the stars

It as usual wasn't
exactly truthful - they
always have to color them
to make it sound interesting.
Was written by "Fearless"
It said you threw a guitar
at me one nite in front
of guests - but I "ducked
it expertly" —
Must be some of Lee
Bowman's tattling from
the nite you broke the
guitar over your knee
be he was so damned

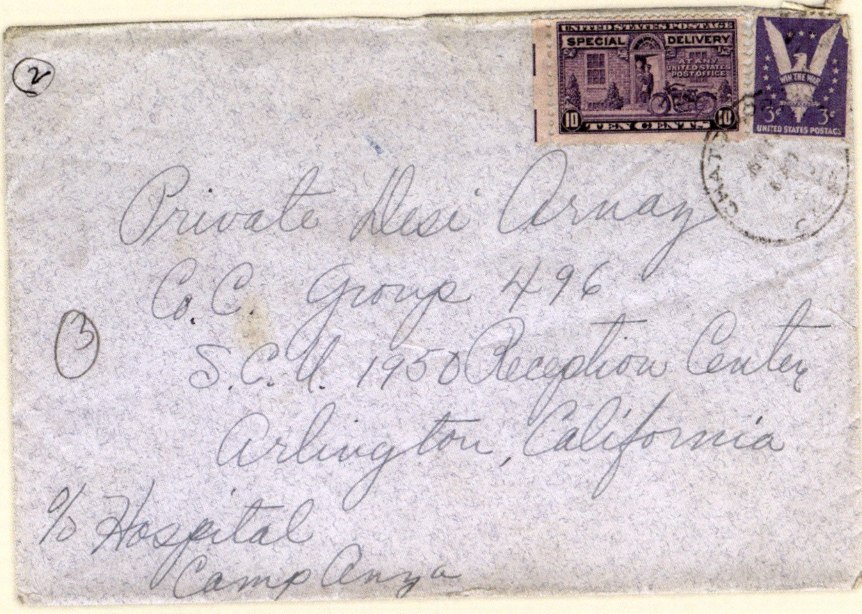

Wednesday

My darling–

Am in our nice big landing field we call a bed—it's 10:44 P.M. Just returned from Father English. S'pose I should have written you before I went but my day has been so uneventful I wanted to wait until I went to bed—I like writing you in bed anyway. As I already told you on the phone I stayed at Mom's last nite. And spent a quiet day at her house sewing on baby clothes. Went to hair dressers at 4:15 and came home + waited for your call.

Glad you were over being frightened and blue about your leg. I'm sure you have nothing to worry about. Just make sure you do everything the Dr. tells you to.

Chatsworth postmark

Magazine article included

Don't be blue darling—we really are <u>very</u> lucky and we know it—and your health is fine otherwise so that's a big help.

Bought a magazine today that had a story in it about us—as part of a lot of other stories about "home life of the stars"—It as usual wasn't exactly truthful—they always have to <u>color</u> them to make it sound interesting. Was written by "Fearless." It said you threw a guitar at me one nite in front of guests—but I "ducked it expertly"—

Must be some of Lee Bowman's tattling from the nite you broke the guitar over your knee because he was so damned objectionable—Anyway it made me laugh—I really got a giggle out of it.

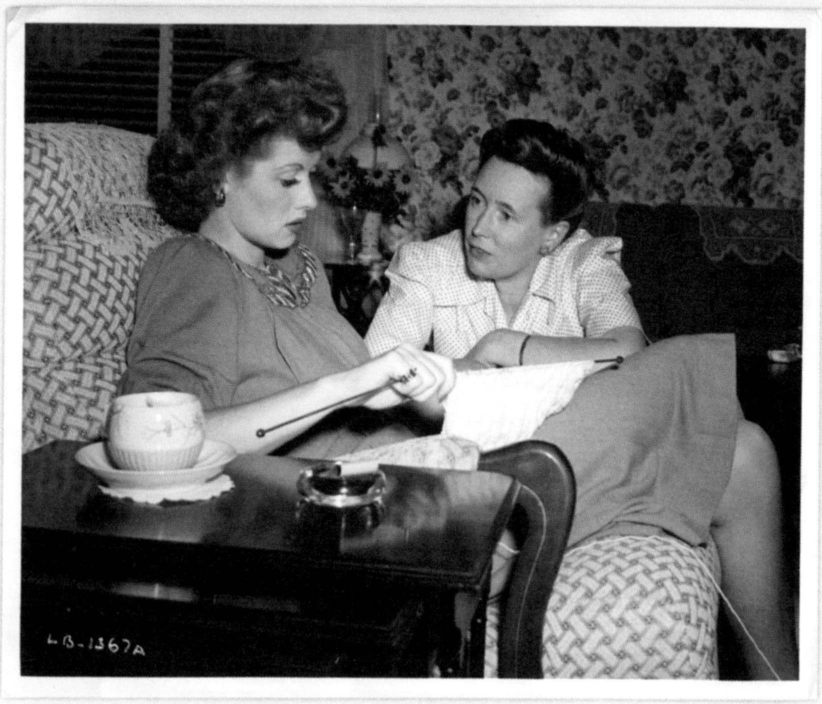

ABOVE: My grandmother DeDe Ball was always a loving and objective ear when any of her brood had worries.

Hate to think of what this driveway is going to cost—3 men working on it. Hope it doesn't take them very long. It certainly needs attention badly—but when we talked about it—you + I—I understood that you were going to put the boards around the circular part—and pour the cement—with Jim's help.

So—the other day when Jim said he was still working on it—trying to get someone with a cement mixer I didn't know whether It was something we had ordered—or what—I was surprised when I got home today + found the driveway filled with equipment, etc.—Am glad to have it fixed but I don't know about Jim hiring so many men etc—Is that right? Could we have managed it some other way—I don'no—what do you think? Or was he authorized to do it—Or did I unwittingly authorize him when I said "yes we should have it fixed."

Hope you get home before the weeds grow up again. John has just knocked himself out cleaning up for your arrival. The ranch really looked beautiful tonite darling. Seemed to be some moonlight struggling to get through too. Walked all around at sundown—waiting for your call—Have a special surprise for you when you get home—and it is not a new building of any sort. A real surprise! It was a surprise to me too. Can you guess?

LUCILLE

objectionable — [illegible]
it made me laugh
I really got a giggle
of it.

Hate to think of wha[t]
this driveway is going [to]
cost — 3 men working [on]
it. Hope it doesn't [take]
them very long. It ce[rtainly]
needs attent[illegible]

I understood that you
were going to put the
boards around the ~~circle~~
circular part - and pour
the cement - with Jim's
help.

So — the other day when
Jim said he was still working
on it - trying to get someone
with a cement mixer I
didn't know whether It
was somethin[illegible]

LUCILLE

driveway filled with
equipment etc — Am gla[d]
to have it fixed but I
don't know about Jim hirin[g]
so many men etc — Is that
right? Could we have
managed it some other
way - I donno — what
do you think? Or was
he authorized to do
it — Or did I unwittingly
authorize him when I said
"yes we should have it

fixed"

Hope you get home before
the weeds grow up again.
John has just knocked
himself out cleaning up
for your arrival. The
ranch really looked beautiful
tonite darling. Seemed to
be some moonlight struggling
to get through too. Walked
all around at sundown —
waiting for your call —
Have a special surprise
for you when you get

The truth about the STARS' HOME LIVES

Home is where the heart is—and where the stars show their true lights. That's why this tell-all treatise is so full of jolts

by "Fearless"

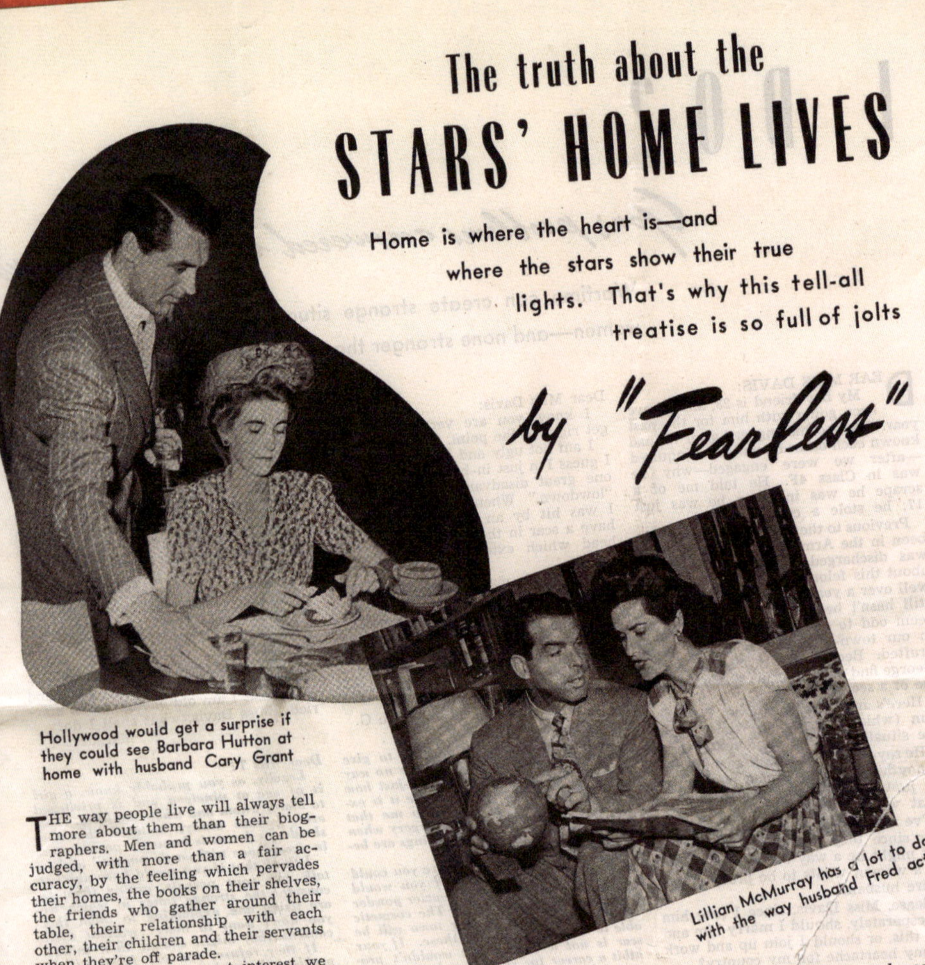

Hollywood would get a surprise if they could see Barbara Hutton at home with husband Cary Grant

Lillian McMurray has a lot to do with the way husband Fred acts

THE way people live will always tell more about them than their biographers. Men and women can be judged, with more than a fair accuracy, by the feeling which pervades their homes, the books on their shelves, the friends who gather around their table, their relationship with each other, their children and their servants when they're off parade.

This explains the great interest we feel in the way our neighbors live, a feeling multiplied tenfold in the case of the stars. The publicity departments of the various studios, well aware of this interest, issue stories about the ideal home lives of their stars. Press agents take costly and elaborate photographs of stars working in their gardens, standing in their doorways, reading by their firesides, playing in the nursery with their children or with their pets on the lawn.

Much of the time all this fails utterly to represent the human beings who live behind the much photographed and publicized star facades. It is the manner in which the stars live, day by day, seemingly unobserved, which serves as a key to their true personalities. Here "Fearless" gives you an over-the-transom look at the stars you know best—yet least.

The intimate life of Cary Grant and Barbara Hutton is a stimulating surprise and proves, beyond doubt, that they are very much in love. Cary and Barbara spend an incredible amount of time at home. It's only rarely they are to be found at parties or night clubs. To many their life would seem dull. It isn't dull to them.

When Cary isn't working he and Barbara entertain at home; mostly Barbara's friends—the so-called international set, titles, rich refugees and many who give evidence of being on the stuffy side.

When Cary is working he comes home, tired, to a late dinner. He reads his paper, plays with Lance—Barbara's son by Count von Reventlow whom he adores—or he and Barbara have a session of gin rummy. Barbara didn't play this game too well when she and Cary were engaged but now she's en expert—to his delight.

Here's something even Grant's pals don't know . . . Barbara has gorgeous, chiffony lounging pajamas and negligees favoring Persian motifs and hand embroidery, made by one of the highest paid and most exclusive designers in Hollywood. She wears these for Cary alone. No one else ever see[s] them. Many a wife would do well t[o] follow her example—not by buyin[g] such fabulously beautiful clothes—bu[t] by looking her best for her husban[d] instead of "for the crowd."

SO often it's the Hollywood coupl[es] who spend most of their time alo[ne] who are happiest.

Strangely enough Bill Powell a[nd] Diana Lewis are in this self-suffici[ent] group. We say "strangely enough" [be]cause Bill and Diana are so differ[ent] because he's so much older—on [the] intellectual and worldly side. W[hen] Bill and Diana aren't working (and most always (Continued on page

19700 Devonshire Boulevard
Chatsworth, California

In the privacy of their desert retreat, teaches husband Bill Powell how to knit For America,"—and that's not the

(Continued from page 68) they arrange to be in the studios at the same time and share the same dressing room!) they live at Palm Springs. When they do trek in from the desert—the last time they came in to buy tools for repairing their fence—Bill looked marvelous and Diana's happiness shines brighter than all the jewels he showers upon her.

Bill tells friends that during the long season they spend on the desert Diana gives him manicures and also touches up his hair. Bill's hair, grey for years, has to be kept darker for the screen.

All of which indicates that Bill and Diana, whose marriage courted such dire prophecies, have already found more happiness together than most couples know in their whole lives.

THE Fred MacMurrays manage many quiet evenings at home. For years Lillian MacMurray was ill and had to guard her health. Many believe this has contributed much to Fred's adoration and loyalty, for they are one of Hollywood's most in-love couples. She's completely well now, but she and Fred continue well content with an occasional small dinner party with their close friends. Fred spends lots of time "tinkering." In his big workroom he has "whittled" about everything from a toothpick to a davenport.

Ray Milland enjoyed home carpentry, too—until he nearly crippled his hands with his cabinet-making pursuits and, pronto, sold his tool chest to Franchot Tone. No mention of the Milland home life would be complete without a report of their bell system. So many gonglike rings which bring the unsuspecting g
out of his chair in
call awaits Ray and
less means it's for
fore this system
housekeeper would
hall that So and So
phone. This bothe
things do. Ray likes
Milland, the charm
who, like so many
sponsibility for her

Lucille Ball and D
other couple who do
Before Desi went in
Lucille definitely pr
home together—hap
way.

At home Lucille
so calm and collecte
in public. They're
quarrel and make u
make up. Desi's jeal
Latin temper. Once
with friends while
guitar in accompani
songs he loves to sin
by something Lucille
Lucille dodged his
Make what you like

Before Desi march
used to work on t
Valley; wear overalls
Literally. Their fri
about the time Desi
house to fix a stove
up, stuck his head in
without taking off
and had it go up i
half his hair and his
the cook put the fire
stood by helplessly s

The servant probl

It was a surprise to me
too. Can you guess?
Lucy the Lovelorn is
getting married. She sa
up on top of the highest
telephone pole and cooed for

get here. Hope they realize
how difficult it is to set
up h

Perhaps
stoves

TARS' HOME LIVES

home life—private life, either—naturally. The Hollywood restaurants are jammed to the doors these days. Some stars, however, are willing to make any effort to preserve the domestic scene. Like Don Ameche. The Ameches haven't had any help for months. With their large brood (cooks are fussy these days!) they have very little hope of getting help for the duration. Don, who used to whip up special dishes for "fun," now cooks the family's dinner in earnest when he gets home from the studios to give Honore a rest from playing nursemaid all day.

Claudette Colbert's given up the big Holmby Hills house where she and Doctor Joel Pressman lived in elegant dignity with a butler in striped trousers and morning coat and English accent. Claudette lives in a Hollywood apartment when she's working. At other times she's in Arizona with Lieutenant Commander Pressman. Whenever she gets away from the studios at a reasonable hour during her Hollywood sojourns she goes over to her mother's French Provincal house out on Sunset Boulevard for dinner. No cook, according to Claudette, ever produced a baked chicken comparable to her mother's.

IMMEDIATELY Ginger Rogers finished "Lady In The Dark" she left for La Jolla and Marine Jack Briggs. It didn't faze her there was a housing shortage. She went to live in a three-dollar-a-day room in a hotel—a far hail from her Coldwater Canyon manse.

Veronica Lake's home address is Seattle, Washington. That's where her husband, Captain John Detlie, is stationed. That's where she leased the charming house surrounded by gardens to which she shipped the furniture she and John have been collecting so slowly and discriminatingly ever since their marriage. This also is where the faithful Clara remains at all times, to look after Veronica's handsome Captain and their baby.

When Veronica is working and can possibly live in Seattle she shares a two-bedroom apartment with Wallace Beery's ex, Rita, and Wally's adopted daughter, Carol Ann. Rita and Veronica divide the various daily tasks and have a cleaning woman once a week.

Dorothy Lamour is trying to rent a little house outside San Bernardino where Captain Bill Howard is stationed. She'll be glad to settle for a cleaning woman once a week, too. She and Bill will cook their own meals very nicely, thank you. Her specialty is Southern dishes. His specialty is broiling steaks. When Dotty's working—and in Hollywood perforce—she'll live with her parents, Mr. and Mrs. O. L. Castleberry, as she did before she married. It doesn't concern her that she has to take care of her room and bath in their (Continued on page 88)

The Truth about the Stars' Home Lives

(Continued from page 70)
big servantless house. She can make a bed and vacuum like mad.

In some cases it is children who dictate the pattern of the stars' lives. But here again the way a star responds to the circumstances of her life and her maternal responsibilities gives a fine off-the-record picture of the star as a woman.

When Anne Shirley and John Payne separated Anne moved out of the Bel-Air house they had built together. But she soon moved back again. For Julie. In Bel-Air, Julie has Deanna Durbin's little nephew, who lives with Deanna across the way, and the Walter Langs' son for playmates.

All of which looks as if the happiness and closeness had drained out of the Shirley-Payne marriage before they ever moved into that house. Anne would be too smart, too sensitive to return, alone, to a place where she and John had once been happy—to torture herself with memories!

For the most part only the girls who are on their own escape complicated lives these days. Take Ann Sheridan and her ranch at Encino, out in the Valley. Annie spends half her time coaxing the grass to grow. She tells all the boys she prefers plants to flowers. Plants can be transferred from their crepe paper fluted pots to the garden. If you think Annie hasn't built up a lavish garden in the two years the boys have been saying it with flowers you underestimate her.

THE house isn't entirely furnished. It's not a large house. It only has two bedrooms. Annie's room, with a canopied bed and perfume shelves but no antiques, satins or brocades, is a room to which any working girl who likes nice things might very well aspire.

The first room to be completely furnished was the playroom. It's Tahitian and Spanish in feeling and features bamboo. If you should ever read about lavish parties being given here be sure it's pure invention. Annie practically never entertains stars in her home. The guests who usually listen to the Capehart play music are her wardrobe girl, hairdresser, secretary and their husbands.

Annie's a smart girl:

She's waiting until she owns the place, free and clear, to install a swimming pool.

The money she gets for her walnut crop pays her taxes.

She invests the money neighbors pay for her eggs in Victory Bonds.

Previously her chickens laid only twelve eggs a day. But Mr. Buick, who runs the ranch while Mrs. Buick runs the house, fed the hens a hot mash stew. Production increased to forty eggs a day.

Ann also has a Victory garden. The mother of Martha Giddings, her wardrobe girl, comes over to do the canning. Come winter Annie's cabbages will be sauerkraut and the tomatoes will be sauces and juices. Ration points? Annie doesn't need them!

This is the first home Annie has owned in Hollywood. She saved the money with which she made a down payment on the house and the four fertile acres while living in rented houses for which she never paid more than seventy-five dollars a month.

Home life in Hollywood, as you can see, very definitely is not what it used to be. But, we repeat, it's exciting—because it's so thoroughly in step with the times and because, as always, it reflects the truth about the stars as nothing else could do!

The End

LUCILLE

time—and I got cold
feet. My God! Everything
is skyhigh! It's terrific.

Marvin Schenk on the set
yesterday. Wanted to know
all about you. You know—
the guy from N.Y.—I
don't know how to spell
his last name correctly.
&
[illegible]

every minute of it. He
gave me lottsa things to
study and talked to
me for over an hour.
I really enjoyed it. Am
to see him in a day or so
again—and will be
ready to be married
again whenever you
come home—he said to
tell you—so hurry darling
I'm very anxious. Ed & Effo
to stand up with us huh?

LUCILLE

Daddy are there they'd
probably disgrace me
but I don't care—

I'm not only just bein
married (you know)—
joining the church
well—is that alright
honey—? Be sure &
me—

I love you with all my
heart—and I wish you
could always love me
Lucill

P.S. This is called "The Strange
Case of the Douglas's"—or—
"Thank God—It Couldn't
Happen Here!"—I don't
think! Anyway ~~~
Gordon Douglas has been home
exactly seven days and hasn't
yet kissed Marion or had
anything to do with her—walks
around in fatigue clothes &
talks about the army—kinda
batty-like—and Marion has
been crying her eyes out but
is mostly bewildered. Gee—hope
you're not ever going to be
that eager to get away from me!
love you—

11:30 P.M. Goodnite Baby—sleep well and please
dream of me—have a nice dream—or else!

Lucy the Lovelorn is getting married. She sat up on top of the highest telephone pole and cooed for a week or more and finally some <u>very</u> nice young dove picked up her message and arrived and has practically moved in. Probably by the time you get here. Hope they realize how difficult it is to set up housekeeping these days. Perhaps they don't need stoves + refrigerators—

Haven't received a call for tomorrow as yet!

Didn't order that liquor from Lucey's as you suggested cuz I got a bill from Schwab's for $92.63 for just that little bit we got last time—and I got cold feet. My God! Everything is sky high! It's terrific.

Marvin Schenk on the set yesterday. Wanted to know all about you. You know—the guy from N.Y.—I don't know how to spell his last name correctly.

Father English was <u>very</u> wonderful tonite—I loved <u>every</u> minute of it. He gave me lottsa things to study and talked to me for over an hour. I really enjoyed it. Am to see him in a day or so again—and will be ready to be married again whenever you come home—he said to tell you—so hurry darling I'm very anxious. Ed + Ebba to stand up with us huh? Of course! If my Mom + Daddy are there they'll probably disgrace me but I don't care—

I'm not only just being married you know—I'm joining the church as well—is that alright honey—? Besure + tell me—

I love you with all my heart and I wish you could always love me—

Lucille (over)

P.S. This is called "The Strange Case of the Douglas's"—or—"Thank God—It Couldn't Happen Here!"—I don't think! Anyway—

Gordon Douglas has been home exactly <u>seven</u> days and hasn't <u>yet</u> kissed Marion or had <u>anything</u> to do with her—walks around in <u>fatigue</u> clothes + talks about the army—kinda batty-like—and Marion has been crying her eyes out but is mostly bewildered. Gee—hope you're not <u>ever</u> going to be that eager to get away from me! Love you—

11:30 P.M. Goodnite Baby—sleep well and please dream of me—but a <u>nice</u> dream—no fights!

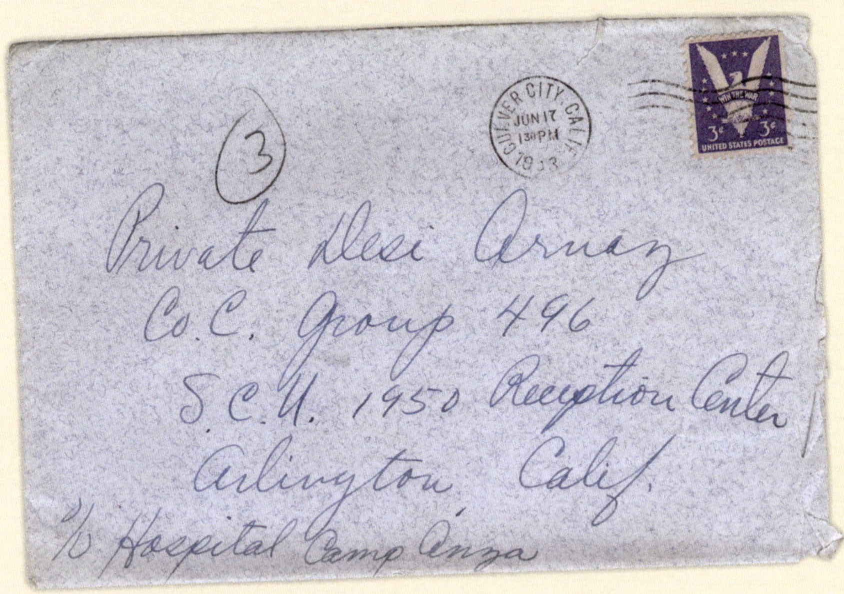

June 17, 1943, Culver City postmark

Thursday
10:35 A.M.
On the set

Dearest:

Well, I made it to work today. Glad I stayed at Mom's or I wouldn't have. Damn these sinus things. Haven't had one in so long thought maybe I was lucky and wouldn't have any more. But here I am again. Sneezing + carrying on—and of course—as always right during my best part of the picture. Anyway—s'awful—and worse than anything else—I'm going to look awful on the weekend and feel awful and I've everything wrong with me! And I do mean everything! But you love me anyway don't you? Hope I can drive down Sunday—have to work Sat. I guess. If you can get a pass—we'll get you home somehow don't worry about that.

Sorry I didn't write yesterday darling. But just couldn't.

Everyone giving me many compliments for you this week—"Bataan" playing now up here.

I think you'd love the ranch even for a couple of days—so really work on it—even though I am a mess!

LUCILLE

Thursday
10:35 AM.
On the set.

Dearest:

Well, I made it to work
today. Glad I stayed a[t]
Mom's or I wouldn't
have. Damn these sinus
things. Haven't had one [i]n
so long thought maybe
I was lucky and wouldn't
have any more. But here
I am again. Sneezing &

during my best part of the
picture. Anyway it
s'awful – and worse
than anything else – I'm
going to look awful on the
weekend and feel awful
and I've everything wrong
with me! And I do mean
everything! But you love
me anyway don't you?
... I can drive down

LUCILLE

get you home someh[ow]
don't worry about th[...]

Sorry I didn't write
yesterday darling. [...]
just couldn't.

Everyone giving me [...]
compliments for you [...]
week – "Bataan" p[...]
now up here.

I think you'd love [...]
ranch even for a co[...]

of days – so really work
on it – even though
I am a mess!

Not going to the preview
tonite. Deffinitely! Going
right home and have
dinner in bed and talk
to you.

Mom talked to Lolita last
nite for me – I was too
sick – She's O.K. – but kinda
lonesome I guess. Hope
Elena gets here soon –
very soon.

LUCILLE

Everyone swell on this pic. Thank God! It's so good to be around congenialness again for a change. Although "Best Foot" was swell too - but I still feel the sting of Skelton in "Du... Can't forget unpleasant... easily can I? Never...

Phyllis is going into defense work - Lockheed - next week. Starts at $45. so she really can't afford to turn it down. I'll miss her though. Wish to God that screwy ... would return to ... senses. In the ... I'll love I guess - ... anyone - ... asks about ... all day long - couldn't

LUCILLE

stop thinking about you every minute - if I wanted to. And I don't want to.

Calling me - gotta go -

I love you Baby

Very much -

Lucy -

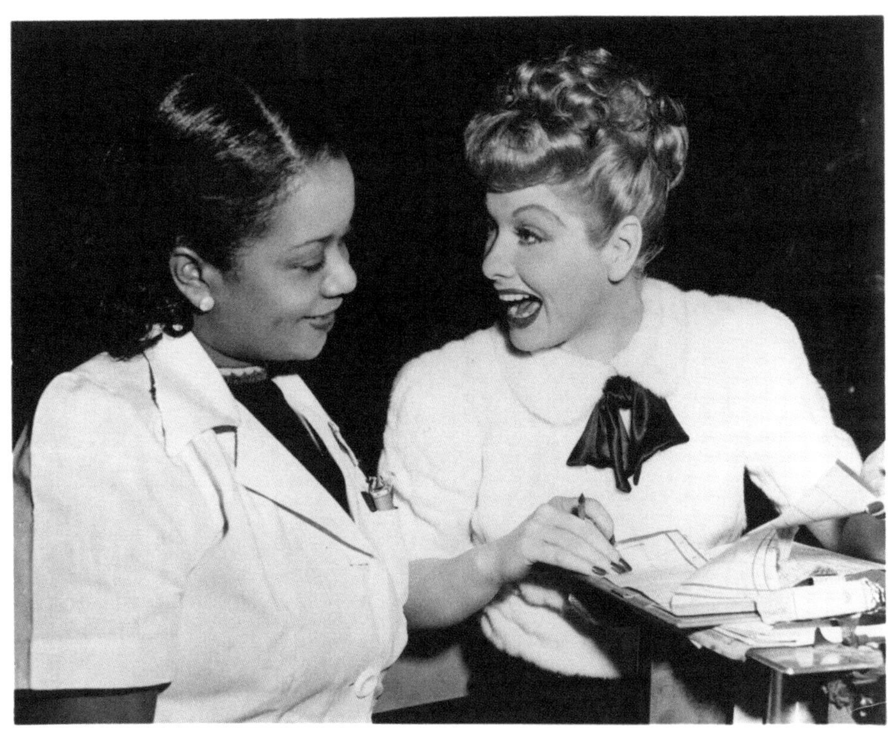

ABOVE: Mom relied heavily on her "Gal Friday," Harriet McCain, and she stayed with us for many years.

Not going to the preview tonite. Definitely! Going right home and have dinner in bed and talk to you.

Mom talked to Lolita last nite for me—I was too sick—She's O.K.—but kinda lonesome I guess. Hope Elena gets here soon—very soon.

Everyone swell on this pic. Thank God! It's so good to be around congenialness again for a change. Although "Best Foot" was swell too—but I still feel the sting of Skelton in "DuBarry" Can't forget unpleasantness easily can I? Never could.

Phyllis is going into defense work—Lockheed—next week. Starts at $45. so she really can't afford to turn it down. I'll miss her though. Wish to God that screwy Harriet would return to her right senses. In the meantime I'll live I guess—without anyone.

Everyone asks about you all day long—couldn't stop thinking about you every minute—if I wanted to. And I don't want to.

Calling me—gotta go—

I love you Baby

Very much—

Lucy—

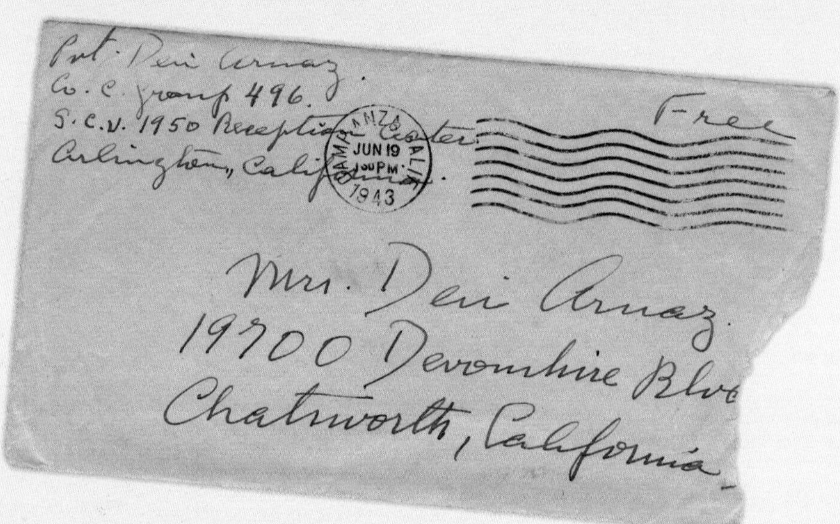

June 19, 1943, from Camp Anza

Friday
9 A.M.

Good morning my darling:

I hope you are feeling better baby, you still sounded sick last nite and I wanted so much to be with you. All through the Rugles's program I was thinking of you and wondering if you have stayed in bed or gotten up to listen to it and if so, which chair you were sitting on finally I decided that maybe you've sat on my chair did you?

The doctor measure my knee this morning and saw the swelling had gone down considerably and that it wasn't much different from my other, I can also bend it all the way back now, so he said, it was really very good and that I would be out in a little while, wouldn't that be great? This afternoon I'll tackle him about the weekend and see what he says.

They really scared me yesterday with that Palm Springs affair, I certainly did a lot of talking in a hurry. When you get to that place is really tough getting out and so far away, I would never get to see you and God that would be just awful. I'm so glad am not going.

I hope I get to go home this weekend am just dying to see it, you have no idea, next Sunday it'll be <u>five</u> weeks since I've been home, and it seems like five months. Will see what happens, I hope I get good news for you when I call you tonite. I hope I hope I hope.

You sounded like a little bity baby last night I wanted to reach through the phone and smodered you with kisses and hugs.

Take care of yourself my darling, I'll call you tonite, and probably will write to you again before the day is over. Say hello to all our dogs and cats. I hope they haven't forgotten me.

Love you with all my heart

Your husband.

DESI

Friday
9 A.M.

Good morning my darling,

I hope you are feeling better baby, you still sounded sick last nite and I wanted so much to be with you. All through the Rugler's program I was thinking of you and wondering if you had stayed in bed or gotten up to listen to it and if so, which chair you were sitting on finally I decided that maybe you've sat on my chair did you?

The doctor was in [illegible] and said the swelling had gone down considerably and that it wasn't much different from any other, I can also bend it all the way back now, so he said, it was really very good and that I would be out in a little while, wouldn't that be great? This afternoon I'll tackle him about the weekend and see what he says.

They really scared me [illegible] with that Palm[illegible] I certainly [illegible]

DESI

to that place is really tough getting out and so far away, I would never get to see you and God that would be just awful. I'm so glad am not going.

I hope I get to go home this weekend am just dying to see it, you have no idea, next Sunday it'll be *five* weeks since I've been home, and it seems like five months. Will see what happens, I [ho]pe I get good news for [yo]u when I call you tonite. I hope I hope I hope [y]ou sounded like a little [k]itty baby last night I [w]anted to reach through the phone and smothered [yo]u with kisses and hugs. Take care of yourself [m]y darling, I'll call [yo]u tonite, and probably [w]ill write to you again [be]fore the day is over. [Say] hello to all our dogs and cats, I hope they [ha]ven't forgotten me.

[I l]ove you with all my [he]art

Your husband.

DESI

Tuesday nite
9 o'clock

Hello darling:

We saw a movie "Reaching for the Sun" with Joel McCrea and Ellen Drew and Eddie Bracken. It started here in the ward about seven thirty and it just finished, and was thinking how much nicer it would have been sitting with you and holding your hand and watching "Best Foot."

I hope it went over big I know it must have.

Like I told you I walked this afternoon for the first time

out any crutches and without help. It felt kind of wobbly the beginning, the muscles my leg are so used to g nothing, but the knee pretty good; the doctor nted to see if it would ll up any, we'll know by morrow. So maybe I'll all right by the end of the eek or by the first days next. I hope.

don't feel so bad this eek, cause the end seems

a very wonderful wife.

Our place looked so bea ful to me darling, tha I can't tell you in wo how much I enjoyed it out in the yard admi it. We are really very l people, you know that, don't you?

Last nite when you le I did feel pretty lonely, bu then I started thinkin of a few other million couples that are so much worse off than we are

and I was ashamed of myself for being discontented and I thanked God for all he has given us together, and for being able to see you and be with you, and the more I thought about it, the better I felt. I couldn't go to sleep until about twelve o'clock so I just laid in bed and thought of you and of our nice 48 hours together.

Good night my baby, love me very much this week as I love you, hope to see you soon.

Considered yourself kissed

Desi

Free

t. Desi Arnaz
. C. Group 496
.C.U. 1950 Reception Center
rlington, California

Mrs. Desi Arnaz
19700 Devonshire Blv
Chatsworth, California

Tuesday nite
9 o'clock

Hello darling:

We saw a movie "Reaching for the Sun" with Joel McCrea and Ellen Drew and Eddie Bracken. It started here in the ward about seven thirty and it just finished, and was thinking how much nicer it would have been sitting with you and holding your hand and watching "Best Foot."

I hope it went over big I know it must have.

Like I told you I walked this afternoon for the first time without any crutches and without any help. It felt kind of wobly at the beginning, the muscles in my leg are so used to doing nothing, but the knee felt pretty good; the doctor wanted to see if it would swell up any, we'll know by tomorrow. So maybe I'll be all right by the end of the week or by the first day of next. I hope.

I don't feel so bad this week, cause the end seems to be nearer and nearer and because I love you very much and you are a very wonderful wife.

Our place looked so beautiful to me darling, that I can't tell you in words how much I enjoyed sitting out in the yard admiring it. We are really very lucky people, you know that, don't you?

Last nite when you left I did feel pretty lousy, but then I started thinking of a few other million couples that are so much worst off than we are and I was ashamed of myself for being discontented and I thanked God for all he has given us together, and for being able to see you and be with you, and the more I thought about it, the better I felt.

I couldn't go to sleep until about twelve o'clock so I just laid in bed and thought of you and of our nice 48 hours together.

Goodnight my baby, love me very much this week as I love you, hope to see you soon.

Considered yourself kissed.

Desi

Wednesday nite:

Hello baby:

June 24, 1943, from Camp Anza

Newspaper clipping about Bataan *included*

I just said goodnight to you over the phone, but wanted to talk a little more so I thought I write a bit before "retiring."

I don't get tired of telling how much higher my moral is since being able to walk. It really feels good after that scare I had.

I'm going to work on that furlough and don't see any reasons why I shouldn't get it, but you know "This is the Army."

I talked to Ben Oakland on the phone today and he said my job is there and they are waiting for me. So unless something comes out of the Mervyn Le Roy deal, at least I'll know I'll be at San Bernardino which is not far from home, and probably would be able to get home most every weekend. All in all things seem to be working out pretty good for us. Thank God.

I knew your pic would go over terrific, you were very good in it and looked terrific and I'm sure is really going to do you a lot of good. It's about time they gave you a break I don't know of anybody that deserves it better than you do, from all angles, including your own beautifully rounded big "angles"? Well you know what I mean I wish I had it here now. Oh mama could I love it!! This kind of talk "ain't" doing me any good lady. It disturbs my peacefull nights, too God damn peacefull.

I am including my great break in the famous newspaper of the amazing and magnificent town of Arlington. Your husband is really getting up in the world, and just the other day I was speaking to you about my lack of publicity, what a guy I am always complaining.

I will call you tomorrow sweetheart, sleep tight, love me much and think of me. I love you terribly and want you very, very much.

God bless you baby.

Desi

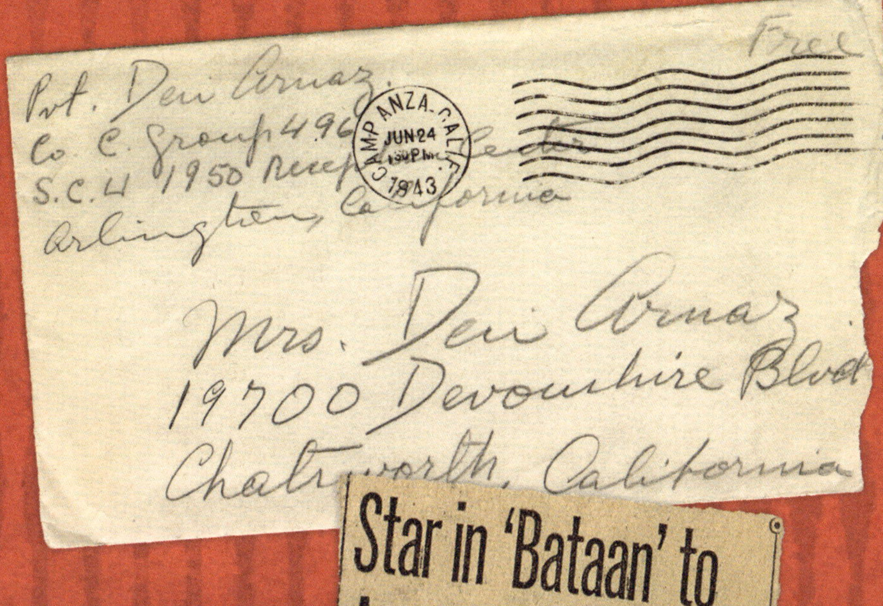

Star in 'Bataan' to Appear in Person

Desi Arnaz, one of the all-star cast featuring also Robert Taylor, will appear in person at the showing of the M-G-M picture, "Bataan," which will be shown at the Chatterbox theater, Arlington, Thursday, at 2, 7 and 9 p.m. Arnaz has the part of Felix Ramirez in the stirring epic.

It is related of Arnaz, who was inducted into the Army at the conclusion of the shooting of the picture, that he started getting himself in training for K.P. duty by giving a party for the cast at his Chatsworth ranch. When the guests arrived, however, they discovered Desi's barbecue pit, which he had built with his wife, Lucille Ball, lacked an opening in which to roast the meat.

Others in the cast are George Murphy, Thomas Mitchell, Lloyd Nolan, Lee Bowman, Barry Nelson, Phillip Terry, Roque Espiritu, Kenneth Spencer, J. Alex Havier, Tom Dugan and Donald Curtis.

Sponsored by the Arlington Lions and 6:30 clubs, "Bataan" is being shown here for the first time as a benefit for Camp Anza, the net proceeds to be used for procuring additional recreational equipment for the camp, where Arnaz is stationed.

DESI

Wednesday
nite:

Hello baby:

I just said goodnight to you over the phone, but wanted to talk a little more so I thought I write a bit before retir[ing]

I don't get tired of t[elling you]
how much higher my [morale]
is since being able to [talk to you.]
It really feels good after t[he]
scare I had.

I'm going to work o[n]
that furlough and do[n't see]
at any reasons why [I]
shouldn't get it, but y[ou]
know "This is the Arm[y."]

I talked to Ben Oakland [on]
the phone today and h[e]
said my job is there a[nd]
they are waiting for m[e.]
So unless something come[s]
out of the Mervyn LeRo[y]
deal, at least I'll know
I'll be at San Bernardi[no]
which is not far from
home, and probably wou[ld]
be able to get home n[early]
every weekend. All in al[l]
things seem to be working
out pretty good for us, Tha[nk]
God.

I knew your pic would g[o]
over terrific, you were
very good in it and looke[d]

DESI

terrific and I'm sure is
really going to do you
a lot of good. It's about
time they gave you a break
I don't know of anybody
that deserves it better than
you do, from all angles,
including your own beautifully rounded big "angles"?
Well you know what I mean
I wish I had it here now,
Oh mama could I ~~love~~ it!!
This kind of talk "ain't"
doing me any good lady.
It disturbs my peacefull
nights, too God dam peacefull.

…ncluding my great break
… famous newspaper
… amazing and magi-
… town of Arlington.
…usband is really getting
… the world, and just
…r day I was squawking
…bout my lack of
…g, what a guy I am
…complaining.
…all you tomorrow
sweetheart, sleep tight, love
me much and think of me.
I love you terribly and
want you very, very much
God bless you baby
Desi

Desilu Productions envelope, 1040 N. Las Palmas Avenue, 1951

To the Vice-President:

Dearest Veepee:

May I take this opportunity to tell you how much I have enjoyed our association for the past eleven years. It has been a great pleasure doing business with you—

I would also like to report that our enterprises are going along fine—

Our T.V. production "I Love Lucy" which showed in tenth place in the Nielsen national ranking has now moved up to fourth in the same rating for the N.Y. area a wonderful indication.

Our first and only Major Production "LUCIE" it has proven to be by far the most outstanding of all our enterprises.

Here's hoping that we will continue to be associated for many years to come—

With all my love
D.A.
PRES.

from the desk of

DESI ARNAZ

To the Vice-President:

Dearest Veepee:

May I take this oppor-
tunity to tell you how
much I have enjo
our association f
the past eleven
It has been a gre
pleasure doing bus
with you -

I would also lik
report that our
prises are going
fine -

Desilu
PRODUCTIONS, INC.
1040 N. LAS PALMAS AVENUE
HOLLYWOOD (38) CALIFORNIA

Our T.V. production "I
Love Lucy" which showed
in tenth place in the
Nielsen national rating
has now moved up to
fourth in the same
rating for the N.Y. area
a wonderful indication
Our first and only
Major Production "LUCIE"
it has proven to be by
far the most outstan-
ding of all our enterprises
Here's hoping that
we will continue to
be associated for many
years to come -

With all my love
D.A.
PRES.

April 20th

I've come to the terribly
realization that my wife
doesn't love me. She loves
her children, her mother,
her family as far as
I'm concerned if I
became well am a nice
guy to have around —
but there's no love —
I've put up with a
million things that she
has done to me in t
past thirteen years b
I love her, many a
these things I didn
like they made m
unhappy she should n
have done them, bu
I forgave her in my
I don't think about
them. Lucy is not
way, she can't forg

me anything, and the
reason why she can't
forgive me anything is
because she really doesn't
love me.

I have a sick feeling in my
stomach. I've had this
feeling before. During the
Cuban revolution, during
Lucy's commie accusations
and now — The other two
times there was something
you could do, something
you could fight, but
you can't fight this
the woman does not
love me

April 20th

I've come to the terrible realization that my wife doesn't love me. She loves her children, her mother, her family, as far as I'm concerned if I behave well am a nice guy to have around—but there's no love—

I've put up with a million things that she has done to me in the past thirteen years because I love her, many of these things I didn't like they made me unhappy she should not have done them, but I forgave her in my mind. I don't think about them. Lucy is not that way, she can't forgive me anything, and the reason why she can't forgive me anything is because she really doesn't love me.

April 20, 1954

I have a sick feeling in my stomach. I've had this feeling before during the Cuban revolution, during Lucy's commie accusations and now—The other two times there was something you could do, something you could fight, but you can't fight this the woman does not love me.

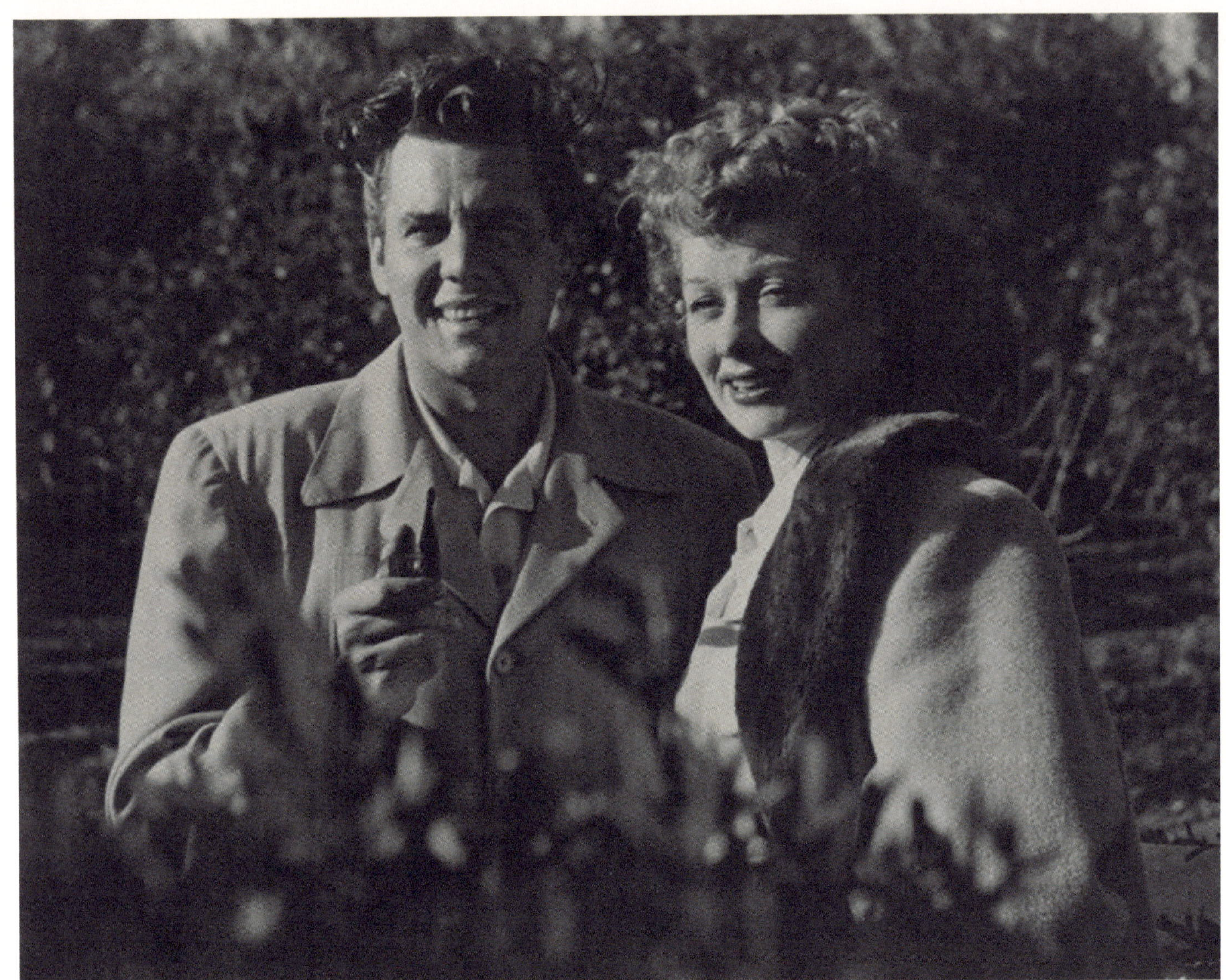

Dearest:

Under the bonus set up of our company I received five thousand as an executive for the past three years—you don't come under that classification—you are a "ham" but I could not have done it without you—so will you please accept half of it with my thanks and my love—

Desi

Lucy

DA

Dearest:

Under the bonus set up of our company I received five thousand as an executive for the past three years — you don't come under that classification — you are a "ham" but I could not have done it without you — so will you please accept half of it with my thanks and my love — Desi

Dearest Desi
Here's a cream cheese sandwich and my love - I'm so in hopes you'll enjoy every minute and come back happy a[nd] healthy as you went away -
Will miss you terribly -
I Love you

P.S.
I'm *so* glad Pepito is with you - I know how happy it makes you -
Give him my love -
Please don't stay away from all of us too long -
Bye Baby -

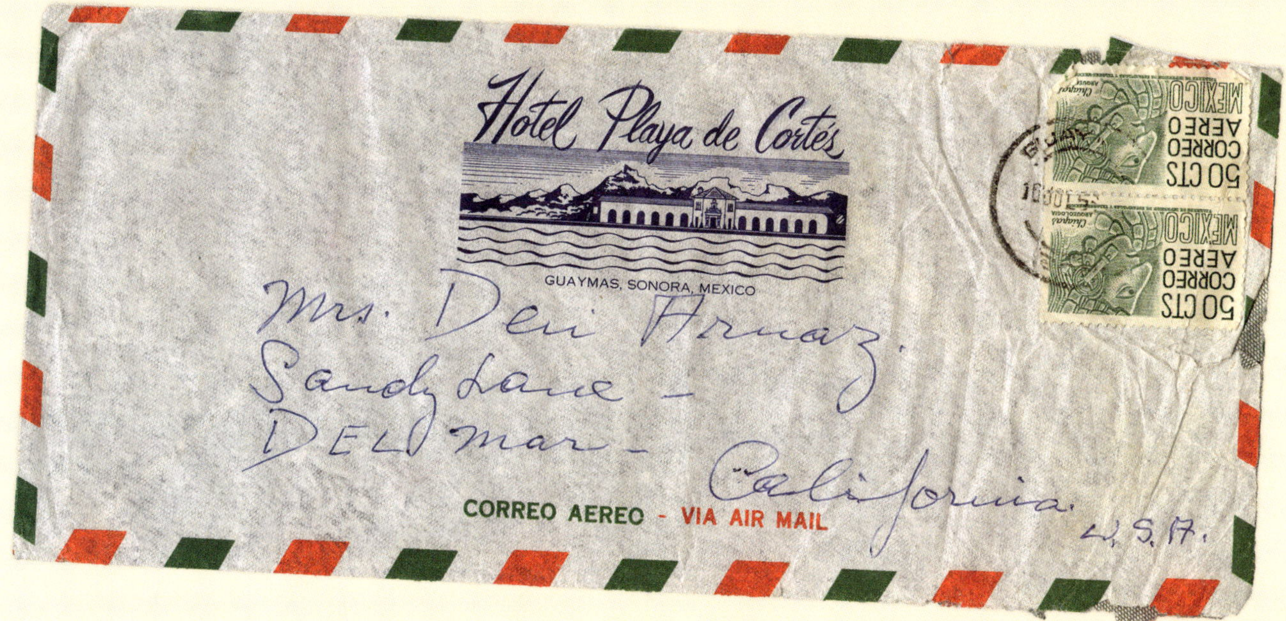

Dearest Desi,

July 1956

Here's a cream cheese sandwich and my love—I'm so in hopes you'll enjoy every minute and come back happy and healthy as you went away—

We'll miss you terribly—

Love you

P.S. I'm so glad Pepito is with you—I know how happy it makes you—Give him my love—Please don't stay away from all of us too long—Bye Baby

W. J. HOLLIDAY
CHAIRMAN
CARL B. ANDERSON
PRESIDENT
MATILDE HOLBERT
VICE-PRESIDENT
IGNACIO SIERRA A.
COMPTROLLER
ELDRED H. TANNER
MANAGING-DIRECTOR

Hello sweetheart:
I just wanted to tell again how much I love you and how wonderful your little note was. I am having a marvelous time the fishing has been great and I hadn't done it for so long — (Hey, look at me, I'm writing a letter, how about that?) Some day I think you may enjoy it if we come down a different time of year when it's not so hot. The food is not too good, but it's not too bad, they don't have

Hello sweetheart:

I just wanted to tell again how much I love you and how wonderful your little note was, I am having a marvelous time the fishing has been great and I hadn't done it for so long—(Hey, look at me, I'm writing a letter, how about that?)

Some day I think you may enjoy it if we come down a different time of year when it's not so hot. The food is not too good, but it's not too bad, they don't have milk, and the service is Mexican, which means slow and lousy but its such a tremendous change from our fast pace that it cannot help but slow you down and relax you

Mailed from Del Mar, July 12, 1956

I'm looking forward to a wonderful and happy summer with my wonderful family. Gosh you don't know how much I miss you all.

Please don't worry about me—I'll be home soon to love you and make you happy—You are a wonderful girl and I'm sorry if I'd made you unhappy at times—

All my love to the kids, Deede, Uncle Ned, Frances, Maddy, the dogs, the cat, etc etc etc.

Desi

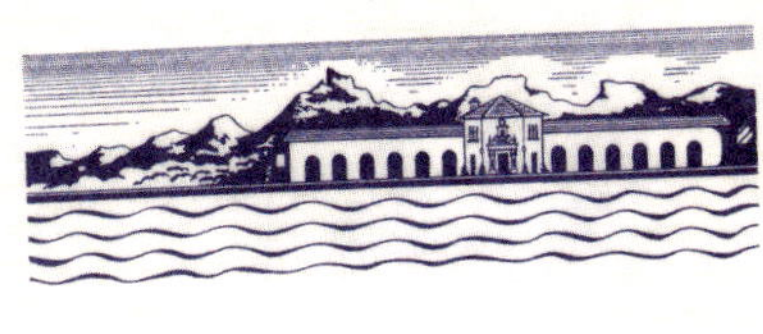

Hotel Playa de Cortés

ON BACOCHIBAMPO BAY

•

GUAYMAS, SONORA, MEXICO

milk, and the service is mexican, which means slow and lousy, but it's such a tremendous change from our fast pace that it cannot help but slow you down and relax you.

I'm looking forward to a wonderful and happy summer with my wonderful family. Gosh you don't know how much I miss you all. Please don't worry about me. I'll be home soon to love you and make you happy. You are a wonderful girl and I'm sorry if I'd made you unhappy at times.

All my love to the kids, Deede, Uncle Ned, Frances, Maddy, the dogs, the cat etc. etc. etc. Don

Nov. 17

Desi Arnaz

Dearest Lucy:

I'm sorry about last nite.
It was silly of me ~~to~~ to make
so much about so little
I am writing you th
because I love you
and maybe I can
things better if I
about them before
them and maybe yo
believe them and
better if you see the
writing—(particularly
this is my second lette
year).

2

Desi Arnaz

A few things about me first.
I have, I admit, been in
deeper ~~in~~ in my work and more
worried about it than ever
before. Believe it or not,
and last nite sure didn't
am coming up
, things are
h clearer, I
some of the
t. and I am
g not to be

ay to Palm Springs
s me tremendously
arous.

3

Desi Arnaz

I had neglected golf too much
and that's not good for me.
I have always had a hobby
Swimming and football when
I was young in school,
horseback riding ~~at~~ at the farm
fishing later on—tennis
then golf—I always took
pride in doing these things
well—so now that I
have all this work it is
good for me to look
forward to a good weekend
of golf—and you know
much I love the house

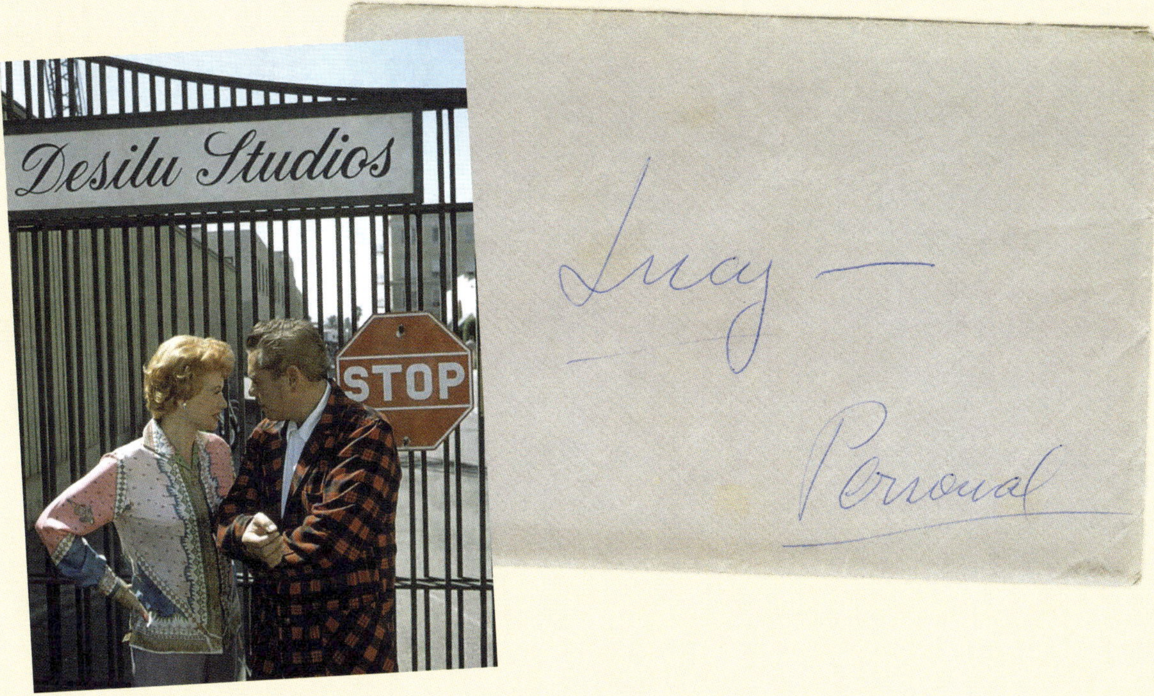

Envelope says Lucy—Personal (not mailed), probably 1958

ABOVE: Just months before their divorce, Mom and Dad spent days posing for a lengthy *Life* magazine article touting the success of their union and Desilu Studios.

Nov. 17

Dearest Lucy:

I'm sorry about last nite. It was silly of me to make so much about so little. I am writing you this note because I love you very much and maybe I can say things better if I think about them before I say them and maybe you will believe them and understand better if you see them in writing—(particularly my writing—this is my second letter in 10 years).

A few things about me first—I have, I admit, been in deeper in my work and more worried about it than ever before—Believe it or not,—and last nite sure didn't prove it, I am coming up for air now, things are looking much clearer, I am getting some of the help I want—and I am now beginning not to be afraid—

The Thursday to Palm Springs situation helps me tremendously for several reasons.—I had neglected golf too much and that's not good for me. I have always had a hobby—Swimming and football when I was young in school, horseback riding at the farm, fishing later on—tennis then golf—I always took pride in doing these things well—so now that I have all this work it is good for me to look forward to a good weekend of golf and you know how much I love the house in the Springs—

When I'm concentrating on playing good golf—it keeps me from drinking too much and from staying out too late—the last two weekends were wonderful examples—I never drank after dinner and believe me I didn't have more than three at the most before—I was in bed before eleven every nite—

I have found out that I can take care of my work by organizing it better when I'm here with regular weekly meetings on different matters. My reading I do most of it down in the Springs—so it works good for me. BUT does it work for you—and the family? I think it would if you plan it—say you and the kids come down every other weekend or such—

A few things about you and me. First, and this you *have* to believe,—I love you very much!! I love my children very much!! I do not want any other way of life—without you all—

The nice things that people say about me are *not* untrue they couldn't be—we could not have done this much and stay together this long if they were—I love you and you must love me to have put up with the many things you have in this first 18 yrs—

So please, my darling, do not despair—things are working out better and I assure you they will be better still—please overlook a silly flare up as last nite's—and look forward to a better life—Do not be sore at me—I hate myself when I make you unhappy—

Please love me—and don't loose your patience I promise you you won't regret it—

This started out as a simple note—and it's wounding up as quite an expossé—

You know me when I write, I write—no moderation.

Love, Desi

Desi Arnaz

When I'm concentrating a
playing good golf - it keep
me from drinking too mu
and from staying out to
late - The last two weekend
were wonderful examples -
I never drank after dinne
and believe me ~~and~~ I
didn't have more than
three at the most before -
I was in bed before eleve
every nite -
I have found out that I
can take care of my wor

Desi Arnaz

meetings on different matte
my reading I do most of it
during in the Spring -
so it works good for
me. BUT does it work
for you - and the family
I think it would if you
plan it - Say you and
the kids come down
every other weekend or

Desi Arnaz

The nice things that peo
say about us are <u>not</u>
they couldn't be - we co
not have done this -
and stay together th
if they were - I love
and you must love
to have put up with
many things you h
in the past 18 ye

So please, my darling
not despair - things
working out better
I assure you they w
be better still - Plea
overlook a silly
as last nite's - and look

Desi Arnaz

forward to a better life -
Do not be sore at
me - I hate myself
when I make you
unhappy -

Please love me - and
don't loose your patience
I promise you you
won't regret it -

This started out as a
simple note - and it's
winding up as quite an
exposé -

You know me when
I write, I write - no moderation

Love Desi

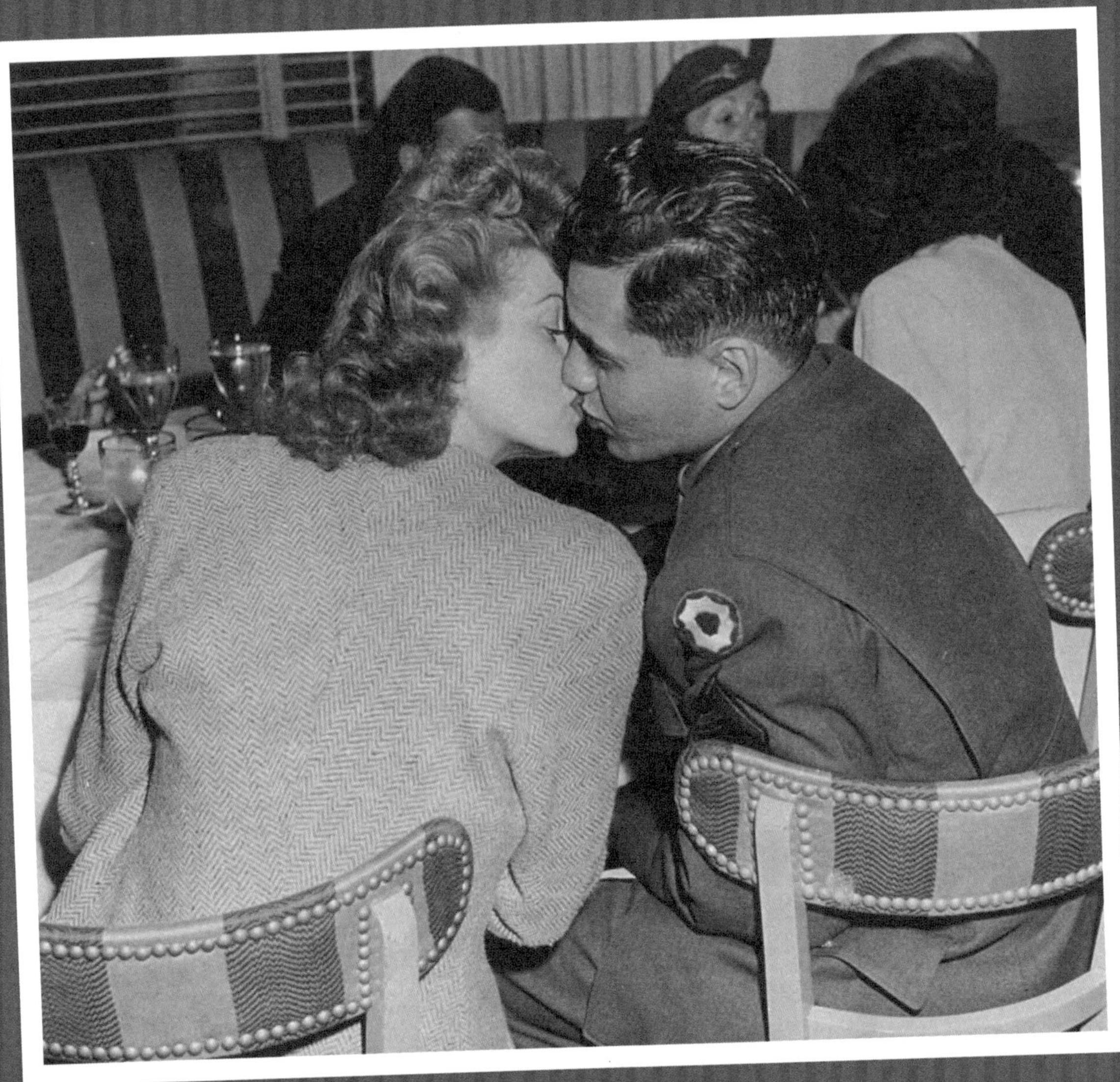

Historical Notes

PAGE 17, *It was wonderful:*

The Hotel Meurice was located at 145 West 58th Street, New York 10019. Desi wrote letters from here in 1940. A prewar property located in Midtown Manhattan, a block from Central Park and 5th Avenue, the hotel was a 13-story building. Sold in 1941 for $600,000, it is now an apartment building.

Eugene Markey (1895–1980) was a writer, producer, and decorated naval officer (World Wars I and II). He wrote and produced dozens of movies, however, none of them with Lucy or Desi.

Dorothy Kilgallen (1913–1965) was a journalist who wrote a column called the "Voice of Broadway" between 1938 and 1965, which featured New York show business news, politics, and gossip. She was also a panelist on the television game show *What's My Line?* Her husband, actor Richard Kollmar, who costarred with Desi in *Too Many Girls* on Broadway, hosted a New York radio show (WOR 710) starting in 1945.

MCA (Musical Corporation of America) was started by Julius Stein in 1924 and originally focused on musicians and bands. It grew from there to become one of the most powerful talent agencies in New York and Hollywood. In 1959, it purchased the 420-acre Universal Studios campus in the Cahuenga Pass, and in 1962 it bought Universal Pictures and Decca Records.

Martin Jurow (1911–2004) was a Hollywood agent and film producer at the William Morris Agency in their film department.

Foyer most likely refers to a talent agent at MCA, and **Marion** is probably someone involved with Desi's act.

Carlson refers to Richard Carlson (1912–1977), actor of stage and motion pictures. He starred in *Too Many Girls* alongside Lucy and Desi.

Too Many Girls is the 1939 Broadway musical that was Desi's biggest break to date. The success and reviews of his stage performances sent him to Hollywood to star in the RKO movie musical where he met Lucille Ball on the set in June 1940.

The **Criterion Theatre** was located at 1514 Broadway in New York. The 1,700-seat movie house opened on September 16, 1936, and during its life hosted world and US premieres of many famous movies including *The Ten Commandments*, *Lawrence of Arabia,* and *My Fair Lady*. The theater closed its doors for good on May 4, 2000.

PAGE 20, *Good morning my Baby—:*

Lucille was very busy making several movies during this time, but "under a dryer" likely refers to the 1941 movie comedy *A Girl, a Guy and a Gob* in which Lucy starred as secretary Dot Duncan.

Max Baer (1909–1959) was a world heavyweight champion boxer and later movie and television actor, and father of Max Baer Jr. of *The Beverly Hillbillies* fame.

Evan Frankel (1902–1991) was a New York builder and developer, and one of the largest landowners of East Hampton, Long Island. Also an investor in Broadway musicals, Frankel was born in Poland and immigrated to New York as a child, where he sold chewing gum and shoelaces on the street to support his parents and nine siblings. He was co-founder and chairman of the Jewish Center of the Hamptons.

PAGE 28, *Hello darling:*

Larry Hart refers to lyricist Lorenz Hart (1895–1943), half of the songwriting duo of Rodgers and Hart, who wrote the music to *Too Many Girls*.

Built as an opera house in the 1920s, the **Versailles** was renovated into a supper club in the 1930s. Located at 151 East 50th Street in New York, the club offered dining, drinks, and entertainment to the well-heeled of Manhattan and beyond. The self-styled "New York's Distinguished Continental Rendezvous" offered musicians such as the very popular Desi Arnaz on a nightly basis.

"**My mamy**" refers to Desi's mother, Dolores (Lolita) de Acha y Socias (1896–1988), who by this time in 1940 had immigrated to the US and divorced Desi's father.

Wasserman was Lewis Wasserman (1913–2002), a high school dropout who became a businessman, talent agent, and eventually president of MCA. He was known as the "most powerful and influential Hollywood titan" during the four decades following the end of World War II. In 1995, he was honored with the Presidential Medal of Freedom, and his statue can be found at Universal Studios Florida.

PAGE 33, *And Good morning my Handsome Little Man–*

Hollywood for Roosevelt was a political radio campaign in support of incumbent US president Franklin D. Roosevelt, who was seeking his third consecutive term in the White House. The campaign consisted of national broadcasts featuring over two hundred actors, producers, writers, and studio executives aired during the week prior to the November 5, 1940, election day (and Roosevelt victory), which places this letter in later October.

Julius Henry "Groucho" Marx (1890–1977) was an American actor, comedian, writer, and singer who starred in vaudeville and on radio, film, and television. Lucy starred in the Marx Brothers' film *Room Service* in 1938.

Perry Lieber (1905–1988) refers to the Hollywood press agent and publicist who worked for RKO. Later he became the PR manager and spokesperson for Howard Hughes.

PAGE 39, *I received your letter:*

"Tabú" is a Spanish-language song sung by Desi Arnaz. It was recorded and can be heard on the *Desi Arnaz and His Orchestra: Babalu* recording.

Composer Richard **Rodgers** (1902–1979) and lyricist Lorenz (Larry) **Hart** (1895–1943) were an American songwriting team. Their impressive collection of stage and film productions includes *A Connecticut Yankee*, *Babes in Arms*, *I Married an Angel*, *On Your Toes,* and *Too Many Girls*.

"Spic and Spanish" is another beloved Desi song, sung in English. He sings it in the Broadway musical *Too Many Girls*.

Paul (1904–1973) and **Grace** (1907–1955) **Hartman** were a married acting team who appeared in vaudeville and on Broadway stages, as well as television and film. Grace won the very first Tony Award for Best Leading Actress in a Musical (1948) for her multiple roles in *Angel in the Wings*.

Peter Lind Hayes (1915–1988) was born Joseph Conrad Lind Jr. in San Francisco. A future stage, radio, screen, and television actor, Hayes got his start in vaudeville and later appeared at the Copacabana in New York. He enlisted in the US Army Air Forces and appeared in the 1944 war film *Winged Victory*.

PAGE 43, *Tuesday aboard plane:*

Picture Play was a popular movie magazine published between 1915 and 1941, when its name was changed to *Your Charm: The Magazine for Moderns*.

PAGE 44, *Back on this damned location:*

Mother refers to Lucille Ball's mother, Desirée (DeDe) Eveline Hunt Ball (1892–1977), who moved from Jamestown, New York, to Hollywood to live with her daughter and son, Fred, in the 1930s. A devoted mother, DeDe supported her daughter throughout her career, helped to raise grandchildren Lucie and Desi during the busy *I Love Lucy* years and beyond, and assembled many of Lucy and Desi's scrapbooks, which followed their lives, family, and careers. DeDe is occasionally referred to as "Des" in these letters.

O'Brien refers to Edmond O'Brien (1915–1985) the Oscar-winning actor who costarred with Lucille in the 1941 movie comedy *A Girl, a Guy and a Gob*.

Harriett [sic] refers to Harriet McCain, who worked as Lucy's "gal Friday" and confidante from the 1940s through the early 1960s. The two became close friends, and when Lucille and her children moved to New York in 1960, Lucy insisted on the racial integration of the elevators in the Imperial House (150 East 69th Street) where they lived, so that Harriet and nanny Willie Mae Barker could ride up and down with the family.

Peggy Carroll was a Hollywood film actress at RKO and a friend of Lucy and Desi.

George Murphy (1902–1992) was an American actor and president of the Screen Actors Guild from 1944 to 1946. In 1965, he became a United States senator from California where he voted in favor of the Voting Rights Act of 1965 and the Civil Rights Act of 1968. He starred alongside Lucy in *A Girl, a Guy and a Gob*, and later served as vice president of Desilu Productions.

PAGE 52, *Wednesday morning Dearest baby:*

In 1943, newly minted US citizen Desiderio Alberto Arnaz III reported for duty in the United States Army. He had applied for entrance into the air force and was set to go to bombardier school, but injured his knee in a baseball game the day before he was set to leave. He spent the next three months in the hospital. After his broken leg healed, he could no longer pass the physical exam for the air force, so he was assigned to the army infantry for the duration of the war. An instructor for a time, he was eventually sent to Birmingham Hospital where he performed and organized the entertainment for severely injured troops and was editor of the *Birmingham Reporter*. He wrote about his time in the service in his 1976 autobiography, *A Book*.

Ed and Eba [sic] refers to Edward Sedgwick (1889–1953) and his wife Ebba (neé Havez, 1899–1982), dear and loyal friends of the Arnazes. Ed was a film director, actor, writer, and producer who directed most of Buster Keaton's MGM pictures. He said to Lucille upon their first meeting, "Young lady, if you play your cards right, you could be the greatest comedienne in show business." Ed gave the bride away at Lucy and Desi's second wedding ceremony on June 19, 1949, at Our Lady of the Valley Catholic Church in Canoga Park, California.

Andy was probably Andrew G. Hickox, Lucy's business manager, and later Desilu Productions' vice president, secretary, and member of the Board of Directors. The 1954 *I Love Lucy* episode "The Business Manager" (season four, episode one) pays homage to Andy by naming Ricky Ricardo's personal business manager and Lucy Ricardo's nemesis (played by Charles Lane) "Mr. Hickox."

Singer and actor **Cully Richards** (1908–1978) was a movie and television actor best known for the TV series *Don't Call Me Charlie!* Stationed at Arlington with Desi, he had probably just just costarred in the film *Let's Face It* with Bob Hope and Betty Hutton.

Free postage: US servicemen could simply write "free" in the upper-right-hand corner of the envelope and the USPS would take care of the rest. During this time in US history, mail was delivered twice a day, so it was possible to send and receive two or more letters from the same person each day.

PAGE 59, *Thursday 9:00 P.M.:*

Arlington, California, is a bedroom community a few miles southwest of Riverside, California.

Camp Anza was a 1,240-acre US Army installation in Riverside, California. Activated in 1942, the camp had over a hundred wooden barracks where over 600,000 troops were processed between 1943 and 1946. It boasted rec rooms, a chapel, a library, a fire station, a newspaper printing room (the *Anza Zip*), a hospital, and a 2,000-seat outdoor theater where Jack Benny and Bob Hope often performed for the troops.

Grant Hotel refers to the historic U.S. Grant Hotel in San Diego. Built by Ulysses S. Grant Jr. (son of the president), it opened in 1910 is listed on the National Register of Historic Places.

Freddy was Lucy's brother, Frederick Henry Ball (1915–2007), who served as Desi's band road manager in the 1940s and early 1950s. He later served on the Board of Directors of Desilu Productions.

Meet the People (1944) was an MGM musical comedy starring Lucille Ball and Dick Powell. Lucy played Broadway star Julie Hampton to Powell's dockworker Swanee Swanson.

Ranch refers to the Arnaz home at 19700 Devonshire in Chatsworth, bought in 1941, and christened the home Desilu.

"The Boys" and **"girls"** refers to the Arnaz family pets.

PAGE 64, *Tuesday 10:00 A.M. Beauty Salon:*

Jean Arthur (1900–1991) was a Broadway and movie actress who started her career in silent films. Best known for her brilliant screwball comedy, she was among many film stars who initially resisted adapting her career to the talkie craze of the late 1920s. Famous among her leading men were Cary Grant, Jimmy Stewart, and Gary Cooper.

The More the Merrier is a 1943 Columbia Pictures romantic comedy starring Jean Arthur, Joel McCrea, and Charles Coburn. The plot revolves around the housing shortage that was prevalent during and after the war, especially in cities such as Washington, DC, that were heavily involved in war and defense work.

Barker Bros. was a home furnishings store based in Los Angeles. Started in 1880 by Obediah Barker, the company grew to 15 stores by 1955, including a decorator store in Beverly Hills. The company closed its doors in 1992.

Lolita was a nickname for Desi's mother, Dolores. He moved her to California from New York when he and Lucy moved there permanently in 1941. An only child, Desi took personal and financial responsibility for her until his death.

Lucy's description of the difficulty of obtaining everyday household items such as furniture and appliances—not to mention the hiring of workers—was an inextricable part of life on the home front during the war. It was difficult to find specific items, as the materials needed to make them, such as iron, aluminum, and steel, were necessary for war material. Gas and food were also heavily rationed, leaving those at home to make do or invent other means to get by. Most towns held drives to collect paper, metal, rubber, nylon and silk stockings, and even record albums, with children going from house to house with their wagons to collect the valuable scraps.

Bill probably refers to Bill Smith who was obviously a good friend, and possibly agent or other professional contact of Desi. Lucy mentions San Bernardino, where it seems they were hoping Desi would be moved for his convalescence.

PAGE 76, *Friday. Dearest:*

Father refers to Desi's father, Desiderio Alberto Arnaz II (1894–1973). A pharmacist by education, in 1923 he became the youngest mayor of Santiago de Cuba. In 1932, he was elected to the Cuban House of Representatives for Oriente Province. Less than a year later when President Machado was overthrown in a revolutionary coup, Desiderio, along with other governmental officials, was thrown in prison, while his teenaged son and wife fled their Santiago home to hide out in Havana. In 1934, he was set free and exiled to Miami, Florida where he was forced to start life over from scratch with his seventeen-year-old son.

Desi writes of Lucy and his mother traveling to visit him in the hospital at Camp Anza. The trip from their home in Chatsworth was about 75 miles.

Grandpa refers to Lucy's grandfather Frederick Charles Hunt (1865–1944). Her own father having died when she was only three years old, Lucy and her brother, Freddy, grew up with their grandfather Hunt and lovingly called him "Daddy." When Lucy began to achieve success in Hollywood, she brought her family from New York one by one. Fred arrived first, landing a job at the famed Café Trocadero supper club on Sunset Boulevard. Together the siblings saved money so their mother and grandfather Hunt could also travel west. For a time the family lived together in a rented bungalow at 1344 North Ogden Drive in Los Angeles.

PAGE 82, *Monday 7:25 P.M.:*

Bataan was a 1943 MGM war movie starring Robert Taylor, George Murphy, Lloyd Nolan, and featuring Desi Arnaz as National Guardsman Felix Ramirez. Set in the Philippines, the plot focuses on the US Army's destruction of a bridge during their doomed fight to defend the Bataan Peninsula from the Japanese.

RKO's 1942 musical comedy ***Seven Days' Leave*** stars Victor Mature as Private Johnny Grey and Lucille Ball as heiress Terry Havelock-Allen. Johnny learns he must woo and marry Terry during the seven days of leave granted to him by the army in order to collect the $100,000 inheritance left to him by his great-grandfather. The movie ends on a bittersweet note with Terry and Johnny marrying before he boards a ship to head off to war.

PAGE 86, *9:45 A.M. Tuesday–:*

The film Lucy mentions will "start shooting Thursday" is probably MGM's *Meet the People*, which was released on June 1, 1944.

Arthur Freed (1894–1973) was an Academy Award–winning producer and lyricist who composed songs such as "Singin' in the Rain," "All I Do Is Dream of You," and "Broadway Rhythm." He produced several of Lucy's films, including *Du Barry Was a Lady* and *Meet the People*, and helped shape the movie careers of many stars, including Gene Kelly, Lena Horne, Frank Sinatra, and Esther Williams.

Bob Young refers to actor Robert Young (1907–1998), star of dozens of films including *Northwest Passage, The Enchanted Cottage,* and *The Mortal Storm*. He is perhaps best known for his television shows, *Marcus Welby, M.D.* and *Father Knows Best*.

PAGE 94, *Wednesday 9:10 P.M.:*

Irene was Irene Lentz (1901–1962), famed Hollywood fashion and costume designer. Known professionally as "Irene," she designed for many of Hollywood's leading ladies, including Carole Lombard, Ingrid Bergman, Lana Turner, and Ginger Rogers. She was inducted into the Costume Designers Guild Hall of Fame.

PAGE 104, *Good Morning "Lovebug"–:*

The **ration board** is a reference to the governmental authority run by the Office of Price Administration. During the war, like most European countries, the United States issued a series of rationing laws so the food and supplies needed for the troops and those on the home front would be available. They managed this through the more than 5,500 ration boards throughout the country. Ration books containing stamps were handed out to each person in a household, and could be used to buy foods such as sugar, butter, and meat. Housewives often saved stamps in order to make large purchases for holidays and other occasions. Other items such as private cars, tires, shoes, stockings, and gas were very limited to civilians. Likely due to her performing for the troops and appearing at War Bond rallies, Lucy received a coveted "C" sticker for gasoline, which were limited to those considered essential to the war effort, and civilians such as doctors. Her good fortune was probably due to her working in films, performing for the troops, and appearing at War Bond rallies to raise money for the war effort. The majority of rationing ended in August 1945, except for sugar, which continued for another year or more. In other countries such as the UK, rationing continued for several years.

Ginny Simms (1913–1994) was a popular singer and film actress. She sang with big bands and with such stars as Ella Fitzgerald, Dinah Shore, and Peggy Lee. She played herself in Lucy's films *That's Right—You're Wrong* and *Seven Days' Leave*. She was married to Hyatt von Dehn, founder of the Hyatt Hotels chain, with whom she shared two sons. The "Broadway" film Lucy mentions was the MGM musical *Broadway Rhythm* starring George Murphy and Ginny Simms as Helen Hoyt.

The **Hollywood Canteen** was a club for enlisted men and women that operated at 1451 North Cahuenga Boulevard in Los Angeles from October 1942 through Thanksgiving Day, November 22, 1945. Organized by Bette Davis and John Garfield, it offered entertainment, dancing, food, and drink to servicemen and women, many of whom were on their way to fight overseas. The price of admission was simply to wear your uniform. The Canteen was often staffed by Hollywood stars and starlets who acted as hosts, busboys, cooks, dishwashers, waitresses, dance partners, and entertainers. Lucy and Desi both donated their services to the cause.

Ida Koverman (1876–1954) worked at MGM for over two decades as Louis B. Mayer's executive secretary, and later as its director of public relations.

PAGE 121, *In the Bamboo Room:*

Aunt Helen (1884–1973) was Helen Orcutt, maternal aunt of Lucille Ball through her grandmother, Flora Belle Orcutt Hunt.

Arthur Lyons (1895–1963) was a theatrical agent, film producer, and manager who is said to have made a star of Jack Benny. Over the years, he and his agency represented stars such as Cole Porter, Joan Crawford, Carole Lombard, and Lucille Ball.

Botsford was probably an agent at Arthur Lyons' agency.

Cecil B. DeMille (1881–1959) was a famed radio and film director, producer, and actor who made 70 feature films, including 52 during the "silent" era. The commercial success of his films contributed to the establishment of Paramount Pictures. One of his most well-known films, *The Ten Commandments*, premiered only three years before his death.

Lucy writes about starting instruction (catechism) in the Catholic religion with **Father English**. A Catholic, Desi very much wanted his wife to join him in his religion, and having grown up without religion, Lucy was happy to please him and his mother. She never did join the Catholic Church, although both Arnaz children were raised in the religion, including being educated in Catholic schools.

PAGE 129, *Hello pretty baby!:*

Lou Maxon's refers to a rustic 750-acre retreat at Black Lake outside Chicago, which ad agency owner and philanthropist Lou Maxon (1901–1971) built in 1932. Lucy and Desi spent some time there right after their marriage (the myth is in Room 222).

The Pierre is a famed luxury hotel located at 2 East 61st Street, facing Central Park in New York. Opening in 1930, the hotel boasts 714 rooms and 41 stories, and cost some $15 million to build. Famed for its *trompe l'oeil* mural in its rotunda, The Pierre has been featured in dozens of books, television shows, and movies and is located within the confines of the Upper East Side Historic District.

Laurel refers to Laurel Canyon, a mountainous enclave in the Hollywood Hills of Los Angeles where many celebrities live.

PAGE 141, *Thursday 10:00 A.M.:*

Bullock's was a chain of department stores in Los Angeles from 1907 to the mid-1990s.

PAGE 149, *Friday–10:00 A.M. In Bed–:*

The Examiner was the *Los Angeles Examiner* newspaper.

Sloane's refers to W. & J. Sloane, a now defunct American department store chain with stores in New York, San Francisco, Washington, DC, and Los Angeles.

Cleo and Kenny were Lucy's beloved cousin Cleo (1919–2012) and Cleo's second husband, Kenny Morgan. Cleo was the daughter of DeDe's sister, Lola, and her husband, George Mandicos. After Cleo's parents divorced, Lola, Cleo, DeDe, Lucy, and Fred all lived together with Grandma and Grandpa Hunt. Cleo grew up as a sibling to Lucy and Fred until her mother died in 1930 and she went to live with her father. As soon as she graduated high school, she moved out to California to rejoin her Hunt/Ball family. Later, Cleo married *Los Angeles Times* television critic Cecil Smith, and was a producer for *Here's Lucy*.

PAGE 153, *Friday. Hello baby darling:*

Marc was Dr. Marcus Rabwin (1901–1988), physician and friend of Lucy and Desi. Dr. Rabwin served as chief of staff at Los Angeles County General Hospital. His wife, Marcella (1980–1998) was renowned in her own right as the executive assistant to David O. Selznick. Dr. Rabwin is famously said to have persuaded Judy Garland's parents not to abort their baby. The Rabwin and Arnaz families were extremely close, treating each other like family.

Attu, Africa, India, China, and the **South Pacific** were places of large, long World War II battles involving American military.

PAGE 156, *Friday nite:*

Movieland was a popular movie fan magazine of the 1940s and 1950s.

Elizabeth Barrett Browning (1806–1861) was a celebrated English poet of the Victorian Age. One of twelve children, Elizabeth's early life was controlled and confined by her overbearing father who did not wish any of his children to marry and disinherited those who did. She eloped with poet Robert Browning and moved to Italy where they were well respected and admired. Her legacy experienced a resurgence in 1934 with the release of the MGM drama, *The Barretts of Wimpole Street*, starring Norma Shearer and Fredric March.

PAGE 166, *Monday night Hello my baby:*

McArthur [sic] refers to General Douglas MacArthur (1880–1964), who served as US commander of the Southwest Pacific Theater during World War II.

PAGE 174, *Tuesday nite My darling baby:*

DeDe Ball was famous for her **goulash** recipe and was famous in her family for saying "the longer it sits, the better it gits!"

PAGE 177, *Wednesday My darling—:*

Lee Bowman (1914–1979) was a film, radio, and television actor who appeared in movies with both Lucy and Desi. He also played the role of Lucy's husband, George Cugat (later Cooper), for the pilot of the *My Favorite Husband* radio show, which aired on CBS Radio on July 5, 1948. Due to other commitments, he wasn't available for the series, so the male lead went to Richard Denning.

Schwab's Pharmacy was located at 8024 Sunset Boulevard in Hollywood from 1932 to 1983. Like other drugstores of the era, Schwab's featured a counter where hamburgers and ice cream were sold. Legend has it that sixteen-year-old schoolgirl Lana Turner was discovered there by director Mervyn LeRoy, but the truth is she was found at the Top Hat Café by Billy Wilkerson, publisher of the *Hollywood Reporter*.

Marvin Schenk (1887–1993) was a Metro-Goldwyn-Mayer executive who ordered the screen test for Ava Gardner, launching her from unknown beauty to $5-a-week contract actress at MGM.

PAGE 184, *Thursday 10:35 A.M. On the set:*

Best Foot Forward (1943) is an MGM musical starring Lucille Ball, Tommy Dix, June Allyson, and Gloria DeHaven. The plot centers around the senior prom at a boy's military academy where movie star Lucille Ball is the guest of honor.

Richard "Red" **Skelton** (1913–1997) was an actor, comedian, and singer on radio, television, and in film. Starting in vaudeville at age ten, Skelton began his radio career in 1937. From there he went to movies, including *Having Wonderful Time* (1938) and *Ziegfeld Follies* (1946) with Lucille Ball. His comedy/variety show, *The Red Skelton Show*, aired on CBS (and later NBC) from 1951 to 1971, and was produced at Desilu Studios. He was also a guest star in the *Lucy–Desi Comedy Hour* episode "Lucy Goes to Alaska."

Du Barry Was a Lady (1943) was an MGM Technicolor musical comedy starring Lucille Ball, Red Skelton, and Gene Kelly. The plot goes back and forth between a modern story and a dream in which Skelton is King Louis XV of France, with Lucy playing his mistress, Madame Du Barry.

Lockheed is the Lockheed Corporation, an American aerospace company based in California whose manufacturing focused on defense, military support, and security. Founded in 1926, in 1995 it merged with the Martin Marietta Corporation to form Lockheed Martin.

PAGE 188, *Friday 9 A.M.:*

Rugles [sic] refers to Charlie Ruggles (1886–1970), a character actor who appeared on Broadway, television, and in almost one hundred films including *Bringing Up Baby* (1938), *It Happened on Fifth Avenue* (1947), and *The Parent Trap* (1961).

PAGE 191, *Tuesday nite 9 o'clock:*

Reaching for the Sun (1941) is a rom-com film released by Paramount Pictures before the United States became embroiled in World War II. It stars Joel McCrea and Eddie Bracken, a stage, radio, television, and film actor who appeared in *Too Many Girls*, both on Broadway with Desi and in the film with Lucy and Desi. He remained friends with the couple for years after. Bracken's other credits include *The Miracle of Morgan's Creek* (1944), *National Lampoon's Vacation* (1983), and *Home Alone 2: Lost in New York* (1992).

PAGE 196, *To the Vice-President:*

I Love Lucy debuted on CBS at 9:00 P.M. on Monday, October 15, 1951, and within six months was in the number-one ratings spot with approximately 11 million families (out of 15 million television sets!) tuning in each week. The "Lucy Goes to the Hospital" episode on January 19, 1953, reaching the astonishing rating of 71.7 with a 92 share.

Lucie is daughter Lucie Desirée Arnaz, born July 17, 1951, days short of Lucille Ball's fortieth birthday and weeks prior to the first full cast reading of the *I Love Lucy* script.

PAGE 199, *I've come to the terrible realization:*

Lucy's commie accusations refers to the 1953 "Red Scare" that saw Lucille Ball accused of communism. It was an incredibly anxious time in the United States with many high-powered citizens—musicians, writers, activists, intellectuals, and Hollywood celebrities—being accused of having leanings toward or working directly with communist organizations or countries. A self-described non-political, Lucy (and other family members) registered as "communist" in 1936 to please left-leaning Grandpa Hunt. At the time, it was not seen as "un-American" to do so, but after the war it became very problematic for many who were caught up in the political and legal chaos.

PAGE 203, *Dearest Desi,:*

Desi Arnaz loved the sea and deep-sea fishing. Being so close to his home in California, he often went to Mexico to escape the stress of work, and enjoy sun, fresh air, and exercise. He eventually built a house at Rancho Las Cruces, a private seaside resort in Baja California Sur, which is still enjoyed by his children and grandchildren.

PAGE 207, *Nov. 17 Dearest Lucy:*

In 1954, Desi Arnaz played a hand of poker and won a parcel of land near the seventeenth fairway of the Thunderbird Country Club in Palm Springs (now Rancho Mirage), California. He hired famed architect Paul Revere Williams to design a home-away-from-home for his wife and two young children. Featuring natural stonework, a "glass-curtain wall" that allowed for viewing of the spectacular Mount San Jacinto, a swimming pool, and lanai, it was the perfect weekend and vacation haven for the busy couple and their family. Ironically, at the time, the Thunderbird was a restricted country club, not allowing Jewish or other minorities, including Desi, to become members.

Acknowledgments

First of all, thank you, Readers, for choosing to share part of your precious moments on Earth with this simple tome. I made it for *you*. I hope it has moved you to embrace whatever love you have in your lives for as long as it lasts.

I want to thank all our friends at Imagine Entertainment, White Horse Pictures, and Iron Mountain Media and Archival Services in Los Angeles for first digitizing all of these precious letters for their documentary *Lucy & Desi*. Having *that* job accomplished made publishing this book so much easier on our end.

I have to thank our longtime friends at Running Press for enthusiastically embracing the idea of publishing these relics. To Susan Van Horn for the extra creative art design and layout. Susan, it's better than I imagined it would be. There are so many others who carried this dream across the finish line, including Melanie Gold, Doug Wolff, Kara Thornton, Elizabeth Parks, Betsy Hulsebosch, Kristin Kiser, Shannon Fabricant, and our guiding star and editorial midwife, Cindy Sipala, for her taste, compassion and delicate care as we birthed this baby together.

A huge thank you to the one and only Mark Sendroff for stepping in to my world a few years ago and making everything clearer, brighter, and more fun, and for jumping in here to tidy up all things legal.

Thank you, always, to Larry Luckinbill, for loving me for over forty-five years and holding my hand through every single triumph and challenge—understanding what it takes to make something of quality.

Finally, and most importantly, an enormous thank you to Elisabeth Edwards for her tireless efforts deciphering my parents' handwriting while transcribing every one of these missives. After thirty-plus years together, I think you have come to know me, my parents, and my life better than I do, and *nothing* I do would be as professional or as much fun without you by my side.